THE CRISIS FOR

WESTERN POLITICAL ECONOMY

and other Essays

The Crisis for Western Political Economy

and other Essays

PETER JAY

BARNES & NOBLE BOOKS
TOTOWA, NEW JERSEY

First published in USA 1984 by
BARNES & NOBLE BOOKS
81 ADAMS DRIVE
TOTOWA, NEW JERSEY, 07512

British Library Cataloguing in Publication Data
Jay, Peter, *1937*
    The crisis for Western political economy, and
    other essays.
    1. Economic policy
    I. Title
    330.9   HD67

    ISBN 0-389-20527-3

Phototypeset by Falcon Graphic Art Ltd
Wallington, Surrey
Printed and bound in Great Britain by
Ebenezer Baylis & Son Ltd
The Trinity Press, Worcester

Contents

Preface   *vii*
Acknowledgements   *vii*
Introduction   1

POLITICAL ECONOMY   31

The Crisis for Western Political Economy
   1. A General Hypothesis of Employment, Inflation
     and Politics   33
   2. The Workers Cooperative Economy   56
A Case for a Select Committee on Economic Affairs   93

FOREIGN AFFAIRS   125

Regionalism as Geopolitics   127
An Arranged Marriage and an Affair of the Heart   158
Britain's New Realism   160
The Four Multipliers of Strife   165
Europe's Ostrich and America's Eagle   168

THE NEWS   189

The Bias Against Understanding
   1. Can Television News Break the
     Understanding-Barrier?   191
   2. Television Journalism:
     Without Pride of Ancestry   196
   3. Television Journalism:
     With Hope of Posterity   201
   4. How Television News Can Hold the Mass Audience   206
Electronic Publishing   219
What is News?   237
Betrayal by Clerks: The Lessons of TV-am   266

PERSONAL AND PHILOSOPHICAL   291

Religion – That's the Only Cloud in Civilisation's Sky   293
Who's Left, What's Right?   298
The Great Fastnet Disaster   300

INDEX   305

To Tamsin, Alice and Patrick

Preface

I am deeply grateful to many people – friends, relations, colleagues and teachers – for the possibility of compiling these essays and putting together this volume. This is not the place to name them all or to detail the debt I owe to each of them. That will have to await a more substantial setting.

But, in addition to the formal acknowledgements that are due, there are two thank yous that I must say for direct help in making this volume possible: to Dieter Pevsner of André Deutsch, for his encouragement; and to my kind and wonderful secretary, Emma Barford, who typed endlessly and, even more importantly, kept me going by her good humour, patience and morale-boosting.

Acknowledgements

Many of the essays in this book were first presented as speeches or articles elsewhere and spelling, punctuation, etc. all adhere to the original versions. The author gratefully acknowledges the permissions to republish them in this volume granted him by the following: for 'A General Hypothesis of Employment, Inflation and Politics', Institute of Economic Affairs; for 'The Workers Cooperative Economy', Manchester Statistical Society; for 'A Case for a Select Committee on Economic Affairs', Her Majesty's Stationery Office; for 'Regionalism as Geopolitics', Foreign Affairs; for 'Europe's Ostrich and America's Eagle', The Economist; for 'Electronic Publishing' and 'Who's Left, What's Right', Encounter; for 'What is News?', The Royal Television Society; for 'Religion – That's the Only Cloud in Civilization's Sky', Illustrated London News; for 'The Great Fastnet Disaster', Washington Post.

INTRODUCTION

This volume of essays is the product of half a working life, which has been haphazardly distributed: between government, journalism and business; between economics, international affairs, politics, management and ethics; between the Navy, Whitehall, newspapers, television, an Embassy and the boardroom; between Britain and the United States; between writing, administering, broadcasting, speaking, negotiating and leading; between 'doing' and 'commenting'. There was no plan in all of this and precious little pattern. It was, perhaps, four-fifths chance and one-fifth inclination, though even then the inclination was in every case prompted or discovered by others. Perhaps the most generous account would depict the author as one who by aptitude and intellectual inclination was, as he started out, a philosopher, but who by temperament could not reconcile himself to the purely contemplative life, who yearned for action, or at least activity, beyond the arm-chair and the panelled 'rooms' while still delighting in the view from the ivory tower.

No respectable moral auditors would certify such a prodigal use of life's resources to the Final General Meeting in the sky; but this volume at least conveniently ties together with a single ribbon the author's spasmodic attempts to wrestle with some of the broader issues thrown across his sinuous and meandering path. If any connecting thread at all runs through the essays, composed, written and 'adlibbed' over a quarter of a century, it is perhaps the author's lasting preoccupation with how and to what ends a society – especially a modern and complex one – communes with itself (and with other parts of the global society) and regulates itself, all resting paradoxically on an obstinate faith that reason and passion can and should be allied to the achievement of useful and noble ends. The author's highest hope is that the essays may be enjoyed by others similarly preoccupied and similarly optimistic.

The essays themselves fall into some convenient groupings, though these do not reflect the dates of their writing, nor any attempt at comprehensiveness or logical sequence within the groups. The groups comprise essays dealing with:–

– Political Economy;
– Foreign Affairs;
– Journalism; and
– Philosophical and Personal Topics.

Each of at least the first three groups aspires to some degree of contemporary relevance, although written over more than a decade. Most of the section on political economy is an attempt, however schematic and speculative, to grapple with what appears to the author more than ever to be the central question of political economy, namely what principle of economic organisation will best permit a society to achieve the goal of prosperity under conditions of real personal freedom without, as seems in the post-War era to have been the case, being wrecked on the rocks of accelerating inflation or intolerable involuntary unemployment. In other words how can a modern free or mixed economy achieve stable and lasting prosperity? The conclusion drawn is that no such solution can be found within the framework of conventional 'Western' economics (whether inclined to capitalist, inclined to socialist or perfectly 'mixed') – still less in the totalitarian 'Eastern' economies – and that the answers have to be sought at an altogether more profound level of political and economic philosophy than that occupied by the familiar debates between rival schools of economic policy (demand-management, monetarism, income policies etc.). What is called for is something that is neither capitalism, nor socialism, at least as they have been understood and practised this century, still less some sort of compromise between them. Intellectually the demand is much greater. It is for the next term in the series: Feudalism; Capitalism; Socialism; X. The essays themselves are chiefly directed to the diagnosis of the instability of existing forms of Western political economy, as found in Western Europe and North America, more doubtfully Japan, and to the demonstration that that instability is inherent, flowing necessarily from the forms of political and economic organisation which define that system: political democracy recognising extensive 'economic responsibilities' of government; an extensive private sector built on the limited liability company as the prime productive and entrepreneurial unit (i.e. on 'capitalist' lines); and an entrenched commitment to free trade unions and collective bargaining. Such a system, it is argued, is like an over-sophisticated toy for children. It can only switch itself off or explode, although the illusion is cunningly contrived that if only the players were more skilful or used better tactics these ultimate failures could be indefinitely postponed. The toy itself has to be redesigned, dispensing with at least some of the features which, in combination, are fated to destroy it and, perhaps, introducing others.

Any reader who recalls the original deployment of the author's arguments in the middle 1970s may conceivably wonder how far the author's analysis needs to be modified in the light of the experience of the period since 1975 or 1976, when the basic direction of the British economic strategy changed and certain 'monetarist' principles became enshrined in official policy. The short answer is 'not at all'. The slightly longer answer is that the economic analysis requires no revision, but that the political analysis – which predicted the progressive de-stabilisation of democratic institutions by the manifest and increasing inability of the economic system to deliver reasonable price and employment stability together – needs to be modified, if only in its time scale. It is necessary to acknowledge the greater short-term tolerance of very high unemployment in Britain, though not everywhere else, than the author (or almost anyone else) thought likely, let alone desirable, a decade ago.

Almost all of what the author would wish to have said to update the analysis given in the mid seventies is admirably and lucidly set out in Mr Samuel Brittan's latest book, *The Role and Limits of Government: Essays in Political Economy* (Temple Smith, 1983). In his preface he writes:-

> In the earlier volume (*The Economic Consequences of Democracy*, 1977), I expressed doubts about the future of liberal democracy because of its inability either to tame interest group pressure directly, or to do so indirectly by abandoning the commitment to full employment – inflation being able to buy only a limited amount of time which came to an end some time in the 1970s. If democracy has survived better than some of us feared, it has been because it has after all abandoned full employment. Am I alone, among members of the non-collectivist limited-Government school, in regarding this as an unsatisfactory and doubtfully desirable basis of survival?

Quite apart from the undesirability (to use a grossly inadequate term for the, in the strict sense, shocking economic and social waste and psychological damage) of permanent very high unemployment, the rational basis for abandoning the belief that it is incompatible with the long-term stability of democratic institutions is so far extremely slim. So far as British experience goes in the recent period, the 1983 General

Election result is just about the only piece of evidence for this proposition; and, properly examined, it falls a long way short of justifying such a conclusion. For a start, elections by themselves cannot overthrow democracy, since they are an exercise in it and lead necessarily to the instalment or continuation of an elected government. Secondly, the accidents of history – the divided opposition, the weak leadership of the Labour Party, the Falklands affair and the mechanics of Britain's 'first-past-the-post winner-take-all' single member constituency system – produced the proverbial 'landslide', but a landslide in which barely 31% of the electorate voted for the result they got, actually less than the 33.33% achieved by the Conservative Party in 1979. (*En passant*, the author may remark that he is not one of those who are persuaded that 'electoral reform', i.e. a different system, would deliver both a fairer representation of the popular will in Parliament and more stable government, defined conveniently enough by those who believe in it as bias towards the political centre. The author believes that the system could either be fairer or more stable, according to which system of proportional representation is chosen, but certainly not both. And he believes that wherever else better government is to be found, it is least likely to occur at the centre of the political spectrum as conventionally described. On the contrary he prefers a combination, carefully selected, of the opinions most commonly found at both extremes of that spectrum – the 'international dateline' antithesis, in spherical terms, of the Greenwich meridian exemplified by the Heath-Jenkins-Healey conventional middle-of-the-road [see page 29 on the 'Balliol years']. Indeed, in matters of political spectroscopy the author's presumption is that truth seldom lies between the extremes, but more frequently beyond them.)

Thirdly, there is a great difference between on the one hand the stability of democratic governments presiding over an economy which is widely believed to be passing through a merely temporary 'vale of tears' beyond which lies recovery, a restoration of high employment and 'a return to normal' and, on the other hand, their stability if and when it comes to be widely recognised that the 'vale of tears' is in fact a permanent condition from which no recovery is likely or possible. The political rhetoric of 1982–3, the atavistic belief that the economic pendulum must swing and a few statistical straws in the wind encouraged a quite widespread belief in 1983 that some form of sustainable recovery really was in prospect without a re-acceleration of inflation. Nonsense though this was, the fact that it was widely believed may have

4

affected the electorate's judgement of the tolerability of the then level of unemployment; and to that extent the result is not evidence of public complacency about indefinite very high unemployment as a necessary structural feature of a non-inflationary economy.

The hypothesis in the essays does not, of course, rule out the possibility of what headline writers will call 'recovery'. It may be, though the author doubts it, that the long-term rate of involuntary unemployment associated with no tendency for the existing rate of inflation to accelerate is somewhat below the level equivalent to the last 1983 official measurement of unemployment at three million. If so, some fall in unemployment could occur, once-and-for-all, before what Mr Samuel Brittan has dubbed the 'non-acceleration inflation rate of unemployment (NAIRU)' was reached. More obviously, output can rise in line with the underlying growth in output per employed man (i.e. productivity) without any fall in unemployment and therefore without any risk of falling below the NAIRU level. Fourthly the NAIRU level may itself shift gradually, as more competitive conditions are promoted in the economy, especially in the labour market. Fifthly, in the short-term wage-push inflation may depend on the perceived direction of change as much as on the level of unemployment and on external 'shocks' like sudden changes in oil and other commodity prices. But these refinements do not weaken the primary hypothesis that there is a NAIRU in Western political economies and that it is far above any level associated with post-War Western definitions of 'high' or 'full' employment. When the author wrote in *The Times* on 1 July 1974, that 'if we are prepared to accept unemployment in the low millions for the rest of this decade, it is possible that inflation will be brought under control, that an incomes policy which offers employment rather than a vague hope of more stable prices in return for pay restraint will prove to have a much longer half-life than its ill-starred predecessors and that the forms of democracy can be preserved', he was universally derided for wild and reckless exaggeration and alarmism; and yet in retrospect it can be seen that he understated the problem by referring merely to 'the rest of this decade'. The author's error was not in the hypothesis, but in his political judgement of the horn of the 'accelerating-inflation-or-unemployment-in-the-low-millions' dilemma on which successive governments would choose to impale themselves, when he wrote, in the succeeding sentences of the same article 'But, of course, that "if" begs the whole question. At this particular moment the posture of budgetary and monetary policy is not particularly inflationary. But the choice will arise very soon when the autumn's pay explosion begins to price large numbers of people out of their jobs and the Government comes under intense pressure to reflate in order to check unemployment. It is hardly imaginable that it will not respond to that call or that, if by some political freak it did not, it would not be rapidly removed from office in favour of some other administration promising quick action against unemployment. So we can take the next plunge into large budget deficit and all-out monetary expansion for granted.' In the event British economic masochism and political courage proved, at least temporarily, both to be greater than the author had expected.

Economically all that has happened since 1976 is that British governments have, willy-nilly, decided to impale the economy up to the hilt on one horn of the 'very high unemployment OR accelerating inflation' dilemma described in the analysis. We have always known that that was possible, though its political consequences remain a matter for observation and judgement. But the experience does not suggest in any way that the dilemma is not as stated or that any means of escaping from it has been found. Because we are currently impaled on the 'very high unemployment' horn rather than the 'accelerating inflation' horn, popular presentation of the problem may have shifted from 'what is the answer to inflation' to 'what is the answer to unemployment'; but analytically the issue is still precisely the same.

Moreover, the fact that, as Mr Samuel Brittan rightly points out in his new book (page 249), 'if one looks at broad strategy and at actions and statistics rather than political rhetoric, it is clear that the fundamental change in policy took place not after the election in 1979, but less than half way through the term of the Labour Government' is yet further evidence of the proposition, discussed later in this Introduction, that all significant issues of public policy, including economic strategy, altogether transcend the stale categories of inter-party debate. The problem is there, not only for Britain, but for all the economies of Western Europe and North America (even the claims sometimes made in the mid seventies that West Germany was an exception are now exposed as hollow); and the need for an answer looms darkly over the demonstrably futile twitchings and turnings of the rats, whether red or blue, in the politico-economic maze from which, as currently specified, there can be no escape.

Anything like a full sketch of what the true solution is – the definition of X – will have to await the separate volume to itself on which the author has been intermittently engaged for some years. But some hints are given; and some of the issues raised are discussed in these essays. Essentially, 'X-ism' proposes to dispense with all three of the salient features of Western political economy, namely the government 'sector', the 'capitalist' firm and free collective bargaining. It proposes to replace the second and third (the Tweedle-dum and Tweedle-dee of the 'tripartite' economy) by the single institution of the workers cooperative and to replace the first (the Tweedle-don't of the government) by the almost universal extension of the market mechanism. It is argued that under these conditions, not merely will the explosive elements of current political economy be separated, but also certain other basic principles of eighteenth- and nineteenth-century economic philosophy, both capitalist and socialist, will once more be restored to their proper prominence. These principles have been perverted and forfeited in the twentieth century by the fatal reliance on large and remote institutions as proxies for the human beings whose interests they are supposed to represent. In the case of capitalism this happened by making 'big capital' – and therefore its corollary, 'big labour' – become the vehicle for enterprise and work; and in the case of socialism it happened by making 'big Government' the stand-in for the citizen. These earlier and purer principles are that the citizen as consumer should be sovereign in the allocation of economic resources and that the citizen as worker should be sovereign in the direction of his and his mates' energies. The two are effectively reconciled and intermediated by the 'hidden hands' of the market place and the 'gain' motive, though some essential tasks always remain for government, notably establishing and upholding X-ism in the first place, correcting manifest discrepancies between private and social costs and redistributing income to fit the needs and taste of each society from time to time.

This is enough advertisement – inevitably over-coloured and over-compressed – of the underlying argument of two of the essays in the section on political economy for the purposes of this Introduction. Suffice it therefore only to add that, whatever may be said in criticism or acceptance of the argument, its whole thrust will have been missed by those who are so committed to the old sterile categories of left-right political economy that they can only reject any ideas which cannot be forced and are not intended to fit into their preconceived mental boxes, who simply see X-ism as either disguised capitalism or revamped socialism or – worst of all – a mixture of the two.

The significance of the remaining essay in this section is quite unconnected with this main theme. This is the essay entitled 'A Case for a Select Committee on Economic Affairs'. It was written at the end of 1969 on the author's return from twelve months based in Washington reporting for *The Times* on the economic policy aspects of the first year of the new Nixon Administration. This had not been the author's first visit to the United States, which had been in 1966; but it was his first experience of living and working there for an extended period. Like all other open-minded Englishmen 'discovering' the United States for the first time he had been enormously excited by America, above all by its experimentalism expressed in the unquenchable conviction that all problems are soluble if only one tries hard and ingeniously enough. Being in America for him, as for so many others, was like having an extra draft of pure oxygen permanently main-lined into one's blood-stream. But it was not, of course, only what was new in America that was new to him. Some of America's longest standing institutions, seen in action first-hand for the first time, were just as exciting. And the same preoccupation with 'how and to what ends a society . . . communes with itself . . . and regulates itself', which, as we have seen at the beginning of this Introduction, represents the connecting thread running through these essays and the author's professional lifetime, stimulated a particular fascination with the operation of congressional committees on Capitol Hill. What grabbed the author's attention was not the minutiae of their activities. Nor was it the very un-British role of those important committees which have both legislative and executive powers, reflecting the fundamental, though little understood in Europe, fact of the American constitution that 'the government of the United States' comprises the Congress and the judiciary as well as the executive Administration. Instead it was the role of certain non-executive, non-legislative committees such as the Joint Economic Committee of both houses of Congress.

These latter committees – and certain of the executive and legislative committees like the Senate Foreign Affairs Committee, whose influence was exerted at that time mainly through its conduct of general hearings on the great foreign policy issue of the period (the Vietnam War) rather than through its formal powers to confirm certain appointments and to consider international treaties for ratification by the Senate – suggested a model which could perhaps be adapted to British purposes without disregarding those fundamental constitutional differences between the United States and Britain which made the executive and legislative roles

8

of many other congressional committees less relevant to the parliamentary system. To the author the essential magic of these deliberative committees was and remains that they provide a unique and prominent forum, under the broad aegis of the nation's deliberative assembly, for the widest possible national debate on issues of great current moment into which could be and were drawn, as invited witnesses, all or many of the most competent citizens, whether or not they happened to be in elected or government positions themselves. This, it seemed to the author, had many advantages both for 'the nation's parliament' and for the nation. Above all it served to bridge the debilitating gap, which has contributed so markedly to the decline of parliament and parliamentary debate in public esteem in Britain and other countries operating a similar system, between the debate in parliament, which is never seen by the public on television and seldom reported in the newspapers, and the debate in the nation whose natural forum is television and the press and which is seen and followed by almost everyone with any interest in these matters other than those who are actively engaged in government and parliament itself. Thus, it frequently seems in Britain that there are two quite separate debates going on, one in parliament for the professionals and one in public for the public. Although occasionally this may enable the debate in parliament – and even conceivably the resulting actions of government – to be more refined and sophisticated, for the most part it diminishes the influence of the parliamentary debate, the standing of parliament, the discipline and coherence of the public debate and, most importantly of all, the quality of the resulting policies and actions.

It seemed to the author, stimulated by the example of the Joint Economic Committee and the Senate Foreign Affairs Committee in Washington, that, if it was possible for a prestigious committee of parliament in Britain regularly and as a matter of course to hold hearings on the key issues of the day, into which were drawn witnesses from all competent walks of life and whose proceedings were widely reported on their merits and, indeed, televised where the interest was sufficient, a useful stride could be taken towards merging the parliamentary and the public debate to the great benefit of both. Parliament would be seen to be the place under whose aegis these debates took place. The disciplines, such as they are, of set hearings, adequate time, opportunities for reply and critical cross-examination would apply. The best brains and the most relevant experience would be seen to be contributing. The parliamentarians and others professionally involved in government would be constrained to pay attention. The public would be aware of and instructed by the hearings. Press and television would be bound (and free) to give proper attention. The whole quality of debate would benefit; and it would be at least an even chance that better, more carefully considered and more widely understood policies and programmes would result.

It did not seem to the author that the two-party composition of parliamentary committees and the essential parliamentary link between the governing party's majority in parliament and its entitlement to govern at all were relevant objections to transplanting this particular American institution to Britain, although some who had not adequately considered the matter seemed to think so. What is important about the activities of such committees and their hearings is not and never has been the contents of the report – or majority report – which they produce, although thanks to the exceptional quality of the individuals, like Senator Paul Douglas, Senator William Proxmire and Congressman Henry Reuss who had dominated the Joint Economic Committee, the subjects chosen by that Committee and its reports over the quarter of a century to 1969 had in fact been of a remarkably high standard. What really mattered was the fact of the hearings themselves and of the opinions and analyses which came out and were widely disseminated under the aegis of Congress as a result. Moreover, the fact, if it were to prove a fact, that such committees would be likely to divide along party lines in writing their reports (something which subsequent history has largely shown not to be a fact) would not matter, again because it would not be the reports, unless they were of exceptionally high quality and enjoyed bi-partisan support, that were important. Again it would be the hearings and debates which preceded them that mattered.

This, then, was what led the author to seek the partnership of his eminent and much-loved contemporary, Samuel Brittan, in presenting evidence to the House of Commons' Select Committee on Procedure, which happened at that time to be considering an aspect of this matter, namely the future of the House of Commons' Estimates Committee. They decided, taking a central concrete example, to press the case for 'A Select Committee on Economic Affairs', which quite explicitly would have terms of reference related to subjects and issues rather than, as with the narrow purview of the traditional Estimates Committee, to the propriety and wisdom with which the taxpayers' money had been deployed in total abstraction from the policies which normally determined the broad pattern of expenditure.

Introduction

In retrospect the author takes modest pleasure in the fact that this initiative is one among some other radical proposals in a number of different fields which he and others have put forward and which, although initially received with scepticism and the usual chants of 'interesting but unrealistic', have within a decade or so become the conventional wisdom of the next era and the blueprints for major practical developments. The work of the Select Committee on Procedure led to the creation of the Select Committee on Expenditure. That Committee's sub-committee (on the Treasury and economic affairs) did increasingly begin to operate, in a small way, like the Joint Economic Committee of the Congress, although the constraining habits of mind of both parliamentarians and professional parliamentary reporters considerably delayed the fulfilment of its real potential. There was a danger of a narrow coterie of specialists monopolising its deliberations and the debates on the Treasury's annual public expenditure White Papers to the exclusion of the broader and more red-blooded political debate which should have centred round the leading issues with which it dealt.

However, it in its turn and the other sub-committees dealing with the expenditure of the main departments of state have led step by step towards the creation of House of Commons' committees on each of those departments; and those committees now regard policy as well as housekeeping as very much within their terms of reference. There is still some considerable way to go before the hearings of these committees come to assume the key role in national political debate which they have at their best played in the United States. But, nonetheless, the trend is an encouraging direction; and some of the pioneering television work done by Granada Television in simulating parliamentary committee hearings – and other hearings drawing on a wide cross-section of competent professionals and others – point in an exciting way to the potential for further fulfilment of this original idea.

Two other themes, not present in the author's mind in 1969, have given new relevance and impetus to the central thought lying behind this early essay. One is the need to give specific and imaginative thought to ways and means of democratising the policy-making process in Britain. The other is its relevance to the chronic problem of the lack of professional advice and support suffered by the Opposition party and its consequent lack, not merely of preparation for government when the electorate so decides, but also of adequate understanding and ammunition with which to conduct an intelligent and effective scrutiny of government policies and programmes.

The first of these two supportive themes raises much too large a question to be examined adequately here. It will have to suffice, therefore, simply to point to it and for the author to undertake that he hopes to deal properly with it on its merits one day. The essential thought behind it is a simple, though for most people, especially in Europe, probably a shocking one, namely that there is and probably should be no automatic, direct and essential link between the electoral process and the policy formation process in representative democracies in general or in Britain in particular. In more homespun language elections are not necessarily and should not be assumed to be about policies, either as the reflection of the electorate's judgement of the policies pursued by the incumbent government or as the determiners of the policies to be pursued by governments in the near future. The myth of representative democracies, even more in Europe than in the United States and elsewhere, is that elections are precisely about policies, that they are the mechanism whereby the people decide what they think of recent policies and what policies they want in the future and that the policies pursued by governments therefore have democratic sanction because they are pursued by governments who were chosen through elections by the voters on the basis of the policy packages which they put forward in their manifestos and otherwise. This myth is damaging both because it is usually false and because it thereby distracts attention from the real and interesting question of how, given that elections do not and cannot fulfil this function, democratic sanction for the policies pursued by governments should be obtained.

There is nothing original about the concept of political parties as competitors essentially for office and for power, with policies being regarded as at best counters they use in their rival bids for the voters' favour. The Austrian economist Joseph Schumpeter spelt it out in his *Capitalism, Socialism and Democracy* more than a generation ago. Unlike some modern theorists in the United States who have tried to carry the idea of parties bidding for votes to the point where they are both – or all – pursuing the same 'representative votes' and so becoming indistinguishable from each other, Schumpeter put the emphasis on the 'issue blindness' of voters and on their inclination to vote for the team, whose job they regarded as being to work out specific policies as need arose. In practice parties can carry a great deal of policy and ideological baggage with them into office, claiming bogusly a mandate for it,

12

provided that they prevail in the primary competition to be seen by the electors as overall the more attractive – or less revolting – group of people. Thus parties themselves, especially in Europe, can be as much as the commentators, victims of the myth that they – or their electoral success – are the vehicles of policy preferences by the public; and, even if the differences between parties on policy matters are not trivial, as they often are not, there is no corroboration in this for the views that these differences provide the electors with a reliable guide to their behaviour in office or that these are the differences which mainly influence voters or that there is any real democratic sanction as a result for the policies which parties in power pursue, even where they are the same as the policies they canvassed before the last election.

It is a simple matter of observation in Britain in the post-War period (and probably even more so before) that there is no systematic connection between the policy postures and general complexion of political parties at election times and the policies subsequently pursued, whether those policies are defined in terms of the stated policy instruments or in terms of their intended results in the betterment of the nation or its citizens. A recitation of Britain's post-War economic history, for example, or of its foreign policy would show that there have been several major and decisive deflections of strategy – from the Butskellite era to the growth-and-indicative-planning era, to the incomes policy and flexible exchange rate era, to the monetarist era (from 1975 to 1979) and recently to the 'there-must-be-life-after-death' era and, in foreign policy, from the imperial to the special-relationship-and-new-commonwealth era, to the 'European' era and now to the 'great little England' era. It would show that none of these key decisions coincided with and none was influenced by the electoral process or by the supposed political 'colour' of the party that happened to be in power. In almost every case the determinants were, as to 85%, the facts of life in the form of the manifest failure of the previous policy and, as to 15%, the success of the next prevailing intellectual fashion in filling the political vacuum thereby created. The possible exception is the end of monetarism in 1979, although since this coincided with what almost every known political commentator persisted in heralding as the *arrival* of 'monetarism' (in their blissful ignorance of what that technical term meant) it would be hard to see it as an example of a major change in economic policy being intentionally caused by the decision of the electorate.

There are, as there have to be, some special 'issues' chosen for their guaranteed total irrelevance to all aspects of national well-being which serve exclusively as ritual footballs in the political arena so that the rival teams can be seen in training and judged as to their likely proficiency. These 'sparring' topics, suitably clad in helmets and bandages of bogus pretentions to seriousness by the David Colemans of the political arena, include such matters as nationalisation and de-nationalisation, and mutual allegations of extreme ideological deviation from natinal norms between the parties.

What is really at issue in all elections, as sane observers like W. S. Gilbert, most Americans, General de Gaulle, Anthony Trollope and Messrs Saatchi and Saatchi have long realised, is a simple competition between two or more rival teams of people for the honour of being the Government. It is a healthy and sensible arrangement that the voters should have the opportunity every few years to chuck out of power whoever is in power, since, as Lord Acton observed, a permanent and predictable tenure of power, or indeed office, tends to corrupt in proportion to the length and certainty of that tenure. This, of course, is also the reason why the electoral system fails in this benign purpose where local circumstances and history make it inconceivable that any but one dominant team will ever be chosen, as in Northern Ireland in the Stormont era. Anyone who retains the illusion that elections can or should normally ever be anything more than a choice between rival teams of people – the blues and the reds – and can, therefore, really be judgements about alternative policy packages (and God help the voter who fails to find all the items he wants in the same package or who fails to detect the broad philosophical coherence of each package which European nostalgia and the lazy labels used by political commentators pretend to postulate) should examine local and 'European' elections in Britain. Manifestly, nothing but a choice between parties on the broadest and vaguest grounds of national personalities and 'image', plus a token opportunity to protest futilely and irrelevantly at the state of the nation and the world, are involved.

This is not only a fact of life, but also sensible. It is as hinted above, not logically possible for millions of people, expressing one choice every five years, to express the infinite variety and gradations of their choices and priorities about the whole range of foreseeable and unforeseeable policy options, great and small, which will arise between elections. Just because political commentators and hucksters find that it consorts better with the extreme paucity of their available means of

14

communication to reduce the whole range of choices facing a society at home and abroad to two ritualistic poles culled from a superficial popularisation of eighteenth- and nineteenth-century European political thought, there is not the slightest reason to think that the real choices genuinely, naturally or spontaneously arrange themselves along any such one-dimensional spectrum or into any such pair of naturally coherent packages. All that the 'left/right' language of political commentary proves is, not that there really is any such useful distinction, but simply that the electoral contest between the 'reds' and the 'blues' (combined with the European compulsion to pretend that elections are about policy) obliges the commentators to invent a shorthand language which compresses the multi-dimensional reality of policy choice into the one-dimensional simplicity of electoral rivalry. This in turn explains why, when political commentators and to some extent politicians themselves stray outside their proper domain of electoral contests between rival individuals and teams into the quite different area of policy, they become so flat-footed and inept, like sports writers trying to deal with the politics of the Moscow Olympics or of South Africa's sporting relations with the world community.

Once, however, the major liberation of recognising that elections and policy formation belong to two quite different worlds – both legitimate and necessary in their own right, but one about which people shall have power and office and the other about what a society shall do about the problems confronting it – is achieved, the interpretation of the electoral process becomes natural and straightforward. With it the nature and basis of party membership and loyalty become clear as an expression of a largely arbitrary early option ('every boy and every gal that's born into the world alive; Is either a little Liberal or else a little Conservative', W. S. Gilbert, *Iolanthe*) which therefore needs no sombre reconsideration in later life. Much more excitingly, it also becomes clear that, if elections provide no democratic sanction for the policies pursued by governments and if it is nonetheless thought important that policies should have democratic sanction, then some other mechanism for sanctioning policies must be found. The referendum and the plebiscite certainly provide possible mechanisms, but only where the nature of the issues makes them suitable. These are normally confined either to issues which are so great and fundamental in their constitutional significance that nothing less than a direct decision of the whole voting body can sanction a new direction or law or to issues which are so slight and subjective, so clear-cut and with so little interconnection with other issues that there is no particular reason not to use a popular vote. Examples of the first might include the decision to join the Common Market and, therefore, to circumscribe the sovereign law-making powers of parliament purportedly for all time; and examples of the second might include whether or not to have 'double summer time' in Britain (or, perhaps, parts thereof).

But for much the greater part of the whole range of policy issues requiring decisions by governments and societies the referendum is not a suitable mechanism. The issues are not so great that the ultimate sanction of direct popular consent is needed. Nor are they so subjective, isolated or clear-cut as to make regular polls sufficiently understandable and practical, sensitive to all gradations of opinion. For this great area in the middle, therefore, something else is necessary, even if closer examination of the American system of ballot 'propositions' shows that rather wider use of plebiscites could be made than is commonly supposed in Britain to be possible or desirable. It is here that the somewhat nebulous, but nonetheless important, concept of the 'national debate' comes into its own. And it is in this context that the ultimate potential and importance of parliamentary committees, each dealing with each of the major subject areas of government, conducting highly visible public hearings on the key issues and drawing the widest possible cross-section of the competent and interested population into the debate, takes on its broadest significance. It is an idea that needs to be worked on and worked out, not merely in great detail, but also with great imagination and with great sensitivity to the differing nature of so many of the problems and policy choices confronting a nation. It will not by itself achieve the direct formalistic democratic sanction of the referendum or the election; and certainly no one in their senses would regard elaborate mechanisms involving national, regional, area, local and grassroots councils and committees as anything but a destructive playground for obsessives and mischief-makers. The quinquennial election of parties and people to parliament and government – and very occasional referenda – are probably quite sufficient formal voting mechanisms. But there have been enough major national debates in recent British political history, with sufficient influence on the ultimate decisions of government and course of the nation, to encourage the belief that, with better leadership and context provided under the aegis of parliament, this informal process could be developed to give a much greater depth and substance to the aspiration of national consensus behind major and minor policy decisions of government.

The second supporting theme is much more modest in its compass. Nonetheless, knowledgeable observers – and particularly those most closely concerned with the realities of government and the substance of policy issues rather than the theatre of politics – have repeatedly returned to the disastrous inadequacies of the staffing and briefing available to parties in opposition, both for the purposes of conducting a proper scrutiny of the exercise of power by the government of the day and for the purposes of preparing the opposition party for itself coming to power. This has from time to time prompted people to suggest that there should be a 'Department of the Opposition' staffed by civil servants or that senior opposition spokesmen should have personal staffs on the scale available to senior American congressmen or the chairmen of important congressional committees in Washington. Neither of these specific suggestions has found favour for both practical and theoretical reasons, some of them connected with the need to perpetuate the European myth referred to above, namely that the parties are, must be and should be divided by deep philosophical differences which make it undesirable, even if it were practical, for both to be served by similar, even if quite separate, teams of civil servants. Since, however, no one seems to object effectively to both parties being served by the identical team of civil servants when they are in government and since, anyway, there is no logical necessity for the two teams of civil servants necessarily to be homogenised philosophical eunuchs, the argument hardly seems valid in its own terms. But, anyway, the problem does not arise, since the concept of two coherent philosophical camps is and always has been utterly bogus in the first place.

A useful and sensible resolution, however, of the reservations which have been felt about the particular solutions that have previously been put forward would be found if the chief opposition spokesman on each of the major government portfolios were by custom to assume the chairmanship of the corresponding House of Commons' committees. There are risks in this, namely that their partisan role would corrupt the substance of the committees' work; but there is the more than countervailing prospect that they, the chairmen, would be educated and restrained by the environment of the committee. As chairmen of such committees they could then have access to a fully competent and professional staff, which would nonetheless be genuinely quite independent of Whitehall. This exposure to competent and professional advice would help to prepare them and their parties for government, as well as beginning to make a reality for the first time of the idea of informed and thorough scrutiny by parliament of the Executive. There are already precedents for opposition chairmanship of key House of Commons committees, most notably in the case of the Public Accounts Committee, which is also the one House of Commons' committee which has a full-scale professional staff supporting it in the form of the Exchequer and Audit Department headed by the Comptroller and Auditor-General. It would be natural and proper – and in accordance with the acknow-ledged constitutional conventions – for the leading opposition spokes-men thus to take the lead in parliament's scrutiny of government, although government back-benchers would have a very full role to play. Thus, the creation of such committees would thereby help to solve this problem, as well as those to which their creation was originally directed.

The inclusion, therefore, of this essay in this volume, while it was itself directed to one specific example, is thought by the author to be justified because of its relevance to these much broader themes for which the public mind now seems far more ready, steeled by the bitter experience of the intervening decade and a half, than it did in 1969, when it was still possible for many people to believe that parliament could, as then structured, provide a serious forum for public debate and that public policy could be adequately and effectively defined and distilled across the floor of the House of Commons.

The section on foreign affairs is slimmer than that on political economy and journalism, reflecting the author's briefer involvement (five years as a television journalist and two years in the Washington Embassy) with that topic. Nonetheless, the pieces do seek, as in the other sections, to grapple with what the author felt to be the basic conceptual issues upon the disentangling of which any specific set of policies would need to be predicated. These issues are in turn:

(a) The global paradox of seeking stability – or at least limiting the excesses of turbulence – at a time when the sources of conflict (population; appetites; politicisation; and weaponry) are multi-plying geometrically, while the instruments of stability (diploma-cy; international law and institutions; and economic resources) are static or increasing only arithmetically;

(b) The proper integration of East–West and North–South perspec-tives in Western global and regional policies, involving the attempt to displace the standard 'either-or' choice (between a cold-hearted, clear-eyed, chess-playing, geopolitical interpreta-

18

tion of all North–South and regional problems in East–West terms and a warm-hearted, high-principled, liberal insistence that all regional problems must be treated entirely on their own local merits) by a true reconciliation of the two approaches in the light of the enlightened self-interest of the West, introducing the notion that the way to win – or at least co-exist in – the unavoidable East–West competition is in fact to align the West's policies with locally or regionally determined priorities and prevailing trends, whenever possible thereby also, on balance, diminishing the quantum of avoidable conflict and war; and

(c) The proper management of West–West relations, calling for greater realism on both sides of the Atlantic about the true division of labour, a rejection of the myth of equal partnership as false and dangerous and a franker recognition that, until such time as 'Europe' becomes capable of accepting the real operational burdens and responsibilities of global partnership (if indeed that is even desirable), the alliance will be better served by accepting the older implicit convention that 'America decides and Europe complains'.

The first of these (the paradox of presuming stability in the face of exploding turbulence) is posed, though not resolved, in the brief address to the University of California at Berkeley on its 'Charter Day' entitled 'The Four Multipliers of Strife'. It is, perhaps, one of those paradoxes that only needs to be stated to be seen; but in the author's opinion it has some value as an antidote to the pervasive beliefs that there ought to be a swift answer to every world problem and that 'crises', as perceived in newspaper and television headlines, are in some way abnormal interruptions of a very normal and natural tranquility and equilibrium in international affairs.

Much the largest and most ambitious theme in the Foreign Affairs section is contained in the article on 'Regionalism as Geopolitics'. This, the author submits, really does contain an important contention in the argument that the standard polarisation of so much debate on international affairs, both general and specific, is artificial, unnecessary and capable of sensible synthesis. If this is true, it is an important liberation because it means that less time and energy need to be devoted to wrangling over the relevance or otherwise of the 'East–West dimension' of regional problems and more time and energy can be devoted to examining and responding to them on their merits. This has assumed new relevance in the wake of President Reagan's increasingly crude demonstration of the effects of pursuing the opposite notion, namely that in order to stand up to the Russians it is necessary to alienate everyone else too.

The essay on 'West–West relations' ('Europe's Ostrich and America's Eagle') can be seen as one example of trying to apply that idea to one particular 'region', namely Europe. But there is a difference. In the case of the European region, the essay is in the first person in the sense that it is written by a European for Europeans, whereas in the case of other regions, whether one is looking at them through European or through American super-power eyes, one is asking how 'we' should relate to 'them' rather than, as in the case of Europe, how the region itself should relate to the super-power. In the author's opinion, although he is aware that this runs counter to the whole suffocating myth of 'European' maturity and unity, much harm to our own European interests is done by the false, indeed the dishonest, pretence that a political entity called 'Europe' is, can and should be some kind of at least aspirationally equal partner with the United States in the conduct of the management of the security of that region and of its relations with the rest of the globe. In the author's submission there can only be even an aspiration to equal partnership if there is an equal capacity and will, not merely for the glamour and prominence of rhetorical postures, but also for the pain and odium associated with responsibility expressed in, where necessary, hard and believable actions. Serious countries and regions of the world are not going to negotiate their future with a debating society whose motto at every threshold is 'after you!' and whose response to every bill is 'I am afraid I have not got any money on me'. There is criticism, too, for those Americans who through excessive deference, whether real or pretended, have indulged these European self-delusions and encouraged the European notion that it is somehow clever or useful to trap the United States into an endless series of 'Catch-22s' whereby the sole guarantor of Western Europe's security is alternately damned for soft, weak, dovish and isolationalist tendencies which will lead it to desert us in our hour of need (note, *en passant*, that the thinking man will ask 'need for what?' and realise that the implied answer is 'need for American protection') and for dangerous 'hawkish' cold war, super-power obsessions which will engulf us all in unnecessary and disastrous conflict. (Students of international and financial diplomacy will immediately recognise the parallel series of 'Catch-22s' thrown at the United States whenever the dollar is strengthening or weakening, its economy expanding or contracting, its overseas payments in surplus or deficit, its interest rates high or low.)

The other pieces on foreign affairs, specifically two speeches on Anglo-American relations given in 1977 and 1978 by the author as Ambassador to the United States, are included for interest as a reflection of the theme of 'new realism' which informed the constant story told on Britain's behalf in America at that time. Since the phrase 'the new realism' was later adopted by Mrs Thatcher, after she became Prime Minister, this provides some further illustration of the author's belief that the supposed profound differences between governments and parties which the 'sports commentator' school of political writer delights to invent bear almost no relation to the reality and continuity of the substance of government policies and actions. It will be noted that all the virtues of financial 'realism' and monetary discipline which have since become associated, whether as virtues or vices, with the post-1979 government were in fact strongly, centrally and officially celebrated as the key elements in the economic strategy of the previous government.

Students of the footnotes of history may care also to note the full context of the notorious 'Moses' gaffe committed by the author in his inaugural address to the National Press Club in the summer of 1977. It speaks volumes about the characteristic sloppiness of British journalism, to say nothing of the irrevocability of such gaffes once they have been uttered, that the author was derisively chided by such eminent commentators as Mr Paul Johnson at the time for having perpetrated an analogy between the then Prime Minister and the prophet Moses without realising that the prophet Moses never actually made it out of the desert into the promised land, when it will be apparent to the reader that that was the whole point that the author was making in the speech, namely that there was much to be said for a national leader who was prepared to work and plan for a national renewal even though its probable maturity would occur so long after the period in which it could be of any possible political benefit to its architect. It has made the author reflect sympathetically on the fate of those (such as his father who perpetrated the phrase, 'the man in Whitehall knows best', Mr Harold Macmillan who coined the phrase 'we have never had it so good' and Mr Harold Wilson who said that 'the pound in your pocket is not devalued') who have become notorious for supposedly expressing a sentiment which was in fact the precise opposite of the main point they were making in the context in which these phrases were used. The phrase, it is evident, is well noted and long remembered, while the point being made is instantly forgotten.

The section on journalism again tries to tackle basic issues, in particular the structural defects of television journalism and the philosophical and ethical conundra involved in the question, in its broadest sense, 'what is news?'. The latter essay is, in the author's opinion, probably the most substantial in the volume. It is, in consequence, very abstract and conceptual. Readers may wonder how all that relates, if at all, to the author's own experiences and involvement, as a manager, in the launch of breakfast-time television on Independent Television, since the melo-dramatic events surrounding the early 'on air' days of TV-am received a degree of public attention way beyond their rather modest merits, though the author has no complaint against the healthy British longing to see the high and the mighty slip on a banana skin. This question is discussed in the one new essay in this volume, on 'The Lessons of TV-am'.

Because 'What is News?' attempts to deal with timeless questions of the definition and status of news and of the 'facts' which supposedly constitute it, as well as with the perennial moral issues of the editor's and journalist's duties to these facts, to his readers, to his profession and to society, because also it does so at rather great length and because, finally, the essay, as a lecture, was composed comparatively recently, it needs no updating or amplification in this Introduction.

Some commentary is, however, needed on the third substantial essay in the section on journalism. It is the author's 1981 MacTaggart Lecture given at the Edinburgh International Television Festival, entitled 'Electronic Publishing', and was in its turn based on – and in parts reproduced the arguments used in – the author's evidence half a decade earlier to the Annan Committee. Although the evidence in its earlier form was published in *Encounter* in 1977, it received very little attention, chiefly because it focused on the – to the author – revolutionary potential of cable technology for broadcasting by the end of the century, whereas in the mid 1970s the main debate was focused on what should be done with the fourth broadcast channel, which was expected to be available by the end of that decade.

It seemed to the author more rational to consider what the position would or could be by the end of the century, when there could be close to an infinity of channels and then to work back to decisions about the 1980s in the light of that longer range perspective. The alternative, and indeed the customary practice, was for rival pressure groups and interest groups to squabble with one another over the spoils of each new channel as it became available, one by one, without regard to any coherent picture of where it was all supposed to be leading. This was, however, an isolated point of view in the mid 1970s. So, when the author was invited to deliver the MacTaggart Lecture in 1981 – and with absolutely no foreknowledge that Government and Whitehall would by the end of that year have put the whole issue of cable and satellite developments firmly on the agenda of national debate, to be followed by rapid authorisation of cable and satellite experiments – he decided to make a further attempt to raise what he still believed was the most important and exciting medium-term prospect for broadcasting, namely the real possibility not much beyond the horizon of what he called 'free electronic publishing'.

That phrase simply meant a world, modelled on a somewhat idealised version of the free print publishing market, where the only decision-makers about what was and what was not 'broadcast' were risk-taking creators on the one side (publishers and authors) and paying consumers (the viewing public) on the other. In this way it would become possible, as it was also in the author's opinion manifestly desirable, to eliminate all other illegitimate fingers in the pie, namely politicians and bureaucrats, QUANGO regulators, unrepresentative producer lobbies, equally unrepresentative viewer pressure groups, broadcast unions and monopoly corporations. This emancipation would not exclude the application to electronic publishing of the same general laws as might also be applied to print publishing (on such matters as libel, sedition, blasphemy, obscenity, privacy, national security etc.). Nor would it prevent governments from subsidising explicitly any particular forms of publication which it judged to be socially beneficial (e.g. news, education and religion) and for which it was willing to pay and to account to parliament.

Two conditions were identified as necessary in order to inaugurate this transformation of Britain's closely regulated and cosy broadcasting scene, namely the creation of a national cable grid capable of carrying an effectively limitless number of channels (at least as many channels as home receivers) and a system of variable price charging at the point of consumption (similar to the method of charging for telephone calls at variable tariffs). The author's message was that this was possible by the end of the century and that it was desirable, but also that it would have to be fought for fiercely, just as the emancipation of the printing press from church, state, privileged crafts and special interests had had to be fought for over the previous three hundred years.

The author did not expect this message to be received with other than horror by the barons of the industry. Nor was he blind to the fact that he was himself at that time a mini-baron (? baron-ette) of a mini-monopoly in consequence of TV-am's success, under the rules of the 'licenced broadcasting' regulatory system, in winning a national breakfast-time franchise. But, as he said, there seemed no incompatibility whatever between operating in the here-and-now according to the rules which society had established and at the same time arguing that in the future those rules could and should be changed for the benefit of society, all the more so since it would not be possible or even sensible to dismantle the system of licenced broadcasting until a sufficiently large investment had been made in new technology to fulfil the two essential conditions for free electronic publishing set out above. These – freedom of entry into the system for any publisher and author prepared to finance the risk and variable price payment by viewers at the point of consumption – could not be physically established, even if the necessary large investment decisions were made, much before the end of the century.

As with other attempts that the author has made (e.g. see the essays in this section on 'The Bias Against Understanding', the essays in the political economy section on the 'Crisis for Political Economy in the West', the essay in the same section on 'A Select Committee on Economic Affairs' and the essay in the international affairs section on 'Regionalism as Geopolitics') to propose radical departures from existing and well-established ideas and power structures, the first reaction was as usual a polite attempt to pretend that one had never said it: 'very interesting, but of course quite impractical . . .' ; 'a nice theory, but quite unrealistic . . .' ; 'logically impeccable, but pragmatically inconceivable . . .' ; 'I agree with your analysis of the problem, but I am not at all sure about the remedy . . .'. The second stage of this process is usually silence for a year or two, followed in the third stage by the original idea resurfacing all over the place as the fashionable opinion, until finally it becomes first the conventional wisdom, then the accepted basis for change and, finally, a new dogma of its own.

In the case of 'free electronic publishing' this standard progression was compressed and accelerated by the government's action (or in-advertence) in leaking a substantial Whitehall discussion paper to *The Economist*, whose excellent report made it suddenly clear that – to the horror of the barons of the industry – the government itself, or at least those within it who were concerned with developing information technology in Britain, had every intention of moving rapidly in at least some of the directions suggested by the author. Then – and this is typical of Britain's craven deference to government in all matters of national evolution – the issues, which had been studiously ignored for the previous half decade and more, suddenly became matters of urgent and pressing debate. Amongst the sourest of the ironies were the endless complaints that the matter was being rushed without full and proper discussion, this from the very people who had cynically and sedulously resisted or ignored all attempts to develop the issues in calm and rational debate well in advance of the opportunity to exploit the new technologies when they became available.

This is not the place to carry the story further forward through the report of the Hunt Committee and the government's eventual decisions on the early stages of cable in Britain, some of which are still awaited at the time of writing. It is enough to observe that in two key respects there seems every prospect that the government, in its preoccupation with employment and investment in information technology rather than with the long-term goal of free electronic publishing (despite the Hunt Committee's endorsement of the 'electronic bookshop' concept), will now fatally jeopardise the direction of future developments at this decisive formative stage. First, they are failing to insist that all early cable installations be compatible with and contributory towards the eventual creation of a comprehensive national fibre-optic grid capable of carrying a near-infinity of channels, without which there can be no freedom of access to all new suppliers. Secondly, they are failing to place adequate emphasis on variable price charging at the point of consumption on the model of telephone charging, without which there can be no true and sensitive consumer sovereignty. Without these two features the experiments will tell us little and lead us nowhere.

The essays on 'The Bias Against Understanding', jointly prepared with John Birt, are included mainly for historical interest, since they had an important impact on the development of news and current affairs in Britain, not only in the organisations with which the authors were directly connected (London Weekend Television and TV-am), but also permeating the BBC, ITN, Channel 4 and other broadcasters. As explained above, a much fuller development of the philosophical basis for the argument is given in 'What is News?'. The original phrase was John Birt's. Its heir, 'The Mission to Explain', was coined by the author on 24 September 1980, on the spur of the moment during a short speech about breakfast television at a public meeting in Croydon. The author's reflections on the subsequent fate of both were briefly given in a letter to

The Times on 4 October 1983, which is reproduced here:

Sir,

Derrik Mercer, in his otherwise excellent article (*The Times*, 30 September) writes:

'As with the more public blood-letting at TV-am, it is the fate of the much-vaunted "mission to explain" that lifts the internal melodrama into something of public consequence.

'It must have seemed so easy in the mid-1970s when Peter Jay and John Birt, now programme controller at London Weekend Television, coined the phrase that came to haunt Jay at TV-am.'

There are three misconceptions here:

(a) the 'internal melodrama' was logically and historically unconnected with the 'mission to explain' (or any other objective programme or business consideration) and should not be dignified as of 'public consequence' by bogus association with such serious ideas;

(b) it did not seem at all easy in the mid seventies to challenge the most cherished preconceptions of the 'green eye-shade and suede-jacket' establishment of television news-and-current-affairs, with its twin inheritance of reflexes from the Gateshead news desk and from Hollywood; and

(c) I am not at all haunted by the phrase (though I would rather people remembered that I always coupled it with 'an equal mission to entertain', that I always spoke of 'a *popular* daily newspaper of the air' and that the model I always cited was Sydney Jacobson's *Daily Mirror*), only by our failure in the first few weeks even to try to make the kind of programmes we had talked about and the undeserved damage which this failure caused to the careers of many excellent and dedicated people – presenters, reporters, technicians, salesmen and others – whose fault it absolutely was not.

The reasons why at TV-am, instead of Jacobson's vigorous and intelligent *Mirror*, we got *The Guardian* without the flair, are too tedious – and too painful – to explain here. Suffice it to say that the captain of the ship should accept, did accept and does accept the blame – for being so preoccupied with the business, sales and operations parts of his ship that he failed till battle was joined to realize sufficiently what was happening (and not happening) in programmes.

What matter now are the lessons for programme-makers. Just as set out in the mid seventies, these are that the idea is valid, that it needs the right resources and that, like most successful long-running television news shows, it needs time (usually a year or two) for success so that the product can be fine-tuned and the public can be accustomed to it.

Derrik Mercer had neither resources, nor time. TV-am (mark one) had resources, but failed to try to implement its mission and, anyway, had almost no time at all. 'Newsnight' has had some pooled news-and-current-affairs resources, has had time – as well as talented pioneers like George Carey and Peter Snow – and has therefore deserved its increasing success.

This letter is quoted here for its relevance to the subsequent experience of the broad ideas discussed in 'The Bias Against Understanding' and 'What is News?' essays. The specific references to the TV-am story are developed more fully in the TV-am essay, 'The Dawn of TV-am'.

The personal and philosophical section is inevitably a rag bag.

The final essay in the volume is sheer self-indulgence, reflecting the author's amateur interest in sailing. But it has one serious theme, which does connect with many of the heavier arguments in the other essays, namely that, when there has been a great failure or disaster, it makes every sense to study and analyse it carefully; but it does not always follow that it makes sense to introduce regulations and controls to ensure that that particular disaster can never happen again. Some acceptance of some disasters, where they have a sufficiently low probability of repetition, will lead to a higher state of human well-being, since the effects of the controls and regulations needed to prevent such a repetition themselves impose a greater loss of well-being than would repetition of the disaster at its probable rate of frequency. In other words, the cure can be worse than the disease. This platitude, however clichéd, frequently needs emphasis and repetition when in the wake of a misfortune all the pressure of press comment and bureaucratic reflexes are for action to 'bolt the stable door', not because this is shown to be useful, but simply as an atonement for what has occurred. The rational spirit and the free spirit should fight against it.

'Our Civilisation', though published in 1970, is an aggressively self-confident assertion of 1960s philosophy and is, again, included mainly for historical interest. Its inclusion also provides an excuse here for a few concluding and thoroughly personal reflections on our times and their changing temper over the quarter century in which these essays were written. At a time when even among intellectuals 'Victorian values' (whether or not there ever was a historical period in which such values were widely practised) are being restored to fashion – and with them the emphasis on authority, on self-denial and self-help, on fear as a salutory and legitimate weapon, on religion, on moral superstition and on 'great little England' nationalism – it is perhaps worth being reminded that there was not so long ago a more expansive and self-confident time (however unsound its economic foundations) when Reason was king and Hope was its queen, when rational argument and common humanity were the only accepted criteria for defining values and charting behaviour and when no man needed to tug his forelock to any person, institution or code which could not base its legitimacy on a reasoned demonstration of its probable contribution to mankind's greater happiness or lesser misery.

These were, to that extent, wonderful days – for all that there was much of pure frivolity and callow love of novelty in the froth and spume of that great breaking wave. The arguments were tough and difficult and their disciplines exacting. But at least in prosecuting them the only thing one had to worry about was getting the argument right – the logic and the facts. There was no need to fear extra-rational reprisals like social censure for non-conformity, like unemployment for questioning authority or like being black-listed simply for holding private political convictions.

An economic determinist would doubtless look for the explanation for this collapse of intellectual self-confidence – and with it the flight from sophistication in economic and social debate, from social conscience and global responsibility, from generosity and magnanimity in human dealings and from serious interest in exciting vistas of amelioration, indeed from hope for progress at all – in the manifest failure of the economy, not merely to deliver the high aspirations of growth nurtured twenty-five years ago, but even to sustain the minimal necessary conditions of economic and political stability in the form of simultaneous price stability and employment stability. Indeed, it is probably true that, when times are bad, fear predominates over hope. The immediate danger predominates over the eventual achievement. The self (and by extension the selfish concerns of one's own family, group and nation) predominates over the common good and the global need. The spectre of authority, both intellectual and institutional, looms more menacingly.

If, despite the essay 'Who's Left, What's Right', there is any political meaning at all to the terms 'left' and 'right', it is perhaps as names for those clusters of human values which tend to predominate, on the one hand, in times of optimism and, on the other hand, in times of pessimism. Certainly, as argued above in this Introduction, these terms have no coherence as classifications of political policies, positions and parties. But there may be some validity in the generalisation that, when dark threats to survival and to prosperity loom more imminently, then cynicism eclipses generosity, scepticism denies idealism, justice has no room for mercy, individualism displaces mutuality, realism frowns on romanticism, the short term becomes the only term, the fittest trample upon the best, vulgarity sneers at cultivation, authority overrides argument, tradition and habit are preferred to inquiry and experiment; and no one rocks the boat. That in short is how the ignominy of the 1970s transformed the hope of the 1960s into the fear of the 1980s.

But there is a paradox. Harking back to the earlier passage in this Introduction about the proper separation of the world of parties and elections on the one hand from the world of policies and government on the other, one could find few clearer illustrations of the irrelevance of electoral ideologies and of the importance of facts and fashion in swaying the fate of nations than the twenty-five years in which these essays were written. For, they embrace the 'twenty years of the two Harolds' (Macmillan and Wilson), the studied flippancy of whose manipulations did so much to destroy the credibility and dignity of national leadership, to be followed by the stark – and much needed – contrast of the 'new realism' (see essay on Anglo-American relations) of the Callaghan-Thatcher years. These were also years, in economics, which saw the hubris of the 'Balliol years' (from 1968 to 1975), when Messrs Jenkins, Heath and Healey believed that central management of the economy, allied to political centrism and tripartite industrial corporatism, could square the circles of inflation, unemployment and growth, displaced from 1976 by the conspicuous modesty and candour of Callaghan's monetarism and Thatcher's TINA ('there is no alternative'). The evidence of moral and intellectual improvement in national leadership may seem to contradict the assertion of moral and intellectual retreat in the nation at large.

And yet . . . and yet . . . one can have been disgusted by the frivolity of the style and methods of the era of the two Harolds and welcome the return to dignity and seriousness under Callaghan and Thatcher; one can have distrusted and disliked the arrogance of the Balliol swashbucklers and welcome the honesty and realism of Callaghan and Thatcher; and yet, still, one can bitterly regret the tawdriness, the sourness, the meanness, the vulgarity and the narrowness of the spirit of the 1980s, which has arisen like some misshapen phoenix – and which holds sway far beyond the confines of politics and economics – as an undeniable reaction to the disillusionment with failure, which was the inheritance of the late sixties and early seventies.

Apologists for the eighties, or at least for their ugly necessity, may argue that it is inconsistent to sigh for the spirit of the sixties, when it was precisely the illusions fostered by the sixties which led to the disillusionment of the seventies and the bitter reaction of the eighties. But this is too fast and too glib. The style of 'the two Harolds' and the *hauteur* of the Balliol men were not inevitable. Nor were they either logically or politically a necessary condition or a consequence of the broader intellectual and personal enlightenment of the sixties. They were, like most things, historical accidents; and, overhanging it all, they leave those persistent romantics who, like the author, still believe that the spirit of the sixties was right, that hard-heads and warm-hearts can inhabit the same frame and that the great human political and economic problems of global and national co-existence and amelioration have not gone away simply because it is no longer fashionable to address them, with the haunting and agonising, though also useless and unanswerable question 'what, if Gaitskell had won in 1959 and lived in 1963 . . .?'

But it is certainly not the overall purpose of these essays to call back the past. On the contrary they are in almost every case proposing radical departures which would take us even further from the political, economic and global patterns of the past, including the sixties, though not necessarily in the same direction that has been travelled in the last twenty years. But for there even to be a chance to move in a worthwhile and rationally determined direction, let alone bold and original ones, it will first be necessary to throw off the paralysing fear of the eighties, to trample down the sudden new undergrowth of smirking vulgarity and indolent cynicism in the place of the intellect and to restore the decent ideals of meticulous thought and benign action as worthy occupations for the intellectual.

December 1983

Political Economy

A General Hypothesis of
Employment, Inflation and Politics

During my eight short years as a newspaperman I have steadfastly and heatedly resisted the notion of journalists undertaking academic and quasi-academic tasks. By whatever composition of general conviction and personal idleness I have been unswervingly persuaded that the writing of learned books, articles and indeed lectures should be left to those who are in fact learned and who have mastered the craft of scholarly inquiry. I have no illusion that I belong to their number; and I have not the slightest doubt that I shall live to regret, very shortly, having been deflected on this occasion from the principles of a lifetime.

In allowing myself to be overpersuaded against my better judgement I was influenced by two thoughts: first, that it was perhaps not for me to substitute my opinions for those of the trustees of the Wincott Foundation and that it would be they, not I, who would be accountable for any manifest error in the choice of Wincott lecturer; and, secondly, that Harold Wincott, whom we honour today, was after all himself a journalist and in that capacity demonstrated over a lifetime of enormous distinction that the newspaper profession, even if in a general way neither learned nor rigorous, need not be ignoble and could occasionally be vouchsafed flashes of contemporary insight. Few can expect to achieve the eminence and authority of a Harold Wincott, distinctions which he also delightfully combined with a talent for entertainment for which he was much loved and admired by his many friends and by his even more numerous readers.

I, alas, never knew Harold Wincott personally; but I was a frequent reader of his memorable columns in the *Financial Times*. I must be honest and admit that I do not actually remember ever reading a column of his with which I agreed; but then I was in those days a youngish man who still believed in the at least theoretical possibility of benign government, a belief which was of course powerfully reinforced in my mind by the knowledge that my own indispensable advice was constantly available at that time at the Treasury. Now, of course, I am wiser; and anyway the Treasury has for eight, and in that context long, years been deprived of the inestimable asset to which I have referred.

A man of middle years tends to gravitate towards the disillusioned view that 'nothing works'; and a certain measure of discount must be applied to the scepticism of people in my stage of life. I look forward, of course, to attaining the more sapient maturity of those of an older generation, some of the most distinguished specimens of which are to be found in the Bank of England, whose position can best be summarised in the proposition: 'You cannot be absolutely sure that nothing works'. Meanwhile, I would ask you to forgive these and other shortcomings of what follows, bearing in mind that it is as best a newspaperman's essay with no pretensions to academic learning. I would ask you to regard what is asserted as being advanced as a hypothesis and not as a proven theory. If it has any plausibility, then others better qualified than I may wish to test it and modify it.

We in Britain are a confused and unhappy people. So are those of our fellows on the continent of Western Europe who have their wits about them. So too are our many friends in the United States who rightly see in the anguish of the United Kingdom the advanced stages of a disease which has already taken hold throughout Western Europe and which is beginning to show its unmistakable symptoms in America.

There may or may not be anything we can do about the grounds for our unhappiness which, as things stand, are thoroughly well founded. But there is no need to be confused. We can at least understand better than many of us do the basis of our morbidity, even if this requires some acutely painful reassessments of cherished institutions and values.

We are unhappy because the foundations of our prosperity seem to be being eroded faster and faster and because we can neither find nor agree upon any sure remedy for this decay. We are confused because we do not clearly understand why all this is happening to us, whether it is due to the malefactions of subversive groups, the incompetence of governments, the errors of economists, the defects of national character, the rhythms of history, the luck of the draw or what.

The search for someone to blame adds to the confusion and the bitterness. Government and governed become more and more alienated from one another. The governors believe the governed to be irretrievably greedy, feckless, idle and recalcitrant, while the governed believe the governors to be stupid, corrupt, power-crazed, self-seeking and unrepresentative. Likewise, class is set against class – the middle classes denouncing the rapacity of the workers while the workers rail at the privileges and the hypocrisy of the better off.

In Britain area is set against area; and separatism gains steady support in Ulster, in Scotland, in Wales and, by reaction, in England itself. Only the Labour Party can any longer claim a vestige of nationwide support; and even the Labour Party could not get even thirty percent of the potential electorate to support it in 1974. And, but for London and Bristol, the Labour Party would be almost unrepresented from the whole of the south of England.

The fissures spread out in all directions like an ice-fall: disintegration in slow motion. Labour unions, business management and City financiers are locked in a triangle of mutual vituperation and incomprehension. Union leaders point to the lack of investment in productive industry. Industrialists complain that the capital markets and the banks do not support them because their time-horizons are too short and their understanding of industry negligible. And the investors ask how they can be expected to put up capital when the unions pre-empt all, or more than all, the potential return on new plant and equipment.

Weak labour unions with low-paid members loudly support same-all-round ceilings on pay increases while their brothers in strongly entrenched industrial positions with higher-paid workers stoutly defend their 'differentials' and angrily compare their lot to the standards enjoyed by bloated capitalists, whom they still imagine to be living like a caricature of a nineteenth-century railway baron – not always wrongly. The media criticise everyone and everything; and almost everyone blames the media for the lack of national unanimity and commitment.

It is an unedifying spectacle and an unprofitable arrangement. Nor does it touch at any point on the true causes of the problem. These causes are deep-seated and general, embedded in the very organisation of our society. They are also complex and abstract. Therefore they are little perceived; and they consequently cannot compete with the more readily intelligible, concrete and enjoyable sport of exposing 'guilty men' and baiting those who are in what is supposed to be 'power'.

There are, of course, no guilty men; and none has any real power. All are corks tossed on the same tempest; and, if some corks are noisier, fatter or uglier than others, that does not mean they have any command over the elements. Let us look then to the pressure systems which determine the storms that throw up the waves which so distress us. For, if we are ever to come to harbour, the recrimination will have to stop and a way will have to be found of riding the waves and of using the winds to our own constructive purposes.

The political and economic organisation of modern industrial societies is founded on the idea of the satisfaction of individual wants as the highest, indeed the only valid, good. However unhistorical this assertion may be, except perhaps in the United States, it still represents the nearest approximation to a widely accepted moral basis of political economy in the liberal and social democracies.

How are we to establish what individuals want? By asking them. How are we to ensure that they get what they want, at least as far as possible? By letting them make the decisions. How do we arrange that? By letting them elect their governments and by letting them spend their money in a free competitive market-place.

This engagingly simple political philosophy may indeed have been a valuable antidote to the depredations practised on mankind by other authoritarian and paternalist regimes in the name of goods higher and other than what the individual thinks he wants. But, alas, it already has built into it the tension – historicists might say the contradiction – which lies at the root of our present troubles.

For, the question of the frontier between the domain of government and the domain of market-place is begged. More precisely – and following the insights of the great Austrian economist, Joseph Schumpeter – two market-places are created which operate in heavily overlapping areas according to quite different and frequently incompatible criteria.

The political arena is a market-place in votes. Rival teams organise themselves to win a majority or at least a plurality of support so that they can exercise power. The only cost to voting for one team is that you cannot vote for another. The teams naturally and inevitably seek to outbid each other by offering more of whatever they think the voters want. There is no mechanism which requires the bids to be internally consistent or which forces voters to balance more of one good against more of another.

The economic arena is – or at least supposedly starts out as – a market-place in money. But here the individual chooses quite differently. He makes small decisions all the time instead of one big decision every few years. Each decision is marginal, to spend his next penny on a little more of this rather than a little more of that. He does not have to pledge all of his income for the next few years to one of a short list of comprehensive packages.

This subjects those who compete for the consumers' favours to quite different incentives from those of the ballot-box. The political entrepreneur must ask himself what people want most. Intensity of wants becomes all-important where the person choosing has to give up something – namely the claim on alternative goods which money represents – each time he chooses.

Secondly, in the economic case the coin in which the chooser casts his vote – the money he pays for his purchases – is also the resource, or at least a claim on the resource, which the supplier needs to continue and maybe to expand the process of supply. In the political case, while votes are the basis of power, they are not the material which power uses. The command over the resources of power comes from the taxing power which is awarded by a plurality of votes. There is no mechanism for ensuring that a plurality of votes implies a commitment by the voters of the quantum of resources needed to fulfil the programme on which the winning political team has won an election.

The pure market-place requires the citizen to exercise his choice and to commit the resources needed to fulfil it in the single act of purchase whereby he parts with his money. This essential feature of the price-mechanism, together with the assumption that individuals will normally seek their own best economic advantage as both consumers and suppliers, is the foundation of liberal economics.

It is the 'hidden hand' which economists since Adam Smith have recognised as the built-in guarantee not only of consistency in economic choices, but also of the optimal matching of available resources to individual wants. Of course everyone is familiar with a thousand and one different ways in which the process does not operate or is prevented from operating in this idealised fashion. Perhaps the most widely quoted of these defects is that purchasing power is unequal and must necessarily be so, post-tax as well as pre-tax, if incomes are to perform their economic function as market rewards for services rendered or risks taken. These imperfections have provided the political pretext, though not the main motive, for intervention by government in the economic domain. It is not necessary here to review the vast literature on the proper scope for and limits upon such intervention. Suffice it to say that there is nothing in the operation of the political market-place which requires that those limits be observed.

Indeed, the essence of democratic politics is a gigantic celebration of the fact that you *can* get something for nothing, or at least that *you* – the individual voter – can get something for nothing, even if as the ancients had it *ex nihilo nihil fit*. For, government, with its legalised powers of coercion, can award benefits here while it charges the costs there. That indeed is the whole nature of the redistribution of wealth and income, an almost universally accepted function of government.

The point here is not to question the legitimacy of this aspect of the political process, but to emphasise that it is a process without any sensitive or automatic regulator. In the very long run indeed, it may be argued, societies would discover that it did not pay them to sacrifice too much of the market – or incentive – functions of incomes to the cause of equality or 'fairness'; but any such feed-back is problematic, slow-operating and highly uncertain.

Nowhere is the feed-back more problematic and less certain than in the central manifestation of the conflict between the different logics of political and economic choice, namely in the relationship between unemployment and inflation. Since Keynes, since the War, since the British *Employment Policy* White Paper of 1944 and since the American Employment Act of 1946 a pledge of full employment has been an indispensable ingredient in any bid by any political party for electoral victory.

After the experiences of the 1930s almost every voter – or so all politicians have agreed in assuming – has regarded the avoidance of mass unemployment as an overriding political objective. After the writings of Keynes and even more after the simplified popularisation of his writings and their endorsement by government, the politicians and the public have also assumed that the means of securing high employment always lay to hand.

Whenever unemployment looked like rising to politically embarrassing levels – and the threshold of embarrassment was extremely low by previous historical standards – the method was to put more spending power into people's pockets, whether by cutting taxes, increasing government spending or easing credit conditions through monetary policy. It was recognised that one might, in theory, go too far in this direction, overheat the economy and cause inflation.

But it was not doubted that there was a safe zone in which something approaching full employment could be maintained without running risks of serious inflation. The exact trade-off within that zone between degrees of full employment and degrees of price stability were thought to be described by a stable relationship known as the 'Phillips curve'.

The economic realities were unhappily different. The belief that, outside the narrow range of the Phillips curve, the regulation of spending power (known as 'demand management') uniquely affected price levels or uniquely affected employment levels, according to whether the pressure of demand was above or below the full employment zone, was false in the long-term and therefore dangerously misleading in the short-term.

The truth was that in the short-term – for the first year or two – demand management mainly affects the real volume of spending, output and so employment while in the longer run it only affects the price level. The notion inherent in the popular understanding of Keynes that an economy could be indefinitely under-employed through deficient demand without prices eventually being forced down sufficiently to clear markets, including the labour market, was a dangerous misunderstanding of the unhappy experiences of the 1930s.

Nonetheless, the belief was almost universal in British economic circles and increasingly predominant in American and Continental European circles that, provided actual overheating of the economy was avoided (and with it 'overfull employment'), budget deficits and the associated expansion of the money supply could be used more or less without limit to head off an incipient rise in unemployment. At the same time there were objective reasons why unemployment was likely to rise rather above the levels regarded as 'full employment' even in the absence of any positively deflationary actions by government and central bank. These were barely recognised and little understood.

They were and are of two kinds: the general imperfections of the labour market; and the operation of what is variously known as 'free collective bargaining' or as 'trade union monopoly bargaining'.

Imperfections of the labour market include anything which has the effect that job-seekers and job-vacancies are not instantly matched to one another. As the pattern of demand and the techniques of supply constantly evolve, different kinds of workers are required by different entrepreneurs in different places. It takes time to convert some workers from one role to another. Others can never be converted and have to be replaced by a new and differently trained generation.

There is a real personal cost in moving location. This makes workers willing to remain, sometimes indefinitely, unemployed rather than take work in a far away place. The natural reluctance to pull up the roots of the family, friendship and all the familiarities of 'home' can be aggravated when, as in Britain, public authority housing works in such a way that a valuable asset in the form of title to very low rent accommodation is automatically forfeit upon the occupier moving to another district.

And there are a thousand and one other major and minor frictions which normally result in a degree of mismatch, at any moment in time, between labour force and work opportunities. This mismatch cannot but be reflected in a margin of the workforce being out of work, or at least between jobs, at any one time. How large that margin is will, of course, also depend on the capital endowment of industry and on its rate of change in relation to the rate of change of the skills of the workforce.

This margin may, as Professor Milton Friedman likes to do, be called the 'natural' rate of unemployment, although this should not be taken to mean that it is established by any law of nature. It is just a catch phrase for all the circumstances *other than the manipulation of monetary demand by governments* which influence the level of unemployment.

The role of free collective bargaining may be regarded either as a second and separate reason why conventional post-war full employment policies were incompatible with price stability – or indeed with a stable rate of inflation – or it can be seen as a special case of the first general reason. The latter way of putting it emphasises the monopolistic character of collective bargaining by labour unions. The effect of charging a monopoly price for labour must inevitably be to reduce 'sales', i.e. employment, below the market-clearing level. Some people will get paid more than they would under perfect competition in the labour market; but others will not get jobs at all.

The effect, therefore, of a widespread pattern of monopolistic bargaining in the labour market will be to increase the numbers unemployed, in other words to raise the 'natural' rate of unemployment. This, as has often been pointed out, is in itself a once-and-for-all effect.

But, like the once-and-for-all effects of other labour market imperfections, it gives rise to an accelerating, indeed eventually explosive, rate of inflation when it is combined with a government commitment to maintain, by demand-management, a lower level of unemployment than the natural level which corresponds to these structural impediments to labour supply. As soon as the higher 'natural' level begins to develop government rushes in with injections of additional spending power, whether by fiscal or monetary means.

The first effect of this is to raise the demand for labour and temporarily to arrest or reverse the rise in unemployment. But before long the overstretching of the labour market in relation to the reserve of unemployed labour which is needed for it to function without strain begins to force prices up (or, in the case of collective bargaining, begins to allow the monopoly price of labour to be raised still further). The real spending power of money incomes is thus eroded; and economic activity begins to fall back to the level which corresponds to the natural level of unemployment.

Whereupon government is forced to intervene again with another injection of extra spending power. Before long consumers and pay bargainers, indeed everyone involved in the economy, get used to continuing inflation. It becomes built into their expectations; and so the stimulative effects of any given amount of governmental 'reflation' are discounted and so eroded. Governments then begin to have to increase the dose; and there is no end to this process of trying to keep the actual inflation rate permanently ahead of constantly catching-up expectations, until the stage of hyper-inflation and breakdown is reached.

It is not strictly necessary, however, to express the role of free collective bargaining by labour unions as a special case of the natural rate of unemployment hypothesis. More simply, it can be said that in anything short of a total buyers' market for labour – which would imply a level of unemployment many times greater than any post-war government has ever contemplated – labour monopolies can progressively force up the price of labour.

Since there is no corresponding increase in the value of output, the extra claims on the available resources have to be neutralised by rising prices, which then become the basis for the next round of any pay claims. It may well be that the sum of all the monopoly pay claims, expressed in terms of the real purchasing power demanded, is greater than the national output available to satisfy them. In that case equilibrium in the short-term can only be maintained by inflation continuously running ahead of the inflationary expectations of the pay bargainers or by the labour monopolies being permitted to price themselves out of their jobs until they are deterred from further exercise of their market power.

Since governments are pledged not to let the second happen, they are forced to choose the other horn of the dilemma and to inflate at an accelerating rate. This 'dilemma hypothesis' is really much the same as the first 'natural rate' hypothesis. For, it critically depends on the assumption of a government commitment to a degree of full employment that is not compatible with the real level of reward which labour is determined to award itself. Only in this way can either hypothesis explain how a once-and-for-all influence such as monopoly bargaining power produces a dynamic and unstable phenomenon like accelerating and eventually explosive inflation.

Surely, it will be said, Western democracy is not going to wreck itself on such an absurd and obvious nonsense. Unfortunately, it probably will, at least on the eastern side of the Atlantic. The problem is only beginning to be recognised very late in the day because it operates transcyclically rather than intracyclically.

Public attention has been and largely remains focused on the intracyclical ebbs and flows of output, employment and inflation. This has enabled lay people and even some economists constantly to deceive themselves that the prevailing economic evil of the moment – inflation, unemployment or balance of payments deficit – is always about to be cured. They have not noticed that from cycle to cycle the relationship between these alternative expressions of the unattainability of 'full employment' has been deteriorating.

It takes more and more inflation (or bigger and bigger balance of payments deficits, which are in some circumstances an inflation substitute) to achieve – or, more often, to fail to achieve – any given employment level. This evidence has been overlooked because we have all been watching the ends of the see-saw go up and down, thus having our attention distracted from the fact that the fulcrum on which the whole contraption rests is sinking steadily into the ground.

Even if and when the danger is fully appreciated it is far from clear that the right action will be possible. The logic of ballot-box choice enables us, indeed almost forces us, to vote for full employment without thereby also voting for the means to achieve it, which must include a willingness to sell one's own labour at a market-clearing price. Even that would not be enough. Everyone else would have to be committed to such individual bargaining; and that would imply the end of collective bargaining and therefore of labour unions in their main historic role.

It would further be necessary to vote for other measures which would reduce the 'natural' level of unemployment until it coincided with our chosen definition of full employment. This would certainly include in Britain an end to subsidised municipal housing (total multilateral transferability of low-rent entitlements being in practice impossible).

It would mean also voting for many other things which, of their nature, make no direct appeal. Since there is, moreover, no mechanism which forces parties to seek support for, or voters to endorse, the means to stated economic aims, there is no political reason why accelerating inflation should be halted, even though, as may well be the case, the voters in the mass dislike inflation-for-all more than they dislike unemployment-for-the-one-in-ten. Even the statesman who fully perceives the nature of the dilemma is debarred from campaigning accordingly. He knows – or thinks he knows – that this would be the road to political extinction, which, as he will say, solves nothing.

Likewise, the fully intelligent citizen is debarred from voting for an option which no party puts forward. Even if the fully perceptive statesman and the fully intelligent voter could somehow establish contact, it is still not certain that it would be rational for the voter to support the statesman. The voter may fear the certainty of a deep and prolonged recession for three or four years more than he fears the eventual crash to which he knows traditional policies must one day lead.

The problem then is that the logic of ballot-box choice does not coincide with, and almost certainly contradicts, the logic of economic optimisation. Government is bound to get drawn into roles and programmes which are bound to reduce economic welfare below the otherwise attainable optimum. The full employment–inflation dilemma is only the most important of these because it produces an explosive chain-reaction which is destructive not merely of a finite quantum of welfare, but of the whole system.

Nor is this dilemma in any way solved by political programmes which would seek to command economic variables to behave contrary to their own nature. Incomes policies, however rational and enlightened they may appear when looked at at the macro-level, necessarily become arbitrary and unacceptable when seen at the micro-level; and that is the level at which they are scrutinised by all the individuals on whose consent, outside totalitarian states, such programmes totally depend. Such arbitrariness is occasionally tolerated for a few months in a fit of national fervour; but it never has and never could last longer.

So we reach the depressing conclusion that the operation of free democracy appears to force governments into positions (the commitment to full employment) which prevent them from taking the steps (fiscal and monetary restraint) which are necessary to arrest the menace (accelerating inflation) that threatens to undermine the condition (stable prosperity) on which political stability and therefore liberal democracy depend. In other words democracy has itself by the tail and is eating itself up fast.

There is nothing inevitable, in the absolute sense, about a process which consists entirely of human actions. We could all decide to travel a different route; but that is an extremely difficult thing for people in groups of many millions to do in the absence of a system which reconciles public and private goods and which harmonises the logic of political choice with the logic of economic choice.

If any nation is likely to escape the dilemma, it is the US because it combines a comparatively mild form of the complaint with far and away the toughest political institutions of any Western country. Inflation is more unpopular in the US than in almost any other industrial country, except perhaps West Germany. The American labour market is markedly less cartelised; and there is a very large sector of genuinely individual pay bargaining in the US.

This means that it is more likely that a government can and will find political support for a strong stand against inflation even at the price of several years of high unemployment by post-war standards. It also means – because the going inflation rate is less and pay behaviour will adjust more rapidly to slower growth in spending power that in the highly unionised economies of Western Europe – that the level of unemployment involved will be less.

It further means that political authority will be better able to withstand any given amount of direct revolutionary challenge which a period of economic adversity produces. And finally, there is the still strong ideological commitment of so many Americans to political and economic liberties as something to be defended beyond any short-term calculation of standard of living.

These advantages may well mean that, as the dilemma matures towards the critical choice between a long recession and the final plunge into hyper-inflation, the US will manage to draw back. By the mid or late eighties price stability may, in the US, have been reconciled with a recovering prosperity; and at the same time Congressmen may still be elected every two years, Presidents every four and Senators every six in accordance with an unchanged constitution.

It is hard to be so sanguine about Western Europe, where the economic weakness is greater and where political institutions have shallower foundations. Countries like Britain, which do have a long tradition of political continuity, face the economic dilemma in its most highly developed form.

Countries like West Germany, which have advanced more slowly along the same road, have the weakest political institutions and are, therefore, vulnerable to even a mild degree of economic adversity. Others like Italy have the worst of both worlds. In consequence they have already slipped over the abyss and presumably must soon be dashed on the waiting rocks of political anarchy and economic deprivation.

No mention has been made so far of the 'socialist' alternative. This is much favoured by those in Western Europe who would accept most of the foregoing analysis, but see it as fulfilling the collapse of capitalism rather than the more general collapse of any civilised attempt to combine a high degree of prosperity with a high degree of personal freedom.

Yet, any alternative must either seek to work through the basic principles of liberal economics, acknowledging the role of prices in balancing supply and demand, or try to override them, presumably substituting either commands or spontaneous altruism by all economic units. The first approach must confront the same difficulties as we face now. The second leads in some forms to totalitarianism – and great inefficiency – and in other forms to paradise. Unhappily the only road to paradise which has not yet been proved to lead somewhere quite different lies through the grave.

I had intended to leave the matter there; but further reflection has persuaded me, even at the risk of carrying my hypothesis yet further into the quagmires of speculation, that the argument must be taken a stage further despite the danger that this will lead me to the suggestion that the contradictions of political economy which I have sought to describe may yet be resolvable, at least from the theoretical vantage point of an armchair at the top of an ivory tower.

If I may briefly summarise – at the risk of over-simplifying – the argument so far, it is this. The political economy of which I speak is one in which governments can periodically be dismissed by the vote of the people and in which the labour market is free except insofar as the principal suppliers of labour voluntarily agree from time to time that that freedom shall be modified for a while. In this circumstance – and given general familiarity with the short-term potentialities of deficit finance – the maintenance in the short as well as the longer run of a very high level of employment becomes a political imperative. This can only be achieved at the cost of an accelerating rate of inflation, which must sooner or later destroy either the freedom of the labour market (with or without the consent of the main suppliers of labour) or the high level of employment. Since either or both of these consequences are outside the tolerance of the electorate, no government will be able to satisfy the electorate; and therefore the system of political economy is inherently unstable.

Accelerating inflation, at least where it can only perform its employment-creating function by running ahead of inflationary expectations which are constantly catching up with it and trying to forestall its next acceleration, is of itself unstable as a basis for policy. Therefore the contradiction of existing political economy can only be resolved either by increasing the public's political tolerance of unemployment or by transforming the economic mechanisms which at present face governments with a choice between politically unacceptable unemployment, politically unacceptable interference in the freedom of the labour market and an inherently unstable policy of inflation accelerating, if not *ad infinitum*, at least *ad* Weimar.

Increasing the political tolerance of unemployment appears only to be a formal option. It is inherent in the description already given of the forms and logic of political choice that an indefinite period of high unemployment cannot become the basis of an electorally successful platform.

It is of course possible that the political tolerance of unemployment is higher than is commonly supposed. It certainly appears to be higher today than it was supposed to be four years ago, let alone thirteen and seventeen years ago. There is, of course, also much learned disquisition designed to show that the official unemployment statistics do not accurately measure the degrees of either economic slack or social misery implied by the current state of the economy.

These arguments do not appear to be sufficiently persuasive in this context. If the political tolerance of unemployment is so much higher than is commonly supposed as to be seriously capable of embracing the level that would be necessary permanently to inhibit inflation without any other changes in the structure and competitiveness of the labour market, then we shall find that out soon enough. It is only necessary that during 1976 and 1977 the government refrains from any fiscal or monetary action which would cause either the GNP at current prices or the money supply to rise at a faster rate than is consistent with bringing the rate of inflation down to negligible levels by the unaided force of market pressures within two or three years.

But the practical need is not for a policy which has an outside chance of succeeding against all odds only if every practical man's judgement of practicalities should prove utterly wrong. What is needed is a policy which offers some real prospect of resolving the basic conflicts which give rise to the dilemmas which afflict conventional policy-making. So, betting on a sudden suspension of the democratic demand for high employment, which appears to have operated with ever-increasing power in all major industrialised democracies ever since the War, appears to be more of a gambler's despairing throw than a serious strategy of political economy.

Nor does a solution appear to me to lie in demonstrating that the unemployment figures are wrong. They may well be wrong – in either direction – in the sense that they do not accurately measure things which official statisticians have never claimed that they do measure. But the range of statistical ambiguity is far narrower than the range of economic uncertainty.

It is far better, in the context of the subject of this lecture, to acknowledge that the levels and duration of unemployment with which government is likely to be confronted if it seeks to extinguish inflation by indefinitely refusing to underwrite increases in factor costs by extra fiscal or monetary stimuli, may well be very large indeed according to whatever conceivable measurement of unemployment is used. The proposition here is that the maximum politically tolerable unemployment level is likely to be well below the minimum level – in both quantity and duration – that would be needed to neutralise the impact on labour costs of monopolistic labour supply. No change in the methods of measurement seems likely to close, if indeed it would even reduce, the gap.

One turns therefore to the question whether there is a way of transforming the economic mechanisms which confront government with the present dilemma between accelerating inflation and intolerable unemployment, either horn of which appears sufficient, over a period of several economic cycles from the beginning and over a few more years from now, to unhinge representative democracy as the accepted basis of government in societies like ours.

I believe that there is an approach which is at least worth considering when things are as desperate as they appear now to be and when anything as important as the survival of the basis of our prosperity and of our political liberties is at stake. This approach contains two elements: first, greatly to extend the role of the competitive market-place as the principal arbiter of the direction and quantity of the application of economic resources in satisfying the wants and preferences of individual citizens, as consumers; and secondly, to take radical steps towards democratising the productive units which present their wares to market.

This is the logical, and potentially the political, antithesis to state capitalism, or corporatism, as now broadly favoured by the central establishment of contemporary political and economic thought, more or less indistinguishable under political parties of either or any colour. It is a plausible starting point in the search for constructive solutions that anything about which those who have been jointly and severally responsible for years of deteriorating performance are agreed is probably wrong. Anything which is the systematic opposite of the highest common denominator of conventional wisdom has a particular presumption in its favour.

We start from a position in which a high level of employment is a politically inescapable desideratum. We confront the fact that, in the face of monopoly bargaining over labour supply together with other avoidable imperfections of the labour market, this high employment can only be achieved in the short-run at the price of a policy – accelerating inflation – which is unstable in the longer run.

Therefore it is the monopoly bargaining over labour supply, together with the other labour market imperfections, which have to change if the other elements in the defined system of political economy are to become consistent so that the system itself can become stable. Yet we have already seen that the attempt to override collectively the dispositions of collective bargaining over pay cannot succeed. For one thing it depends on the voluntary consent in practice of national trade unions.

They are scarcely likely to consent voluntarily to a programme which would forever extinguish their principal role. Trade unions were historically called into being in a capitalist environment to balance the bargaining power of private capital at a time when labour was still comparatively plentiful and capital was still comparatively scarce.

Those conditions have long since changed. But, having once established their powerful positions in the economy and society, trade unions can hardly be realistically expected to surrender that power – or, if they can prevent it, to permit Parliament to abridge it – if at the same time government policy is asking for their active cooperation in restraining their members, and if those members are not being offered any comparably credible alternative protection against what they still see as the bargaining power of employers, especially employers on whose interests the sun seldom if ever sets.

Yet so long as national trade unions remain as principal bargaining agents the labour market can never function in such a way as to ensure a high rate of matching of men to jobs without inflation. Equally, the economic and political power of national trade unions is such that there is no foreseeable prospect of dealing with them in the kind of way that more traditional monopolies were dealt with by anti-trust and anti-monopoly legislation earlier in the development of industrial societies.

Trade unions can mobilise a political resistance to such legislative action which conventional monopolies could never muster; and, even if their political support fails, their industrial power is something which conventional monoplies, who depended heavily on the rule of law for the exploitation of their advantages, could never have deployed. So a simple direct attack on trade union power offers no harmonious solution within the constraints of our present political economy, even if it is supposed that the advantages of curtailing collective bargaining would outweigh the other real social costs of seeking to deprive a sophisticated public of other benefits which it believes it gets from trade union membership.

The incomes policy option is also closed by the theoretical impossibility of centrally controlling the movement of an average while allowing full freedom of market determination to all the constituents which give rise to that average. There is manifestly no way of indefinitely settling pay relativities by central decision unless quite egregious inefficiency is to be tolerated.

So what is needed, against the indispensable background of a fiscal and monetary policy which provides only for as great an expansion of monetary demand as the real increase in the productive capacity of the economy warrants, is a system under which the labour market will work more efficiently and, in particular, labour will refrain from pricing itself out of jobs at the given level of monetary demand, but which will not involve a crude frontal onslaught on the industrial rights and powers of working people. They need somehow to be 'disalienated' enough to become infected with the entrepreneurial realities which confront their present employers so that they will accept a non-inflationary market-determined environment as setting the level of rewards that can be afforded.

This is never likely to be accepted in large enterprises, where the individual worker, whose voice is decisive in pay bargaining processes, feels no general loyalty to or identity of interests with the enterprise for which he works, and where there is widely believed to be a gigantic leakage in the commercial arithmetic called private profit. It matters not that this beast is as near to extinction as the Loch Ness monster, if all working people believe that at the margin any restraint shown by them disappears into the bottomless pit of shareholders' dividends.

But might it not perhaps be different if those working people themselves were the entrepreneurs of the firm, in the sense that it formally belonged to them, that its broad policy was decided by them and that it hired and fired the professional management and decided the terms on which it wished to reward itself, its managers and those who supplied finance?

There is ample evidence that working people in general are willing and indeed eager to justify their jobs and earnings in a competitive market-place, provided they are sure that the wool is not being pulled over their eyes and that no mystery middle-man is making off with the lion's share of the swag. In the circumstances suggested such suspicions would be finally laid to rest. What is more, the terms on which capital is rewarded would be much better understood. They need not be very different in practice from those which operate today (some long-term creditors being rewarded on a share-of-profits basis); and more general appreciation of the economic and social importance of savings and financial investment might be achieved. The traditional middle classes might lose their illusion of direct commercial power which equity ownership is supposed in Marxist literature to confer upon them; but that would be a modest price to pay for the opportunity to save and to earn without penal taxation in a prosperous and stable economic environment. The only losers would be those whose economic position genuinely depends on accidents of wealth which no economic liberal would see any need to justify.

It will be said that such an arrangement would put national trade unions out of business just as much as the incomes policies and the outlawing of collective bargaining which have already been rejected partly on that account. But there is a great difference. It is one thing to seek to put trade unions out of business by simply abolishing their function and leaving their members otherwise, as they will perceive it, defenceless. It is quite another to allow them to wither away because a different and better way has been found of securing not only the direct financial interests of their members, but also a much wider range of advantages – such as a direct say and involvement in the conduct of the enterprise to which you belong – as well.

Of course the leadership of national trade unions will tend to resist. But it is much harder to fight against a programme which effectively transfers power from the national leadership to the general membership than to fight against legislation which seems directed against the whole union. Both politically and industrially the trade union bureaucracies would be outflanked.

There remain, of course, a thousand and one very loose ends; and I do not propose to try and tie them here and now, though I have considered them and as yet have not found any of them fatal to the conception. There clearly need to be some limits on the right of workers to liquify the assets of the firm, distribute them and join other firms, especially perhaps in the case of employees of banks. It needs to be shown in detail that an effective and strong capital market could indeed work perfectly well under the supposed circumstances.

It may be that the formula would not be applicable to certain reserved sectors of the economy such, for example, as the public utilities. There are also extremely difficult issues, well developed in the substantial literature on the subject, about the ownership of the assets of such cooperative ventures. So long as the enterprise is a going concern, and particularly if it is expanding, the difficulties are less acute. There is a straightforward incentive to the members of the cooperative to invest provided that the return will cover the cost of raising finance and leave a surplus for the payment of higher wages and salaries. Investments which would merely allow the same wages and salaries to be paid to a larger number of people may be less attractive to a going concern; but these opportunities should appeal to those who are unemployed or who are employed in lower paid activities.

There is a substantial problem about the rights and obligations of those who leave and join going concerns. If a departing worker carries any rights of ownership with him or can cash them in, then presumably a new entrant would have to buy himself in; and this would both create an intolerable impediment to the proper functioning of the labour market and tend to recreate the gulf between capital and labour. It is therefore more natural to vest the formal ownership of the enterprise in its supervisory board, as elected by the members of the enterprise.

Problems do then arise when the firm is contracting or when the opportunity cost of important assets comes to exceed their present-use value to the cooperative. Presumably the enterprise should be free to sell them, if the 'hidden hand' is to function properly in securing the optimal use of assets throughout the economy. What then does the cooperative do with the fruits of the sale? If they are reinvested in alternative productive assets, there may be no insuperable problem, though even here an element of economic rent could be created on behalf of those who belonged to the enterprise; and this in turn could create an undesirable premium on securing membership for the favoured friends of those already within the fold.

More seriously, there may be no alternative productive investment to make. The supervisory board could find itself becoming the holding

51

company for a valuable portfolio of investments whose fruits would belong to a shrinking work-force – in the last resort to a single clerk who kept the books of what would have become a pure investment trust. This result might be avoided if the redundancy provisions for those leaving the enterprise, as its productive activities were run down, were arranged so as to consume the financial investments of the cooperative pro-portionately to the reduction in the labour-force. Alternatively, the surplus financial assets might be surrendered progressively to the state. There would still be real difficulties about laying down such a combina-tion of redundancy and surrender provisions as to distort neither the incentive to realise productive assets when, but only when, there was a higher-yielding alternative use for them nor the incentives to hire and to be hired consistently with the efficient operation of the labour market.

It is also necessary to meet the argument that such a system will lead to systematic under-investment because the time-preference of the employees of an enterprise will be systematically shorter than the time-preference of society as a whole. This might to some extent be met by an appropriate structure of tax incentives. Certainly, this must not become a pretext for reintroducing the evils of state interference through the back door, since it is of paramount importance that consumer preference and market forces remain the principal determinants of economic activity.

Realistic provisions also need to be made for new and small enter-prises. It is probably not sufficient to leave the creation of new enterprises to the spontaneous initiative of unemployed or underem-ployed or underrewarded groups of workers getting together to strike out in a new direction, though this might well happen. On the other hand if, as seems desirable, enterprises employing less than some maximum number of people are exempted from the general provisions for collective ownership and control, a kind of 'smallness trap' will be created inhibiting desirable expansion when the employment threshold is approached, unless there is an effective transition mechanism which properly reflects the interests of the original entrepreneur. Yet if there is such a mechanism, there is again the danger of recreating the capital-labour split though, in practice, this may mean no more than that those who are good at starting new enterprises will become compara-tively rich without coming to own or exercise direct control over the means to other people's livelihoods.

As I said, it is not my purpose here to prove that such a system is flawless or even wholly practical. My only wish is to draw attention to the possible relevance of this kind of approach to the resolution of the particular crisis of political economy which I tried to describe in the first part of the lecture. If that crisis is as deeply rooted in the basic political and economic institutions of contemporary industrial societies as I have suggested, if we are as near as I have suggested to the time when the tensions within the system must overthrow it and if the consequences of such overthrow are as politically and economically grim as I have suggested, then it is legitimate to examine alternatives, not with a perfectionist eye, but with a view to seeing whether they can be made to work well enough to be better than the literally awful alternatives.

It needs, of course, to be proved that industrial workers as a whole would indeed prefer a combination of democratic units of production with a market-dominated wider environment to the seemingly easier option of collective extortion from governments.

Certainly, the time for the change has not yet come. The remaining two or three years of phoney crisis, while our present Prime Minister (Harold Wilson) continues to preside like a paper over the cracks, ably anaesthetising constructive political and economic thought and action, have to be endured before the breakdown of our present political economy becomes sufficiently manifest to sufficiently many people for genuinely new approaches to become practical.

But imagine when inflation is thirty percent and rising towards fifty percent, even at a hundred percent; when unemployment is falling at a snail's pace from levels still close to a million and a half; when the most recent incomes policy episode lies in the inevitable ruins at the government's feet; when the pound is falling out of bed in the foreign exchange markets and even the Chancellor of the Duchy of Lancaster acknowledges that reserves and credit are exhausted; when eighty of the government's supporters in the House of Commons rebel against the Cabinet's remedial measures; when whatever form of government then follows is confronted with determined and desperate industrial opposition, not least in the public sector, as trade unions fight to protect the living standards of their members which are being eroded by raging inflation. The phoney crisis will then become a hot crisis. If the only alternatives at that stage are more state capitalism and control with the rump of the Labour Party or mixed capitalism under a resurgent Conservative Party, it is hard to see how total conflict and breakdown of parliamentary government can be avoided.

But if those who basically believe that individuals must predominate over organisations, that man should be master of the machines and institutions which he has created, all join hands to demand a restoration of the sovereignty of the consumer in the market-place over an extended area of national life and at the same time to demand the sovereignty of the members of an enterprise within it, then the electorate might yet be offered a way out of catastrophe without suspension of political freedoms. Indeed, those for whom individual freedom and fulfilment have always been the major premises of political philosophy will see such a programme as evolutionary and in a sense conservationist. Only those for whom the essence of economic liberalism has been the same as the essence of Marx's caricature of it, namely the special power and privileges conferred by the private ownership of capital, will regard it as revolutionary.

As one who has never found the concepts of pure ownership or naked power very relevant to the political economy of modern industrial democracy, but who has always been impressed by the importance in practice of designing structures in which the maximum amount of individual freedom can operate benignly, I make no apology for suggesting to you at such length that, if we wish to escape a totalitarian fate of one kind or another, then the true economic liberals must join hands with the true socialists against those who have conspired to make government, usually by themselves, a universal placebo for all ills.

Here then is the proposition. Our existing political economy is inherently unstable because it insists upon a level of employment which is unattainable without accelerating inflation under existing labour market arrangements. There is no reasonable prospect of persuading the electorate to accept the continuing level of unemployment which would be associated with non-inflationary fiscal and monetary policies under existing labour market arrangements. Therefore those arrangements must change in such a way as to remove the general influence of collective bargaining and to enhance the general efficiency of the labour market.

The latter would involve extending market principles to areas of national life which have been gravely distorted by well meant but ill considered state intervention, most notably the whole area of housing. It is moreover essential that the whole apparatus of state subsidies to industry, where these are essentially attempts to compensate for excessive collectively bargained labour costs, should be retired, though the simulation of regional devaluations by way of general payroll taxes and subsidies would remain a proper market remedy for the geographical imbalances caused by state-imposed common currency arrangements.

54

And it would still be a proper function of government, within the framework of an unswervingly non-inflationary fiscal and monetary policy, to correct by tax and subsidies the crude operation of *laissez-faire* where a systematic divergence of private profit and common good can be established.

At the same time the general influence of collective bargaining can only be removed by offering working people an alternative and better protection than national trade unions can offer. The only potentially acceptable alternative is a change in company law which gives ownership and ultimate control of enterprises to the people employed by them. They would then have to sink or swim in a market environment. Inflation would subside. Employment would be high. The sovereignty of the consumer would be assured. The 'hidden hand' would continue its benign dispositions. The corporate state and its handmaiden, the national trade union, and the bureaucracy of the mixed economy, would wither away. The democracy of the ballot-box, of the market-place, and of the work-place would prevail over the otherwise impossible power of giant organisations, most particularly of government itself. It is at least an alternative to the anarchy followed by the strong man to which present arrangements are inexorably leading us.

Wincott Lecture, 4 December 1975

The Workers Cooperative Economy

The purpose of this paper is to raise for discussion certain theoretical and practical questions about a market economy in which the predominant enterprises are workers cooperatives. By workers cooperatives I mean business enterprises in which the freehold ownership of the assets of the business is vested in the members collectively, in which the sovereign body is the members each having one vote and in which all employees and only employees are members. The rest is negotiable.

By an economy in which workers cooperatives predominate I mean, for the sake of argument, an economy in which by law all enterprises employing more than say a hundred people are workers cooperatives as defined above. By a market economy in which workers cooperatives predominate I mean an economy as above in which the relationship between enterprises and between producers and consumers is regulated by free competitive markets, in which monopolistic tendencies are effectively discouraged under law and in which the activities of government are confined broadly to the traditional foreign and domestic functions plus interventions by way of taxes, subsidies and regulation in the manner developed by Professor James Meade to correct clearly defined and established market imperfections involving public goods and other externalities.

My interest in this economy has arisen neither from academic curiosity nor from socialist idealism *per se*. I have no ambition to improve upon, for example, J. Vanek's classic *The General Theory of Labour-Managed Market Economies* (1970). Nor am I primarily concerned to build directly on the heritage of syndicalism and those sub-plots in socialist theory which have emphasised workers in their work place rather than the state as the proper embodiment of the public or society for the purposes of the public, common or social ownership and control of productive activities.

My concern is more with policy and practicalities, even though at this moment the perspective may appear heroically futuristic and, as today's politicians might see it, unrealistic. In my 1975 Wincott Memorial Lecture, later published by the Institute of Economic Affairs under the title *A General Hypothesis of Employment, Inflation and Politics*, I argued that our present political economy suffered a central contradiction which portended a catastrophic failure of the system within a finite number of years.

I suggested, but did not develop at all far, the notion that the contradiction might be resolved and the catastrophe therefore avoided if and only if labour were in general to replace capital as the entrepreneur of the predominant productive unit, dealing at arm's length with the workers in the labour market (with the one important difference that monopolistic practices would and could be more effectively prevented in the capital markets under such conditions than they can now be in the labour market).

This is not the place to go again over the same ground. But the briefest summary of the hypothesis is needed as background to the present discussion.

Our present political economy was defined as a system with government dependent on renewable consent on the basis of universal manhood suffrage and with widespread free collective bargaining in the labour market. It will be seen that political economies satisfying this definition are broadly coterminous with the membership of the OECD, in other words the so-called 'western industrial democracies'.

The fact of renewable popular consent to government entails, it was argued, a political imperative to deliver some approximation to full employment and a general stability of the inflation rate, if not actual stability of prices. If this imperative were breached in either or both respects and if the breach appeared to be indefinite without an early prospect of rectification, then the basis of consent to government – to any government based on the representative democracy, not just to this or that coloured administration – would dissolve and, after such lags as were implied by the political process, some or other sequence of anarchy and authoritarianism would ensue.

The fact of collective bargaining in the labour market entails, it was argued, a high equilibrium rate of unemployment, certainly higher than any conventional post-War interpretation of full employment as implied by the political imperative. This arises because collective bargaining is of its nature an exercise in monopolistic supply, the essential character of which is that a higher than market-clearing price is charged and a smaller quantity than under perfect competition is supplied to the market.

Under these conditions governments are confronted with a threatened breach of that part of the political imperative which requires full employment. If they move to meet this by stimulative fiscal or monetary policies – and for these purposes it matters not whether you prefer the monetarist or the Keynesian canon – the only effect beyond a temporary rise in economic activity will be a rise in prices while employment remains at its low equilibrium point.

If governments keep stimulating by fiscal and monetary means, after a rather long lag, equilibrium will be found with a higher rate of inflation and the same high level of unemployment. If governments try to beat this, as they will be obliged to do, by constantly increasing the fiscal and monetary dose, they will in theory be able to maintain or at least approach the target employment level at the price of continuously and logarithmically accelerating rates of inflation. But in the end either this breach of the other leg of the political imperative will force abandonment of the policy or hyper-inflation will be reached. In the latter event money illusion will break down; and the temporary stimulative power of expanding monetary demand faster than people are discounting inflation will evaporate because it becomes literally impossible. Either way, there will then be a catastrophic rise in unemployment, almost certainly far over-shooting the long-run equilibrium point. Either way, government is then seen to be in breach of either or both aspects of the political imperative; and its previously supposed remedies against such evils are exposed as ineffective. Then the basis of political consent to government disintegrates.

In support of this hypothesis it was argued that what have come to be known as incomes policies offer no escape from the explosive nature of the model for basic economic reasons as well as for practical political and industrial reasons. You cannot indefinitely abolish collective bargaining without either establishing a totalitarian state or abolishing trade unions by law, it was argued. The first takes one outside our present political economy as defined, while the second appears inconceivable in a modern democratic state.

The historical evidence was said to corroborate the hypothesis. In all the main OECD countries, though most graphically in Britain, a steady logarithmic acceleration in inflation rates (abstracting from the usual four-year cyclical movements) is detectable from the middle or late 1950s.

This has, however, been diluted by a progressive rise in the average level of unemployment through each cycle; and it has been temporarily distorted or alleviated from time to time by exporting the problem to each other and to the third world.

This is not observed in the pre-War period only because the political imperative did not then effectively exclude in all countries (though it clearly did in Germany and perhaps in Italy) a very high level of unemployment. It is not observed pre-1914 because collective bargaining was not then the pervasive norm of the labour market.

So it is argued that, if the OECD countries, with Britain in the lead, are not to suffer the fate of Germany between the wars, some way must be found consistent with the constraints of political democracy and free societies of eliminating collective bargaining other than either outright legal prohibition of trade unions or incomes policy. It was suggested that only the conversion by law into workers cooperatives of all enterprises, other than the technical monopolies, above a certain small size could achieve this and that it would.

The questions to be discussed here are not how valid that argument is, but, given that it is broadly valid, how an economy of workers cooperatives would work. Would it lead to the withering away of collective bargaining and would it have such other grave defects as to outweigh any benefits it might have of the kind advertised above?

Among the questions to be asked are:

(a) How would a workers cooperative raise finance for investment?

(b) Would there be a general tendency to under-investment by the standards of optimal capitalism?

(c) Would there be a tendency to under-employment by the standards of optimal capitalism?

(d) What is a maximum practical size for a workers cooperative – how would an economy of workers cooperatives cope with much larger firms of the kind which account now for an increasing proportion of national output?

(e) What arrangement should be made for the present statutory monopolies in the public sector?

(f) What about the 'technical monopolies'?

(g) Why should labour behave differently in respect of its monopoly power under such conditions?

(h) Would governments be any more able than they are now to

confine their functions and to abjure discretionary fiscal and monetary policies in the way suggested?
(i) In what directions could the market economy be extended?
(j) Why is the record of workers cooperatives so poor?
(k) Does it work in Yugoslavia?
(l) Is there an evolutionary route to market socialism?
(m) Do workers want cooperatives?

Sources of Finance

Once the employees of a firm collectively rather than the suppliers of capital are the entrepreneurs of that firm it will no longer be reasonable to expect capital finance to come from the entrepreneurs individually. For one thing, employees individually do not have personal access to savings in the necessary quantities. For another, even if they did, it would be unwise for them to invest their individual savings heavily in the enterprise on which their employment and earned income also depended. For a third thing, they will not have individually differentiated and realisable stakes in the enterprise; and, if they did as a result of putting up money for new investment, the character of the cooperative as a collectively owned enterprise would be modified. Moreover, if there were individually owned stakes in the enterprise, either departing workers would take away their entitlement with them, in which case the spectre of the capital shareholder would rise again from the ashes of conventional capitalism or departing workers would have to be bought out by newly arriving workers or by the cooperative itself.

Either arrangement would impose unacceptable cash burdens on the buyer to the detriment of the vitality and flexibility of the enterprise.

Indeed, it would be a misunderstanding of the whole concept of workers cooperatives, defined as an enterprise in which the supplier of labour is the entrepreneur, to try to reimport the concept of the limited liability company in which the entrepreneur is supposed to supply the capital. Capital and labour are distinct factors of production; and it would be surprising if it were appropriate for both to be supplied by the same group.

Instead investment would be financed, as now, from a free capital market and from retained surplus earnings, with banks continuing to play the role in short- and medium-term finance which they play now. The main novelty will be in the terms on which workers cooperatives deal with the capital market, since *ex hypothesi* they will not be in a position to offer investors an equity in the enterprise where an equity implies a freehold ownership of the assets and the right to appoint the directors.

It is likely that two main forms of investment in cooperatives will be used: fixed interest and 'equity type'. Fixed interest investments will be modelled on the present form of obligations and present no new problem. 'Equity-type' investment will be new in that it will entitle the investor neither to appoint the board of directors nor to realise the net worth of the enterprise on liquidation.

'Equity-type' investors will be entitled to receive all of the 'profits' of the enterprise; and it may also prove desirable to assign them a mortgage on the relevant assets. The 'profits' will correspond to the distributed earnings of a limited liability company and will amount to whatever the board of directors, appointed by the employees, says they amount to. This is likely to work more similarly to present arrangements than is supposed by the many who believe that distributed profits are the residual earnings of a company.

Distributed profits, though in the long run inevitably influenced by the success of the company, are at present whatever the board of directors decide they should be, whether this means drawing on reserves or adding to reserves. The reserve movement is the true residual on a short-term view. The motive now to make a distribution of suitable size is essentially to maintain a reasonable price for the company's obligations on the capital market, though at present the shareholders can petition to have the company wound up if the directors' distribution policy dissatisfies them.

This motive – of maintaining a reasonable price in the secondary market for the cooperative's obligations – will continue to apply. For on that will depend the cooperative's ability to raise new finance in the future at reasonable cost. It is true that the additional spur of warding off threatened takeovers will not apply; but in the presence of one adequate motive to reasonable distributions secondary motives are not needed.

It would be possible to include in the legislation establishing the cooperative economy a provision giving 'equity-type' investors an entitlement to petition for foreclosure on the assets mortgaged to them in specified circumstances of inadequate distribution. But it is hard to see why this artificiality should be needed to reinforce a natural market equilibrium between those who lend and those who borrow, unless it were to overcome irrational hesitation during the initial stages of transition or because there was some public interest in the encouragement of 'equity-type' investments. There probably is such an interest, since the alternative of either over-gearing the cooperatives or forcing them to excessive dependence on received earnings for financing future investment would tend to damage the financial resilience of the new structure and perhaps to inhibit investment which could show a good social as well as private return. But this is what might be called a 'committee-stage' point on which either view is tenable without being integral to the principle of the scheme itself.

Another committee-stage point on which either of the opposing views seems tenable is whether the cooperative economy would need to surround itself with tight exchange control regulations in order to prevent savings which need to be invested in the cooperative economy at home flowing overseas in pursuit of the more familiar form of capitalist investment in which, at least at first, investors may be expected to have greater confidence. The argument for it is obvious and, in effect, as just stated.

The argument against is more subtle. First, insofar as all the free industrial economies are supposed to be suffering the same morbid condition the attractions of capitalist investment overseas must be presumed to be diminishing and, if they exist at all, only to reflect the differing stages of morbidity of the various conventional economies. So at worst the need for exchange controls would probably only be temporary.

Secondly – and quite apart from what may be happening in other economies – the existence of alternative investment outlets offering attractive returns abroad may be regarded as a necessary and proper protection of savers at home and as a desirable incentive to workers cooperatives to earn and make reasonable distributions. Thirdly, it is a technical fallacy to regard home and overseas investment as direct alternatives, however much it may look like that to the investor. The quantum of home investment is constrained by the quantum of home savings, in the sense of available non-consumed resources. This quantum may or may not be affected by overseas investment whose direct impact is on the balance of payments, short-term capital movements, the reserves and the exchange rate.

On balance it seems desirable to seek to avoid exchange controls as anything more than a transitional measure. But, if it should prove necessary to retain them longer than this, there is nothing in the nature of workers cooperatives which makes that impossible; and certainly it would involve no loss of freedoms and efficiency now available.

In sum then the expectation is that the financing of industries and enterprises would be less different from present arrangements than may at first blush have been supposed. The essential and desirable character of a market relationship between savers and entrepreneurs is conserved. Moreover, all of this is in relation to the free enterprise concept working as it is supposed to work, not working in the warped and sickly manner which the essential contradictions of our political economy have in practice made inevitable, with society earning little or no apparent return on its productive assets, with savers – including pensioners and small insurance beneficiaries – suffering manifest injustice, with new investment disastrously depressed, with employment and international competitiveness increasingly threatened and with a growing dependence on government as the only large source of new investment funds. By that comparison the arrangements for investment and capital markets under the cooperative economy may be expected to work much better. The entrepreneur has legitimacy, which contemporary opinion does not allow to the capitalist entrepreneur. Competition between cooperatives will provide an incentive to new investment, as will the natural desire of each cooperative to maximise its income per head and to protect future employment. Governments will have been extracted from their heavy industrial involvement by the nature of the market socialist settlement here considered. The motive force behind the progressive acceleration of inflation, of a kind which is necessarily destructive of private investment, will have been removed by the withering away of collective bargaining.

It is even tempting to speculate that in the new environment the taxation of savings and capital should become less penal. In a world of workers cooperatives the people will hardly thank the government for raising the cost of capital finance by taxation, more particularly when the conventional capitalist against whose excessive wealth such measures are supposed to be directed has been removed from the scene, or at least from the mythology of the society.

Moreover, with the government's role severely restricted its revenue requirements will be correspondingly reduced. This too may create a better environment for savings and investment.

Will Cooperatives Under-invest?

A workers cooperative seeks, to the extent that it conforms to the archetype of the economically rational unit, to maximise income per head of its members. This is a different, though substantially over-lapping, maximand from the conventional limited liability company's maximand of profit for the shareholders.

An investment which would show a good return to capital by, for example, building a new factory employing new workers at the same rate of reward as existing workers, but no return per head to labour would appear to be more attractive to a privately owned enterprise than to a workers cooperative. Conversely an investment which raised rewards per head of the labour force, for example by equipping the workers with more efficient machinery, without necessarily earning any return to capital would seem to be more attractive to the workers cooperative than to a firm where the decisions are made in the interests of the owners and providers of capital.

But this analysis is too simple. The reality is more complex. All returns to new investment are by nature returns to capital; and, if in the event labour partakes of part or even of all of the benefits, under capitalism this can only occur either because trade union bargaining is in a position to scoop a large proportion of any new surplus earnings or because more generally throughout the economy investment is raising the demand for and therefore the opportunity cost to each employer of the labour which he needs to operate new investments.

Both the capital and the labour entrepreneur has to pay the cost of capital finance, whether it is the actual cost of market borrowings or the opportunity cost of using retained earnings to finance new investments.

If there is a surplus return on the investment, then it belongs naturally to the entrepreneur, whether capital or labour is playing that role.

The capital entrepreneur will be interested in any investment which produces such a surplus return. The labour entrepreneur will only be interested in investments which produce a surplus return per head of workers. The second category appears to be more limited than the first. In other words in an economy of workers cooperatives the kind of investment which creates new employment at the going rate of pay seems not to be attractive to existing enterprises, though it should be attractive to those who are unemployed if they can organise themselves to go into business.

But this leaves out the distribution of the surplus which the new investment has earned. Under a capital entrepreneur this is distributed, or at least attributed, to the shareholders. With a labour entrepreneur it can be distributed amongst the workers; and therefore there will always be a return to labour per head where there is a return to shareholders under the traditional arrangements. It may on occasions be very thinly spread; but then so it is also when there are very large numbers of shareholders, who indeed can often outnumber the employees.

This analysis, however, assumes that the cost of capital to a workers cooperative would be the same as to a capital entrepreneur. Yet this can hardly be so when the different distribution of risks and benefits are considered. If, of course, all investment were to be financed by fixed interest borrowing or retained profits, then what has been said would be true. But that would be a very unsound arrangement. External finance is likely to be needed; and in a healthy market economy an efficient market in funds between savers and investors is important for efficiency in the allocation of capital resources. Total reliance on fixed interest borrowing to finance new investment, which is sometimes called 100 percent gearing, leaves an enterprise extremely vulnerable to bankruptcy in a trading recession because capital's reward has to be paid whether or not any trading surplus has been earned.

Some 'equity-type' finance will certainly be needed by workers cooperatives if they are to survive such recessions. This means that the risk which the investor accepts in making such an investment – and it is greater where he does not own the freehold of the assets created and does not appoint the directors who will manage the investment – will have to be rewarded by the prospect of at least a share in the surplus earnings from the investment.

This indeed was the arrangement already described in the first main section of this paper. Market forces in the capital market, if they work in textbook fashion, will tend to drive this share up towards 100 percent of the surplus earnings, because it will always pay any workers cooperative to outbid its competitors for investment funds up to this limit. In practice workers cooperatives will begin to lose interest in this auction as the share approaches the level which would leave the return to workers per head at what they would see as a negligible level.

If investors are left no other outlet, then equilibrium will probably be found with rather a lower level of effective interest rates in the capital market, a rather lower rate of savings in the economy and a rather lower rate of investment than under conventional capitalism. Or so again it would appear. But even this leaves out of account the interest of unemployed workers. If there are such and if they can overcome the inertial difficulties of forming themselves into a new cooperative, then it will pay them to enter the capital market and offer investors up to 100 percent of the surplus earnings from new capital.

If investors are free to invest overseas in conventional capitalist enterprises, then domestic cooperatives will indeed have to offer close to 100 percent of the potential surplus earnings in order to attract the funds they want for new investment. If they do not, savings will flow overseas and the exchange rate will eventually move to restore equilibrium by reducing the real value of the monetary rewards which the cooperatives are rewarding themselves.

There is still a problem. The investors have no stake in the capital appreciation of the assets of the enterprise, although they may have a fall-back mortgage at historic real cost on the assets and they may well enjoy capital growth in the market value in secondary markets of their conditional stake in the enterprise. This difference may be more apparent than real. If the enterprise is a going concern, then what matters is the value of their 'equity-type' shares in the secondary market. If it is not a going concern, then the mortgage at historic real cost on the assets may well be as good a protection as a freehold in a bankrupt enterprise would be under traditional arrangements.

Even so the risk to the 'equity-type' investor is clearly greater to the extent that he cannot appoint the management and that he cannot, except perhaps under limiting conditions, petition for liquidation of the enterprise. If, therefore, his prospective return is only as great as under existing arrangements, the investment will tend to be less attractive.

The difference may be very small once investors have become accustomed to the new system, although during the period of transition, before workers cooperatives had demonstrated that they have the same interest in appointing and the same capacity to recruit professional management which conventional enterprises have, suspicion of the new enterprises may create a larger temporary confidence gap.

But there are two other very important factors to be taken into account before reaching a definite conclusion about the investment behaviour of an economy of workers cooperatives:

(a) The effect of cooperative organisation on labour productivity; and
(b) the effect of cooperative organisation on collective bargaining.

So far we have been comparing the rational investment behaviour of workers cooperatives with the rational behaviour of idealised capital enterprises working according to textbook optimisation. If we actually lived in the latter world, we would hardly be considering the problem discussed in this paper at all.

The classical texts on producer cooperatives, mainly written in the late nineteenth and early twentieth centuries, tended to argue that workers cooperatives would suffer lower productivity than their capitalist contemporaries and so would fail to survive in competition with them. The historical evidence in both Western Europe and North America tended to confirm this view.

The failure was blamed mainly on less efficient management and deficient investment, arising from failure to amortise past investment properly, leading to lack of finance for capital replacement. This view of the history, especially in North America, has recently been challenged by Professor Derek Jones, who puts more of the blame for failure on an artificially hostile legal and political environment.

Certainly I would reject on an elementary point of logic any inferences drawn about the systematic characteristics of an economy of workers cooperatives from the experience of particular workers cooperatives operating in the framework of a conventional private enterprise economy. There is no private advantage from behaving in the jungle as if the rule of law applied; but there may yet be advantage for all jungle-dwellers in establishing together the rule of law.

It is in fact an open question whether the favourable effects on productivity of better motivation and enhanced credibility of managers under a system of workers cooperatives would outweigh the unfavourable effects – which are not inherent, but possible – of any disinclination on the part of the cooperative to accept or pay the market price for good professional managers.

Even if the advantages to productivity – and the recent cases of Meriden, Kirby and the *Scottish Daily News* have not been in business long enough to substantiate the first favourable impressions – did outweigh the drawbacks, workers cooperatives still might not prosper in a capitalist economy.

Capital markets might still discriminate irrationally against them. Trade unions might well discriminate against them, perceiving them quite correctly to be in the long-run a threat to the existence of trade unions, since the abolition of private enterprise would eventually destroy the *raison d'etre* of collective bargaining. In other ways the law and the tax system might discriminate against them; and certainly the existing system of patents, marketing and sophisticated corporate finance makes it difficult for workers cooperatives to get off the ground in areas where large conventional enterprises predominate. Moreover, the tendency for workers cooperatives only to come into existence where a conventional enterprise has collapsed suggests that the seed has been sown on peculiarly recalcitrant soil.

Against the visceral feeling that sceptics may have that workers cooperatives will tend to be less productive per head of their work force is the fact that for a workers cooperative the direct interest is in maximising labour productivity, because that determines income per head which is the natural maximand of a workers cooperative. A conventional firm seeks to maximise capital productivity because maximising returns to shareholders is its natural maximand.

As Professor Jim Ball and others have pointed out, the discrepancy between the overall economic interest in maximising labour productivity and the private interest of the enterprises which comprise the conventional economy in maximising capital productivity can under certain conditions be a source of sub-optimal performance by the economy. An economy of workers cooperatives would not suffer from this apparent conflict of private and social goals.

Another possible reason for predicting lower productivity in workers cooperatives is their presumed soft-heartedness about laying off redundant workers. The cooperative will prefer, unless faced with literal bankruptcy, to carry surplus workers as a form of disguised social insurance for and between the members of the cooperative.

This seems undeniably true; and historical experience seems to confirm it. On the other hand, for the very reasons discussed above in relation to possible reluctance of workers cooperatives to invest in employment-creating expansions unless this can be shown to produce more income per head for the existing members of the cooperative, they can be expected to be more reluctant than conventional firms to take on new labour. Therefore, where cooperatives are expanding they may well be more inclined and able to stretch the productivity of the existing work force than a conventional firm.

The whole question, however, becomes very much less moot when we drop the artificial comparison between the workers cooperative and the idealised capitalist firm of free market textbooks and compare the potential performance of the workers cooperative in the workers cooperative economy with the performance of the capitalist firm in the capitalist economy as it has in fact developed. For, the moment that the comparison is extended to the macro level from the micro comparison of disembodied enterprise units, one confronts the pervasive fact of trade unions.

Trade unions are a natural and probably political inevitable response of the suppliers of labour in a capitalist market economy to the opportunities, if not indeed the exploitative tendencies, of a *laissez-faire* labour market. It is theoretically arguable that combinations should be prohibited by law, as in parts of the nineteenth century they were.

Beyond much doubt the common interest would be served by such a prohibition, just as the common interest is also served by the prohibition of other forms of monopoly and cartel. The greater efficiency and dynamism of the economy would make up within a very few years for the once and for all reduction in labour's share of national income; and from there on it would be pure gain, at least in real income terms.

But that is hardly consistent in practice with the assumptions of universal suffrage operating in the wake of the political heritage of the last hundred years. To any individual group of workers a combination will always be a superior option to free individual bargaining so long as black-legging can be prevented by force, industrial strength or custom.

The perception of a social advantage in general abstention from collective bargaining is too remote from the circumstances of the individual worker for him even to support through the ballot-box a general prohibition on trade unions, let alone to abstain privately from their immediate protection in a world where there is no reason to expect other workers to confer a reciprocal advantage on him by similar abstention. Since workers and their families predominate in the electoral process, it would be an extraordinary triumph of abstract macro-economic reasoning over concretely perceived private realities to secure a political mandate for the suppression of collective bargaining in favour of free individual bargaining; and the occasional political support for incomes policies offers no counter-evidence because, while it bespeaks a popular appreciation of certain macro-economic realities, the consent is given strictly on the assumption of some principle of fairness in its application which necessarily implies an administered control rather than perfect competition in the labour market.

So, it is right to regard free and independent trade unions as an inherent feature of real world market capitalism, even if they are a gross disfigurement of the original ideal of a private enterprise economy. It is therefore also right to compare the workers cooperative economy with the capitalist economy on the assumption that the latter works not as in the classical textbooks, but as it does in the second half of the twentieth century.

We then confront a quite different standard of performance although it is more pronounced in Britain than in most of the other OECD countries and although the very rapid and in some ways geometrically accelerating advance of technology in the post-war era has engendered more rapid growth even in Britain than in almost all previous eras. If the argument in the preamble to this paper is accepted, then we are at the end of the era in which we can expect on the basis of the characteristic institutions of post-war political economy sufficient stability in the economy for these impressive growth achievements to continue without an insupportably accelerating rate of inflation.

This arises not because of any restraint imposed by the physical environment, as the Friends of the Earth would argue, nor because of any exhaustion of technological novelties or super abundance of savings forcing down the rate of return on capital as contemporary neo-Marxists argue, but quite simply because collective bargaining has advanced to the point where there is no, or virtually no, return on the capital assets employed in industry and commerce. The effects of money illusion disguised this fact from us for some years, until the techniques of inflation accounting were properly applied; but the recent NEDO study leaves us in no doubt, cyclical fluctuations apart, that industry in Britain is now earning virtually no return at all.

This does not of course mean that there is no social return, in the sense that we should all be equally well or better off, on a conventional present value calculation, discounting future benefits for society's time preference, if we were to consume our existing stock of capital, although we are now in fact very close to doing just that because of the alarming discrepancy between private and social goals which collective bargaining has caused. It does mean that there is very little incentive under existing arrangements for capital entrepreneurs to undertake even those new investments which would show a return to workers and shareholders added together, because the whole or more than the whole of the return would be taken by labour under pressure of collective bargaining. The current position over the introduction of new technology into Fleet Street is a classic case in point and may well now lead not merely to the cancellation of the new investment but also to the liquidation of the existing assets and widespread closure of newspapers.

It is a symptom of this condition that more and more enterprises find themselves driven to turn to government for investable funds; and it is not surprising that workers cooperatives born of the collapse of conventional firms under these pressures (as well sometimes as under the pressure of normal market forces) also turn to government when private investors are so demoralised. But this offers no permanent solution to the problem of under-investment because government is prevented from simulating the behaviour of a competitive capital market by the political constraints under which it operates. Even if it could – which would depend not merely on all voters being wholly rational and wholly informed but also on their having entered into an enforceable mutual contract to refrain from seeking to press any sectional advantage through the political process (itself a quite breathtaking exercise in constitution-making) – government would still confront the difficulty of financing its lending without either coercive taxation, which impairs the efficiency of the labour market and final markets, or a formidable burden of fixed interest borrowing.

There may be certain formal schemes which could theoretically reproduce through government the operation of a perfect capital market without unacceptable fiscal and monetary side-effects.

But the government would still be faced with the yet further problem of how to recognise investments which would yield a positive return to workers-cum-shareholders in a world where profits as conventionally defined were always nil. The problem might not be unanswerable in principle if there were a limitless supply of virtually costless teams of government cost-benefit accountants and economists to examine and compare investment propositions put up by every enterprise in the country. But the mind and the heart recoil from such an extension of bureaucracy; and any realistic consideration of the fallibility of government congruent with the widely celebrated fallibility of markets puts the matter beyond serious doubt.

So, we are back comparing the likely investment performance of the workers cooperative economy with the investment performance of the private enterprise–trade union economy as we know it. If there is adequate force in the earlier argument that the workers cooperative economy, from which *ex hypothesi* collective bargaining is absent, would only perform slightly less well than the idealised free enterprise economy without trade unions, then it follows that it would perform a great deal better than an economy in which, once its internal contradictions have fully matured, no one will invest at all.

As an afterthought it may be added that, insofar as investment is regarded as important because of the contribution it makes to growth, any tendency of the workers cooperative economy to under-invest by the standards of idealised capitalism is less serious to the extent that growth is less highly regarded as the sovereign aim of economic processes or to the extent that growth is seen as a subordinate objective to or predicated on the stability of employment and prices which, as we have seen, our present political economy cannot deliver.

Would the Workers Cooperative Economy Tend to Under-employ?

This is two questions disguised as one. The first is, 'Would the workers cooperative, at the micro level, tend not to recruit new employees and members where a conventional firm would?'

The second is, 'Supposing that the answer to the first is "yes", would that imply a tendency to higher unemployment at the macro level of the economy as a whole?'

The first question has already been discussed at some length in the context of the kind of investment which workers cooperatives might be expected to reject where a conventional firm would go ahead. The conclusion was that to some degree the workers cooperative would be less inclined to make the kind of new investment which would increase employment without increasing distributable rewards per head of the pre-investment members of the cooperative.

Whether there would as a result be a macro tendency to unemployment as a result – and some observers have claimed to identify such a tendency in Yugoslavia, though we may wonder how they distinguish this element in the observable unemployment from other causes such as structural and frictional unemployment, regional unemployment, voluntary unemployment, unemployability and so forth – entirely depends on the efficiency of the mechanism for forming new enterprises.

If we assume that the combination of a neutral fiscal and monetary policy, in Professor Friedman's sense, with access to technological improvements and an initial level of incomes sufficient to engender an adequate savings potential will always guarantee the possibility of employment for all those who are not the victims of structural, frictional, regional, or voluntary unemployment or of unemployability or the collective enforcement of a higher than market-clearing price for labour – in other words that there can be no long run demand deficiency in Keynes's sense – then anyone who is unemployed could be employed provided that a new cooperative could be formed to exploit the market opportunity which, *ex hypothesi*, is there and would have been exploited by lateral expansion of existing enterprises under pure market capitalism.

This then is purely a problem of friction in enterprise formation. But it is a real problem.

It is for this reason – and in order to preserve the important competitive condition of freedom of entry for new enterprises – that I have suggested in *Employment, Inflation and Politics* (1976) a threshold size of enterprise, measured by number of employees, below which conventional capital entrepreneurship would continue to operate. The assumption behind this is that the creation of new enterprises to fill market gaps and to exploit new technologies is by its nature more easily undertaken (and therefore more likely to be undertaken) by an individual than by a spontaneous workers cooperative sprung ready-made from the dole queues.

As a direct corollary of this, provision has to be made for the conversion of a privately owned enterprise into a workers cooperative when the threshold size is reached. This is made significantly easier than it might otherwise be by the form of relationship described already between workers cooperatives and those who supply its capital. The founder-owner would himself be the owner of all the 'equity-like' obligations of the new workers cooperative; and he might also be entitled to a mortgage on the assets at their historic real value.

He might choose to sell his rights in the ordinary secondary market. He might be offered and accept a post as a senior manager in the enterprise by the new workers cooperative. He might choose to go and found a new venture, if that were his temperament. He might decide to rest on his laurels and his share in the future 'profits' of the cooperative.

It may still be argued that a tendency to under-employment in the workers cooperative economy will persist because the change in the company law whereby the new era would be accomplished necessarily introduces a friction into the operation of the classical labour market which was not there before.

However nearly this friction can be eliminated by simulating the mechanisms of captialism for absorbing unused labour into commercially viable activities, the full efficiency of the classical labour market cannot be reproduced.

The shortest way with this objection is to accept it. Indeed, the experience of Yugoslavia, for what it is worth, tends to corroborate the conclusion of *a priori* reasoning.

But, once again the point must be made that the comparison here is with the capitalist economy working with text-book perfection. Anyone who has accepted the argument on which the case for the cooperative economy is predicated must accept that that is not the choice that actually has to be made. Anyone who has not accepted that premise must be met on that ground anyway.

If, as is implied by the diagnosis of instability in our existing political economy, the choice for conventional capitalism, with its inevitable corollary of strongly developed collective bargaining, is between stability of a kind with a permanently very high level of unemployment and a progression towards hyper-inflation and then even higher unemployment, a considerable tendency to underemployment in a stable and workable alternative political economy may still be acceptable.

A direct quantitative comparison of the levels of unemployment implied by the alternative systems is not possible, since both magnitudes are unknown and extraordinarily difficult to estimate. But judgement may be assisted by the reflection that, whereas the unemployment implied by capitalism with conventional bargaining is inherent and structural in the sense that it is the direct counterpart to the fact of monopoly in the labour market, unemployment in the workers cooperative economy is inertial and frictional and will constantly tend to yield to market opportunities for new enterprises.

How Big can Workers Cooperatives Afford to be?

This is a large issue and cannot be adequately treated here. There is no question that experience and *a priori* reasoning both suggest that workers cooperatives work best when they are small – up to maybe a maximum of 1,000 members – and that their supposed advantages tend to evaporate as size rises much above that level.

These impressions need to be assessed rigorously and critically to establish how far they are universally true, to identify the precise reasons why they are true and to consider how far modifications of the design – including possible federal and confederal arrangements – may be able to raise the acceptable limit on numbers.

Of the 18 million people employed in the UK private sector in 1973 just over 7 million were employed in firms employing more than 1,000 people, of whom over 5½ million were in enterprises employing over 5,000 people and over 3,700,000 were in enterprises employing over 20,000 people. This is the picture given by the Bullock Report (Table 2 page 7).

Another 2 million are employed in public corporations, including nationalised industries, which tend to be large employers. A further 5 million are employed in central and local government administration and services. This leaves about 11 million people employed, predominantly in the private sector, in small enterprise units.

So, on the face of things about 9 million people appear to be employed in enterprises which may well be too large for effective workers cooperative functioning; and another 5 million government employees are not in the market economy at all, but may require in varying degrees and ways to be brought into it under the general concept of market socialism.

The question of the public corporations will be discussed in the next section. The question of marketising existing public services is briefly discussed under a later section in this paper. So, attention here is focussed on the 7 million or so private sector employees in enterprises which may at present be too large for easy conversion into workers cooperatives.

The first question which naturally arises is whether or not the present size of existing enterprises (and as Bullock very carefully acknowledges the Committee had to make some pretty heroic definitional stipulations in order to reduce the chaotic heterogeneity of the real world of diverse corporate structures to the neat categories of their statistics) reflects an objective industrial and commercial logic which could only be disturbed at great real cost.

This is a subject on which the literature is extensive and by no means unanimous. It is worth bearing in mind that the number of establishments in which more than say 2,000 people are employed on a common enterprise is small and accounts for a small fraction of the 7 million private sector employees in large companies.

The new study this year by Professor S.J. Prais, *The Evolution of Giant Firms in Britain*, tends to throw doubt on the industrial objectivity of the reasons for high concentration of employment in large firms. Instead it emphasises the role played by artificial financial factors, to say nothing of the natural temptations to monopoly wherever government policy and the law do not stand in the way (let alone where they actively encourage concentration, as in Britain during the post-1964 craze for restructuring British industry to meet the alleged competition of foreign-owned super-corporations).

Professor Prais concludes with the view that 'the encouragement of a progressive and competitive economy now requires a systematic series of policy measures aimed at tilting the balance throughout the range of firm-sizes; measures are required to offset the private financial advantages enjoyed by the largest firms, *to encourage individual plants to be run as independent businesses rather than as subsidiaries of a distant head-office*, and to foster an increase in the number of smaller independent firms to the level found in other economically advanced countries' (my italics).

Certainly, many conventional managements of large enterprises regard it as most efficient to run their component enterprises as if they were independent firms, with head-offices merely monitoring financial performance and intervening only to supply new capital and to ensure consistency on certain broad questions of corporate policy and strategy, labour relations commonly being an important head-office issue. In a world where the present artificial financial incentives to size and concentration were removed and where the conventional problem of labour relations had been replaced by the mechanisms of a workers cooperative, the need for firms to be larger than the appropriate size for individual plants might well appear weaker than it now is.

Nor have I involved any of the broader social, and social psychological, arguments for smaller units in which the individual feels less lost as a meaningless cog in an unintelligible, even hostile, machine. For what they are worth, they appear to favour smaller self-directing groups against giant hierarchical and remote structures.

The only general conclusion to be ventured at this stage is that the present state of knowledge does not warrant the automatic assumption that workers cooperatives cannot work above a certain size, which size is too small to accommodate modern industrial realities. There remain very important questions of fact and analysis to be investigated, including the degree to which there may be important economies of scale in marketing, research and design even where there are no real economies of scale in production. Even here it will be important to know how far these economies could not be equally well realised on an inter- rather than intra-enterprise basis, and how far the economies are specific only to the environment of a conventionally structured economy.

Finally, we have to remember yet again that the standard of comparison being made, when the pure artificialities have been excluded, is with an idealised free enterprise economy, not with the political economy we actually have.

What About the Statutory Monopolies?

This question can be quickly answered, so far as issues of principle are involved. Insofar as existing statutory monopolistic public corporations (and indeed public services) are so structured for reasons other than the effective impossibility or absurd diseconomies of competitive enterprise in the activity in question, then they should be split into competitive enterprises. The question whether such component competitive enterprises would be too large for organisation as workers cooperatives is no more than a special case of the general question of size already discussed.

Insofar as existing statutory monopolies are so structured because competitive enterprise would be impossible or absurd – say in sewage and some few other public utilities – then they must so remain. The question whether and to what degree they could then be organised as workers cooperatives can then be put on one side as a genuinely special case, the treatment of which does not have any critical significance for the general viability of the workers cooperative economy. My personal leaning would be against trying to establish workers cooperatives in such cases, preferring instead to adopt the model of, say, the police force where employment by such a public monopoly carries with it certain natural and widely accepted restrictions on the scope for collective bargaining.

What About the Technical Monopolies?

This question has now been considered as a special case of public monopolies.

Would Trade Union Monopoly Power Really Wither Away?

This is a critical question for the whole argument for a workers cooperative economy as a viable alternative to our present supposedly doomed political economy.

The case to answer has been well posed by Mr Samuel Brittan in a late draft of a volume of essays due for publication this year, of which he has been kind enough to afford me a preview. He writes:

> There is. . . no reason to suppose that industry-wide monopolistic behaviour by organised workers would stop. It would, of course, take the form of raising prices rather than wages, but the distinction would be one of form.

Indeed, workers coops could more easily combine directly with each other to raise return by limiting output, if they did not have to go through the inconvenience of threatened or actual strike behaviour first. Nor is there any reason to suppose that the tensions produced by an unstable balance of power between different groups of workers, and the resulting threat to employment and temptation to inflationary policies, would be any less than they are today. The most difficult wage issues and confrontations have even under the existing system been in the public sector, where the issue of profits has not even arisen and where the argument is clearly one with the rest of the community over relative shares.

If this view were correct, then indeed the thesis presented in the final part of my *Employment, Inflation and Politics* would fall to the ground. But this critique appears not to give sufficient weight to the following points:

(a) Strict competition between cooperatives in final markets is an essential element in the market socialist new political settlement, as I have proposed it;

(b) Effective anti-trust enforcement of this condition by law will be politically possible in a way that anti-combination laws are not enforceable, because, in the face of the threatened collapse of existing political economy, the political settlement itself will be able to command general assent in a way that what would look like a union-bashing capitalist counter-revolution would not, because individual cooperatives will have assets against which legal sanctions can be enforced and because of point (d) below;

(c) Small government, balanced budgets and Friedmanites' 'neutral' monetary growth are also essential features of the new settlement so that government will not be, and will be seen not to be, available as a universal provider and supporter of commercial enterprises;

(d) Once working people are organised, willy-nilly, into cooperatives the natural forces which tend eventually to undermine producer cartels of all kinds can begin to work, which is effectively impossible so long as the only perceived group identity of working people is as members of their union. Rival unions do not commonly produce close substitutes in final markets for each other's particular products and their sense of solidarity against capital in general prevents them from competing to supply cheaper labour to employers – but once the cooperative identity has been established the temptation to break ranks and undercut any collusive cartel price which might be illegally proposed will operate directly on the members of the cooperative wishing to extend its market share. If it did not, the provisions for new entry into the industry already described would put heavy pressure on them to do so and would anyway undermine the cartel price; and

(e) The arrangements already described for transforming public corporations into competitive workers cooperatives, technical monopolies apart, and the proposed marketisation of other public services are other integral elements in the political settlement and so dispose of the danger of special difficulties in the public sector except in the cases of the technical monopolies, where the proposed adoption of the police model of industrial relations would be easier in the context of the general settlement proposed.

In short, my answer to Mr Brittan is that there are indeed reasons to suppose that industry-wide monopolistic behaviour by organised workers would stop. These are that:

(a) it would be politically possible to make such behaviour illegal (in the sense of collusive price-setting);

(b) it would be politically and operationally easier to enforce such anti-trust legislation;

(c) it would be politically possible drastically to reduce the government's role as direct employer;

(d) workers organised into cooperatives would perceive much less need for trade unions (which are essentially a response of labour to the capitalist entrepreneur); and

(e) whether they perceived this or not, collective bargaining would disintegrate under the pressure, that eventually breaks all cartels, of the free-rider temptation which will operate on cooperatives as on conventional producers – though perhaps to a weaker degree because of the cooperative's interest in maximising income per head rather than the conventional profit and because of its acknowledged hesitancy over increasing its membership – because the imposition of a cartel is bound to mean reduced output and employment which each participating cooperative has an interest in minimising.

I am puzzled by Mr Brittan's reference to 'an unstable balance of power between different groups of workers'. He would be the last person to describe the relation between firms in a competitive market as an unstable balance of power, although of course he would not expect it to be static. The relationship between cooperatives is congruent with that between firms on the conventional competitive market.

Lastly, he misconstrues, I am sure through unclarity in my original exposition, my contention that workers 'need somehow to be disalienated enough to become infected with the entreprenurial realities which confront their employers, so that they will accept a non-inflationary market-determined environment as setting the level of rewards that can be afforded', if he thinks that by that I meant that workers are alienated by the fact of private profit as such.

I meant that as employees of enterprises, often large and remotely managed, the residual effects of whose financial successes and failures fall upon third parties (either shareholders or the government), employees have little perceived direct interest in the commercial performance and viability of those enterprises, except in certain moments of extreme crisis when it is usually too late. They simply want better rewards and have no opinion about how their employers will meet the cost. This point applied at least as much to public sector employees as to private; and therefore Mr Brittan is wrong to infer that the behaviour of public sector employees can only stem from a conscious claim on the rest of the community for a larger share (though that of course can be the only reality in what they are doing, just as it can be the only reality in the private sector except where profits can indeed be squeezed).

Mr Brittan also raises the spectre of all the cooperatives in a particular industry banding together to confront the government with a demand for privileged treatment – say, authorisation of a cartel – on pain of stopping all output. Why, he asks, would they be less likely to do so under market socialism?

This leads one into an important discussion of the differences between the economic realities of trade union behaviour and the purposes of such behaviour as perceived by the people who are instrumental in leading and supporting it.

It is certainly true that the only rationally predictable consequence of some forms of trade union behaviour in stateable circumstances would be, if that behaviour were successful in its declared purposes, to divert claims on the real disposable national income from the rest of the community to the affected members of the trade union in question. It does not follow that this is the purpose of the action as those members see it; and to make this distinction it is not necessary to suppose that the trade unionists in question are any less rational, informed, well-motivated, patriotic, altruistic or healthy in mind and body than those of us who presume to comment on their behaviour.

It is perfectly rational and ethical for any given group of producers or suppliers, who are allowed by law to operate a monopoly or cartel to do so to the limits of their self-interest; and this remains true even if it is not sensible or even morally right for a society to allow people in general to behave in this way. Of course, the monopolist's profit can only be secured at the expense of the rest of the community, since there is nowhere else for it to come from. But the people who exploit such an opportunity are merely seeking to promote their own legitimate advantage without harbouring any particular opinion about what the distributional effects diffused throughout society may or should be.

It may be said that every man is morally accountable for the foreseeable consequences of his actions, whether taken individually or collectively. But we do not expect a man in a queue to keep moving to the back because this confers a benefit on the rest of the community in the form of other people in the queue. We merely expect him not to jump the queue because that is the rule established by society for balancing self-interest against group interest in that situation. If queues as such are evil, then it is up to society to change the rules, not to rely on individual sacrificial gestures.

It may be said, taking for example a hypothetical threat by the massed cooperatives in the coal mining industry to refuse the nation supplies of coal until the rules of market socialism are abridged in their favour, that when the coal-miners defied the Heath government in 1973/74, they showed themselves willing to break explicit rules established by society in the form of an incomes policy law passed by Parliament. Leave aside the technicality that they only asked the executive to exercise a discretion which that law specifically provided to the executive.

Leave aside, too, the economic fact that what they sought was certainly no more than their economic value following the quadrupling of the price of oil.

Leave aside thirdly the tempting observation that this was precisely the kind of nonsensical situation which incomes policies breed and which market socialism would stand a better chance of avoiding by promoting a more effective and more probably acceptable form of market criterion for setting rewards to labour. The important point is that the miners maintained throughout and evidently believed that theirs

81

was essentially a conventional dispute about wages with their employers, the State, and not a dispute with parliament about the general framework of industrial and commercial law.

Obviously, there can be no way by law of ensuring that no one will ever break the law. What Mr Brittan imagines could happen. But in the wake of the new political settlement supposed – and that could not occur without general political consent having been secured to the settlement and consequent legislation – the mining cooperatives, if they were to fulfil Mr Brittan's speculation, would have openly and directly to demand a change in the framework law, not merely a modification of government policy, on pain of denial of supplies. It would explicitly be a demand on the rest of the community.

They would be seeking legal easement to charge monopoly or cartel prices which would fall directly and immediately on the rest of the community as individual and cooperative consumers of coal, without any muffling mediations through the Exchequer. They would also face the consequence that even coal has imperfect substitutes; and the community could decide, each man and cooperative for him and itself, how far they wished to pay the price of such special cases or how far they preferred to economise or switch to alternative fuels.

It may be said that there is nothing to prevent the government under present arrangements from passing on the effects of excessive public sector pay settlements and that private sector employers naturally have to do so and that this does not deter collective bargaining.

But this does not mean that the blame is necessarily attributed as it would be under market socialism. For, in advance of a new political settlement we live in a world which expects the government to extract quarts from pint pots, which is indeed frequently encouraged by actual and aspirant governments to expect such results and which accordingly blames governments for any disappointment of such expectations. The attribution of blame matters because it ultimately affects the enforceability of those laws where, as in this area, enforcement depends heavily on support not merely for the principle of the laws but also for the necessary sanctions against those who break the law.

Thus, it is seriously doubtful, at the very least, whether the avowed and conscious purpose of trade unionists as at present organised is to hold the nation to ransom in the customary headline writer's sense; and so they would more probably balk if forced to make their choice in that form. It is also clear that the enforcement of competition laws in the political context posited here would, again to say the least, have a better chance of success than the enforcement under present conditions either of wage control or anti-combination laws.

Would Governments be Able to be Any Less Inflationary?

As already stated, the political settlement which would inaugurate the world of market socialism under discussion here would commit governments to orthodox fiscal and monetary policies. There would be no discretionary demand management, no countervailing contracyclical judgements (though certain automatic fiscal stabilisation might be permitted, if it could be defined in a water-tight way) and no scope for financing government outgoings from the literal or metaphorical monetary printing presses.

So the question is whether there would develop insupportable political pressures to break these rules. Strong pressures could certainly develop.

Even if the system of competitive workers cooperatives was wholly successful in suppressing the evil effects of collective bargaining on real labour costs and so on employment, a sharp rise in world commodity prices would certainly cause a transitional domestic recession until other prices were forced down sufficiently to restore the previous average price level. If the rise in such world prices is real and not just a reflection of domestic inflation in supplying countries, then the effect cannot stably be absorbed by adjusting the sterling exchange rate.

In those circumstances, so long as what may for brevity here be referred to as the Keynesian illusion (though unfairly to Keynes) lingers in the public mind, pressure for reflation may well develop. But there are certain advantages in the new situation. There will be *ex hypothesi* much less prospect of the effects of the higher import prices leading into a domestic pay-price spiral because there will be no such spiral once pay is effectively market determined rather than determined by collective bargaining. If government does seek to accommodate the higher level of import costs by increasing monetary demand through fiscal or monetary means, the effect will be to drive down the sterling exchange rate in such a way as to achieve a new payments equilibrium at the new terms of trade; and with no pay-price spiral waiting to be aggravated that could be the end of the process. There will have been a once-and-for-all price increase at home, but no permanent increase in the inflation rate, still less any prospect of accelerating inflation of the kind inherent in trying to maintain full employment by expanding monetary demand while labour monopolies seek to earn a monopolist's return.

So, economically as well as politically it should become easier for governments to abjure the horn of accelerating inflation because the other horn of the current dilemma, namely an inherent domestic tendency to high unemployment, has been removed; and occasional disturbances from abroad can be accommodated without embarking again upon the old vicious circle.

This leaves out the possibility of a domestically generated recession. Since government policy is *ex hypothesi* neutral, this would originate in an imbalance of domestic savings and investment. A modern monetarist may incline to scepticism about the likelihood of such a development and be willing to rely on automatic monetary stabilisers, in the form of falling interest rates, to correct the recession.

There is also the possibility, once the new political settlement is established and working well and collective bargaining has faded away more or less entirely, of permitting a cautious revival of Keynesian ideas.

Once the effects of monopolistic bargaining have been eradicated the notion of demand efficiency becomes much less dangerous. A modern monetarist might at least accept that the natural level of unemployment (i.e. the non-inflationary level) would be much reduced by the elimination of the monopoly effect and that therefore the inflation-generating gap between the natural level and likely governmental employment targets would be reduced.

A modern Keynesian, who had nonetheless accepted that incomes policies could not solve the unemployment-inflation problem, would certainly argue that the way was now clear to resume discretionary demand management, provided only that the available quality of forecasting was sufficient to give a substantial probability that action would in practice tend to be contra- rather than pro-cyclical. The modern monetarist will still worry that official employment targets will be set above the natural or sustainable rate and that therefore accelerating inflation could be reborn, because even in the absence of collective bargaining there are plenty of other structural and frictional reasons why full employment will not be fully attainable.

If unemployment does tend to settle down at an uncomfortably high level, affected in part by any tendency of a workers cooperative economy to under-employment as already discussed, then this condition will have to be carefully and empirically examined. Monetarists will tend to argue that such a tendency is evidence of a high natural rate of unemployment and therefore of the presence of structural and frictional causes which may or may not have been identified. Keynesians will tend to suspect demand deficiency.

A careful and jointly monitored experiment might throw light on the correct interpretation. Let the government take up by fiscal or monetary action all or some part of the demand gap as estimated by the Keynesians. Then wait five years. If the employment position improves markedly without any strong tendency for prices to rise correspondingly and for the level of economic activity to fall back after the first stimulative effects wear off, then demand deficiency will appear to have been the right diagnosis and may be acted upon on subsequent occasions.

Whither to Extend the Market Economy?

The short answer is in the direction of what is now government activity, including those areas which, though technically in the private sector, are so heavily regulated or dependent on government aid and custom that market criteria do not in effect determine behaviour.

It includes the provision of social services as well as the mainstream industrial and other productive activities such as agriculture. It implies that distributional policies, however egalitarian or inegalitarian, will be seen mainly as an operation affecting cash incomes; and, while in some areas it may be convenient for the government or some statutory agency – or even a state promoted workers cooperative – to continue to provide some or, in the absence of any other entrants to the field, all of a particular service, the concept implies that the consumer would acquire the service on market terms and that the signals so given of consumer preference would determine the scale and direction of future service. The cooperativisation of nationalised industries has already been discussed; and the main thrust under this heading will be in areas not traditionally regarded as primarily economic, such as education, housing, health, personal services and broadcasting.

This is not the place to be more specific, although in the case of broadcasting I would draw attention to my evidence to the Annan Committee (*Encounter*, April, 1977) which seeks to explain how the principles of the present print publishing market could and should be applied to electronic publishing when the next generation of spectrum technology becomes available towards the end of the century. Much work done by the Institute of Economic Affairs has opened up a number of interesting avenues for investigation of the possible application of market principles to education, social, health and personal services in ways which need not conflict with the original compassionate and social purposes of those services. In the context of a market socialist political settlement these would become germane, just as many of the ideas developed over many years by Professor James Meade for correcting specific and ascertained market failures in areas involving public goods and external diseconomics would be even more obviously necessary than they already are, as well as being more easily distinguishable from extensions of state intervention which have quite other rationales.

Why is the Record of Workers Cooperatives so Poor?

There is a popular knock-down argument against almost all claims on behalf of the workers cooperative economy, namely that if cooperatives had the advantages attributed to them they would, as Samuel Brittan and Peter Lilley imply in their book this year *The Delusion of Incomes Policy*, spread 'like wildfire' through the economy without benefit or statutory imposition. And they have not. Therefore, either they cannot have the advantages claimed or there must be other, more than offsetting, unconsidered disadvantages.

This is a little too fast. For one thing there have been and are a number of impediments to such a spontaneous combustion. More importantly, the argument for the workers cooperative economy is an argument for a change of system because of systematic defects in the present political economy; and it is often the case that the switch to a better system is not self-propagating, as for example with the adoption of a 'Keep Left' or 'Keep Right' rule of the road.

This is not the occasion to review the evidence of producer cooperative successes and failures in North America and Europe. Experience is concentrated in the two hundred years from the middle of the seventeenth century to the middle of the present century; and in very broad terms it leaves an impression that producer cooperatives have tended to be small, to be short-lived and to have difficulty surviving in the prevailing environment, although there are some important exceptions.

But this evidence has to be interpreted with great care, if morals are to be drawn about the viability of market socialism. The American evidence and literature have been usefully examined by Derek C. Jones (of Hamilton College, Clinton, New York) in a privately circulated paper, *The Economics and Industrial Relations of Producer Cooperatives in the United States 1791-1939*. He throws considerable doubt on the conventional view that American producer cooperatives failed through inherent internal weaknesses.

He draws attention to the extent to which many American cooperatives were not truly workers cooperatives in the sense in which self-management is defined by J. Vanek (the chief modern theorist of labour managed market economies, see his *The General Theory of Labor-Managed Market Economies*, Cornell University Press, 1970), namely enterprises where all control, management and income remains in the hands of those who actually work in the given enterprise on the basis of equality of vote.

The European experience has some similar features, although there are also many differences of which the most important is that the record is by no means so seemingly dismal as in North America. There is little doubt that in Britain the extreme hostility from the end of the nineteenth century of trade unions and socialist intellectuals to workers cooperatives discouraged their development.

The Webbs were peculiarly fierce against them on the dubious grounds that workers cooperatives were necessarily an element in a world of producer sovereignty to which they quite rightly preferred consumer sovereignty as the only coherent basis of legitimacy for any economic activity (see their 'Cooperative Production and Profit-Sharing', *New Statesman* Special Supplement, 1914, and *A Constitution for the Socialist Commonwealth of Great Britain*, Longmans, 1921).

But the stronger point is the purely logical one that nothing necessarily follows about the rival merits of labour- and capital-managed economies from the experience of individual cooperatives operating in the context of a capital-managed economy. Insofar as the crucial advantage urged for the labour-managed economy is that it would cause collective bargaining (in which incidentally the Webbs and the classical American consumer supremacists strongly believed) to wither away, so dissolving the catastrophic dilemma of high unemployment or accelerating inflation, that cannot be tested by examining the experience of individual cooperatives in a capital-managed economy where the general need for trade union organisation and collective bargaining is bound to be strongly felt.

We have already discussed whether and why collective bargaining would wither away in a labour-managed economy. Manifestly it would not do so just for the benefit of an odd cooperative here and there. Trade unions with a powerful base in the conventional sectors of the economy will take good care to see that it does not, unless they regard the individual case as too small to matter, as has occurred with some small or commercially doomed cooperatives. One only has to reflect on the attitude of the TUC and key national trade union leaders to the forms of industrial democracy urged upon and accepted by the Bullock Committee to appreciate what would be and indeed has always been their natural and inevitable attitude to the creation of a genuinely independent expression of workers' power.

Obviously so long as the main power-base of collective bargaining remains, as it is bound to do in a free society with a capital-managed economy, ways would be sought and probably found of preventing any serious tendency for workers cooperatives to undercut union labour prices. What is more, the entrepreneurs of potential workers cooperatives, themselves workers, are virtually reluctant to embark upon ventures which could and would be represented as anti-union and therefore, under our present political economy, anti-labour and anti-working class.

In these circumstances it will seldom pay any individual enterprise to become a workers cooperative, overcoming all the substantial inertial and transitional problems at the same time. It follows that the lack of evidence of a general tendency for workers cooperatives to propagate themselves except in circumstances of total commercial failure of the conventional enterprise proves nothing about the potentialities of a workers cooperative economy. As every social thinker knows, in a theatre on fire it does not pay the individual to behave unilaterally as it would pay him to behave if he had good reason to think that everyone else would so behave on condition of his so behaving. For the benefit to him, in the form of a better chance of escaping the theatre unharmed, flows, not from his own orderly restraint, but from the orderly restraint of everyone else; and orderly restraint on his part would be irrational, albeit heroic, if it were not the price of the orderly restraint of others from which he can expect to benefit more than he expects to benefit from disorderly self-assertion in the absence of a mutual restraint agreement. In other words, conduct which in the context of a changed system of rules would benefit the whole community and all or most individuals in that community is not self-propagating merely by the individual's pursuit of private advantage as perceived in an unchanged context. This phenomenon is a cliché and should not need to be laboured.

Yugoslavia

The description 'market socialism' has commonly been applied to the economic system which has prevailed under Marshal Tito in Yugoslavia.

It is natural to inquire, when market socialism is proposed for other economies, how it has fared in the one place where it is supposed to have been tried.

I am not able here to answer that question. Impressions of tendencies to under-employment, inflation and under-investment have certainly been reported by some observers. Others have detected some successes. Any final evaluation must allow fully for the differences in the circumstances and system of Yugoslavia from any other economy to which the model of market socialism might be applied.

Yugoslavia is far from having a fully developed industrial economy. It is poor. It is under authoritarian Communist rule, though it is not part of the Moscow-dominated Communist bloc in Eastern Europe. It relies heavily on state planning as the predominant mode of resource allocation; and the outside capital for investment by cooperatives comes mainly from the state, not from private savers through a free capital market. It is most doubtful whether free trade unions would be possible in the Western sense, whether or not cooperative forms of enterprise management made them otiose.

In these circumstances it is uncertain how much could be definitively learned about the potentialities of a workers cooperative economy in Western Europe and North America from the experience of Yugoslavia, but clearly it should be examined more thoroughly than it yet appears to have been by English-language economists.

Can We Go Step by Step towards Market Socialism?

The argument already presented for regarding the change to market socialism as unlikely to be self-propagating because the private and social advantages will only be enjoyed after the system has been changed must tend by parity of reasoning to weaken the idea of a step-by-step approach. If it is an all-or-nothing choice, then it cannot be had bit by bit.

This is a real difficulty, because any practical politician who sees merit in the general thrust of the argument will want to find ways of moving gradually towards the goal, that being the nature of non-revolutionary politics. Moreover, others who see *prima facie* merits in the argument, but who would like more evidence from hard experience before trying to turn a whole modern economy inside out, will naturally and properly look for some limited experiment.

Alasdair Clayre, writing (in *The Economist* for 5–11th March, 1977) sympathetically to the idea of self-managed enterprises, explains his own preference for 'self-management as one sector of a mixed economy'. Any sensible man would prefer at least to start out by this route, provided that the general systematic advantages of a workers cooperative economy could be expected to be given a fair trial in a mere sector of a conventional capital-managed or mixed economy.

It may be that experiments could be conducted in some fairly self-contained sector, where the existing trade union organisation and collective bargaining procedures are specific to that industry or sector alone. Coal mining is a tempting example. Schools, postal services, newspapers, professional and technical services, railways, fisheries and parts of the entertainment industry may be others. But the heart of the matter is manufacturing industry, where general and craft unions predominate over industrial unions and where, even if they did not, it is hard to see how one could bite on a mere part of the bullet without forfeiting the prospects of a transformation of the patterns of pay determination.

There is also a real danger that in the next few years the creation of a cooperative will become the standard response of workers to the bankruptcy of their conventional employers and that, as a result, the idea will be put on test in hopeless circumstances in which neither the systemic nor even the internal benefits of cooperatives will have a fair chance. *The Scottish Daily News* and the Meriden Cooperative are a warning. The Plessey plants at present under threat of closure may be other cases in point.

The central argument is for a workers cooperative economy and should continue to be pressed as such. If ways can be found to conduct genuine and fair experiments, so much the better. But the advocate of a market socialist solution to our macro problems will have to be vigilant against the real danger of unfavourable conclusions being drawn from partial and biased contexts which do not and cannot test the main thesis.

Do Workers Want Cooperatives?

They may or they may not, according to the prospects as they see them for job security, living standards and influence over those aspects of their working lives which most concern them under conventional and alternative management. They cannot reasonably be expected to appraise the macro-economic arguments for a workers cooperative economy on the basis of the information at present given them by their employers and trade union leaders; and, even if they could so appraise the arguments and did appraise them favourably, that would be very far from giving them sufficient reasons of private advantage in each or any of their particular employments for preferring a cooperative form of management. Anyone who is in a position to rip off the taxpayer, negligent shareholder, indulgent proprietor or exploitable consumer is clearly well advised to continue doing so as long as people are foolish or kind enough to let him get away with it.

But the argument here, unlike that in the Bullock report, in no way depends on what the currently expressed or even eventual preference of workers may be. It is not to be done because workers want or demand it. It is to be done whether they prefer it or not, although of course subject to the basic democratic sanction of the ballot box and the Parliamentary majority, because this is the only or best way of preventing a calamity for the whole community.

An unintelligently hostile expression of the underlying thought would be, 'OK, you've fought capitalism to a standstill and it won't work anymore; the government's cupboard is bare and it can't play sugar-daddy so now you run it, but without coercing consumers, taxpayers or savers.' That would be unintelligent because it confuses in the word 'you' working people as organised in trade unions with working people as such and because it imputes either folly or malignity to them, where the fault lies not in the intentions of any man, but in the institutional framework for expressing his intentions.

The problem would not be essentially different in character from what it is if every single participant in the economy had a Ph.D. in economics, was a devout supporter of the traditional principles of the United States Republican Party and was as fully concerned for the welfare of his neighbour as is commonly thought to be desirable. It would, of course, be different if every participant were a saint and an ascetic because in that case there would be little call for any economic activity at all.

In the circumstances of a community of wise, understanding, well-motivated and normally materialistic individuals, they will and must behave broadly as they now do, so long as they are organised into pressure groups and sectional lobbies, because in a world of what Samuel Brittan has called 'collective extortion' the loner is a sucker and his dependants suffer.

But in such a community the individuals would also jointly decide, if they perceived the option, to abstain by collective agreement from mutually stultifying and eventually destructive modes of pursuing sectional advantage. That would be a political and not an economic or industrial decision; and in that decision the voices that count are the voices of every individual as a total human being, not just the voices of one economic category, however large, expressing only one aspect of themselves.

It would pay every motorist to get free petrol; and the overwhelming majority of the adult population are motorists. Yet, we are very far from providing free petrol. No more can the opinion of workers *qua* workers, still less trade unionists *qua* trade unionists, supposing it were sceptical about cooperative organisation, be decisive if it conflicts with the general interest of the community, although as has been said no political action can be taken until the democratic conditions are fulfilled. To fulfil them is the political task for market socialists.

Paper for Manchester Statistical Society 17 March 1977

A Case for a Select Committee
On Economic Affairs

Contents

I.   Introduction 1-5
II. Nature and Role of a SCEA 6-14
III. The Joint Economic Committee of the United
     States Congress 15-23
IV. General Case for a SCEA 24
     A British Council of Economic Advisers 25-27
     SCEA and Select Committee on Expenditure 28-34
     Whitehall v. Who? 35
     Parliament, NEDC and Accountability 36
     Diagnosis Before Cure 37-40
     Bringing in the Outsiders 41
V.   Objections 42-3
     Manning 44-5
     The Floor of the House 46-9
     A Para-Executive 50-52
     American Transplants 53-57
     The Treasury's Evidence 58-74
VI. Conclusion 75-78

I.   Introduction

1. A Parliamentary Select Committee on Economic Affairs (SCEA) would make a major contribution both to the vitality of Parliamentary democracy and to the conduct of economic affairs. Recent events to do with Parliamentary scrutiny of public expenditure have prepared much of the ground for such a further large initiative.

2. The purpose of this memorandum is to sketch the general case for a SCEA and to examine some of the familiar objections to it. The shape of the paper is:

(a) to define the nature and role of a SCEA;
(b) to describe briefly the partial analogy of the Joint Economic Committee of the United States Congress;
(c) to state the general case for a SCEA in Britain; and
(d) to examine certain objections which have been brought against it.

3. We are aware that the Treasury, in both written and oral evidence to the Select Committee on Procedure last year, evinced an unmistakably negative attitude to proposals such as those in this memorandum. We are not unduly dismayed by this. For, we have noted that in evidence to the same Committee last year the Treasury showed some enthusiasm and took much credit for the idea that the public expenditure side of the Government's medium-term planning should be brought under closer and more systematic study. The previous history of this proposal suggests that Treasury opposition at an early stage need not invariably prove fatal to a soundly based idea. For example, on 20 May, 1958, Sir Norman Brook, the Joint Permanent Secretary to the Treasury, gave oral evidence to the Select Committee on Estimates which was examining Treasury Control of Expenditure. The Committee subsequently issued a highly critical report which launched the long progress of the public expenditure review culminating in December's Treasury White Paper (Cmnd. 4234) setting out expenditure plans to 1973–74 and in the two-day debate on 21–22 January 1970, on the White Paper. Replying to a question (Q. 3108) suggesting that 'in the present age the system of annual estimates is really rather out of date and that there ought to be a longer term view taken', Sir Norman remarked 'in some ways there would be advantages if a longer period could be taken for certain purposes; but I doubt myself whether it could be accommodated in our Parliamentary procedures and our annual budgeting'. This, of course, was precisely what the Treasury's Green Paper (Cmnd. 4017) of April 1969, proposed should be done and is now being done.

4. Three years after Sir Norman's testimony, the Plowden Committee, which in other respects took the second large stride forward in the development of the public expenditure review, reported (Cmnd. 1432):

It is therefore doubtful whether any government will feel able to place these surveys before Parliament and the public. To do this would involve disclosing the Government's long-term intentions of a wide range of public expenditure; and also explaining the survey's assumptions about employment, wages, prices and all the other main elements in the national economy. It would be surprising if any government were prepared to do this.

Surprising it may have been to the Committee. But Governments were already doing it less than thirty months after the Plowden Report was published – namely in the Maudling White Paper of December 1963 (Cmnd. 2235); and they have done – more or less – in seven subsequent publications: The National Plan (Cmnd. 2764) in September 1965; the Callaghan White Paper (Cmnd. 2915) in February 1966; the Wilson statement (Cmnd. 3515) in January 1968; the Department of Economic Affairs report 'The Task Ahead' and the first Jenkins White Paper (Cmnd. 3936) both in February 1969; the Jenkins Green Paper (Cmnd. 4017) in April 1969; and the second Jenkins White Paper (Cmnd. 4234) in December 1969.

5. We wish to make one other introductory point. We believe that the conduct of public policy and the quality of politics improves or deteriorates in direct relation to the quality of public debate about it. The quality of public debate in its turn varies directly with the quality of information and understanding deployed, not by the government, but by its chief interlocutor. For, the level of debate, like that of tennis or chess, tends to be set by the weaker participant. On the ability of Parliament to conduct a serious dialogue with Government depends, not merely the vitality and effectiveness of Parliament itself, nor even just public respect for politics, but also the ability of the Government itself to improve the quality of its own conduct of policy. For too long, in too many areas of too great importance, too much of this task has been left frankly to the Press, who perforce make a sorry job of it. Indeed, the press might do its primary job of reporting and commenting on the news very much better if it were not also having to stand in for Parliament as watch-dog and interlocutor of the executive.

II. Nature and Role of a SCEA

6. We envisage the staple diet of the SCEA as being of three kinds:–

(a) current economic assessment;
(b) consideration of the long-term economic, fiscal and financing implications of the Government's annual public expenditure White Papers; and

(c) investigation of special topics, e.g. poverty economics, international monetary reform, trade policy and multi-national companies.

7. The only formal product of the SCEA's activities would be reports. These would not be expected to judge or to recommend policy as such. But they would be expected to serve as convenient sources of information and as clarification of the issues with which policy has to deal–in other words as useful briefs for MPs taking part in ensuing debates on either side. Without prejudging the debates, the reports should enhance their quality by disposing of red herrings, by highlighting known facts, by elucidating new facts and by refining issues to the point at which political controversy can and should most usefully begin.

8. The SCEA would, of course, have no formal powers of legislation, resolution or appointment. How far it should have control over its own choice of subject, in addition to its obligatory annual tasks, over its own procedure and over its own staff can be left to be decided later. These questions are not central.

9. The SCEA would need a substantial staff, including perhaps five professional economists, as well as the ability to retain consultants *ad hoc* when required.

10. The SCEA would normally be expected to take written and oral evidence from any whom it thought professionally or otherwise qualified to give it, as well as from Ministers and Government servants. We would hope that, in so far as Parliamentary custom and the nature of matters under examination could be made to permit, the SCEA would hold most of its hearings in public with access afforded to the Press. The thought here is that this would substantially enhance the chances that the activities of the Committee would achieve the purpose of raising the level of public debate and understanding about economic policy and at the same time of reflecting credit on Parliament as the natural and most effective focus of such debate and information. We recognise, however, that private hearings would suit the proposed Committee's convenience better on some occasions. Officials would be normally expected, so far as they were able without impropriety or impairing their primary duty to Ministers, to assist the SCEA in its task of gathering information and clarifying issues. The conventional constitutional doctrines about the role of officials would be scrupulously observed. Equally, the contention that the executive should inform and consult Parliament would be borne somewhat more actively in mind.

11. Subject to the availaibility of staff and funds, the SCEA would be permitted to undertake and commission research which was directly relevant to and needed for current enquiries. But it would not become a patron of economic research for the sake of the art.

12. The SCEA should have a sufficiently large membership to enable it to man up to half a dozen sub-committees pursuing simultaneous enquiries.

13. Special Parliamentary time might be needed to debate some of the SCEA's reports, if they excited sufficient special interest amongst Members for there to be a demand for this. But normally the SCEA's reports would serve as valuable material for the existing apparatus of economic, budget, expenditure and other debates on whose contents the reports would frequently bear. It would be understood informally that an almost equally important benefit from the SCEA's activities was its role in initiating, sustaining and enhancing public debate on a range of economic issues.

14. At present much depends on the Press and on a few learned institutes to bridge the gap between on the one hand the deliberations of Government, including its private and quasi-private exchanges with industry, labour and other vested clients and on the other hand the work of academic economists in universities and elsewhere. There is also a wider public in Parliament and outside it which needs and wants to know more about what these two groups are doing and thinking and to see the two confront each other. A SCEA would be uniquely well placed to conduct (in the orchestral sense) such a discussion, thereby simultaneously enhancing the standing of Parliament itself, promoting public information and understanding and almost certainly improving the conduct of public affairs.

III. The Joint Economic Committee of the United States Congress

15. The analogy of the American JEC is only partial. But certain basic facts are worth recording about it.

16. The JEC was established by the Employment Act of 1946. It was the third of three innovations in that Act. The other two were the obligation on the President of the United States to make an annual Economic Report to the Congress and the creation of a Council of Economic Advisers to the President within his Executive Office. This tripartite constellation was interdependent and was designed to sustain

the policy declaration set out in the second section of the Act. This, which was the nearest US equivalent of the British Employment Policy White Paper (Cmnd. 6527) of May 1944, read:

> Sec. 2. *The Congress hereby declares that it is the continuing policy and responsibility of the Federal Government to use all practicable means* consistent with its needs and obligations and other essential considerations of national policy, with the assistance and cooperation of industry, agriculture, labour, and State and local governments, to coordinate and utilize all its plans, functions, and resources for the purpose of creating and maintaining, in a manner calculated to foster and promote free competitive enterprise and the general welfare, conditions under which there will be afforded useful employment opportunities, including self-employment, for those able, willing and seeking to work, and to *promote maximum employment, production, and purchasing power.*

17. The main function of the Economic Report was to set out a programme for realising this policy. The Council's main job was to help prepare the Economic Report and otherwise to help in developing policies in accordance with the Congress' declaration of policy. The task of the JEC was to receive the Economic Report of the President, to study matters relating to it, to study means of coordinating programmes in order to further the policy of the Act and to report by 1 March each year on the President's Economic Report. It was also enjoined to make such other reports and recommendations as it thought advisable. In 1949 it was further authorised to issue a monthly publication entitled *Economic Indicators.*

18. The membership of the JEC was to be drawn equally from House and Senate reflecting the party majority in each. At present the Act, as amended, provides for ten members from each chamber, six of whom shall come from the majority party in each case. The chairmanship and vice-chairmanship alternate two-yearly, with one coming from each chamber. Thus, at present, Senator William Proxmire and Congressman Wright Patman take turns Congress by Congress in taking the chair.

19. The Act also provides carefully for the JEC's minimum logistic requirements:

> . . . (d) The joint committee, or any duly authorized sub-committee thereof, is authorized to hold such hearings as it deems advisable, and, within the limitations of its appropriations, the joint committee is empowered to appoint and fix the compensation of such experts, consultants, technicians, and clerical and stenographic assistants, to procure such printing and

binding, and to make such expenditures, as it deems necessary and advisable. (The cost of stenographic services to report hearings of the joint committee, or any sub-committee thereof, shall not exceed 25 cents per hundred words.) The joint committee is authorized to utilize the services, information, and facilities of the departments and establishments of the Government, and also of private research agencies.

(e) To enable the joint committee to exercise its powers, functions, and duties under this Act, there are authorized to be appropriated for each fiscal year such sums as may be necessary, to be disbursed by the Secretary of the Senate on vouchers signed by the Chairman or vice-chairman.

20. The JEC has eight sub-committees (with between seven and thirteen members on each) on the following subjects:

Economy in Government.
Economic Progress.
Inter-American Economic Relationships.
Foreign Economic Policy.
International Exchange and Payments.
Economic Statistics.
Fiscal Policy.
Urban Affairs.

21. The JEC has no legislative functions, in the sense that it does not like other operational committees draft laws for presentation to the floor of the Senate and the House. Nor does the JEC confirm Presidential appointments, the second executive responsibility of major Senate committees such as the Senate Foreign Relations Committee. Indeed, the JEC's role is essentially educational. The regulation of government spending, of tax rates and of banking is all under the executive responsibility of other committees.

22. To the end of 1968 the JEC had issued over four hundred reports. It is proud of the fact that, unlike the taxing and appropriations committees of both chambers, it looks at both sides of the fiscal balance in an economic light rather than merely measuring the degree of popular enthusiasm for a particular item of expenditure or taxation in isolation from the total budget picture into which it may fit. Over the years the JEC pioneered public discussion of such topics as:

Inflation (1946–49) when full employment was still widely expected to be the greatest post-war problem;
Economic poverty and techniques for alleviating it (1949), a lively topic twenty-one years later;

Automation (1954), before it became fashionable;
Monetary Policy Reform (1951–52), years before Radcliffe;
Full employment, growth and price levels (late '50s), before President
Kennedy called it the 'new economics' when his first Council of
Economic Affairs chairman, Walter Heller, espoused it from 1961.

The JEC also took early interest in the role of the money supply, taking
evidence from Professor Friedman more than ten years ago. Again it was
very early into the field on the question of greater exchange rate
flexibility, well before the Nixon Administration and the 1969 annual
meeting of the International Monetary Fund made it respectable officially. They have already been looking for a few years at the question of a
link between the creation of international liquidity by means of IMF
Special Drawing Rights and increasing international aid flows to
developing countries. This is still some way from becoming officially
respectable amongst leaders of the international monetary world. Again,
it was the JEC that was one of the first even in Washington to take a real
interest in the output budgeting method of planning and evaluating
expenditure programmes in the public sector. The list could go on and
on.

23. Beyond question much of the JEC's great distinction in the 1950s
(when it outshone the Council of Economic Advisers in US economic
policy formation) was due to the exceptional talents, energy and
economic intelligence of one man, Senator Paul Douglas of Illinois. But,
even since 1961, when the Kennedy Council began to claw back much of
the limelight, the JEC has continued to play a vital part both in opening
up new topics and in engaging the Council of Economic Advisers in a
level of debate normally worthy of the steel of men like Jim Tobin,
Walter Heller, Gardner Ackley, Arthur Okun, Paul McCracken and
Henrik Houthakker. Two recent chairmen of the Council have strongly
confirmed to one of us the importance of the role of the JEC as a foil to
their own work within the Administration, even though on occasions
they have been locked in surprisingly bitter controversy with the JEC.
Most officials know, we think, how hard it is to make confident and
effective policy in complete isolation from any critical interrogation
from the outside world. This is strongly confirmed by the American
experience; and it will emerge as one of our particular reasons for a
SCEA in Britain.

IV. General Case for a SCEA

24. The general case for a SCEA rests on the following main points:

(a) it would be a necessary counterpart to any move to create a formal Council of Economic Advisers in Whitehall–the case for which is explained in paras 25-7;

(b) it would be a necessary counterpart to the Select Committee on Expenditure proposed by last year's Select Committee on Procedure Report, which was endorsed by almost every speaker in last month's debate;

(c) the conduct of economic policy is unlikely to be as good as it should be so long as Whitehall is not matched by another constitutional body with the authority of Parliament itself and equipped to discuss economic policy at least at the same level of sophistication;

(d) the standing of Parliament requires that Parliament itself should not surrender to the unelected National Economic Development Council and the rest of the official network for consulting interest groups its fundamental duty of scrutinising and questioning government policy in the vital area of economic affairs–indeed, the problem of 'industrial interference in government' through the operation of official non-elected bodies and committees is, we believe, one that should soon receive Parliament's particular attention;

(e) a SCEA would be uniquely well placed to open up to rational public inquiry new areas of possible economic policy, to marshal facts and arguments and to promote wider public discussion before Government has made up its mind – in the past it has too often occurred that, after resisting a new policy for many years, the Treasury has suddenly adopted it as a result of internal deliberations whose nature is inevitably concealed from the public; and

(f) more generally, a SCEA would be well placed to serve as a focus of public discussion at a high professional level on the major unsolved questions of how economic systems work, thereby drawing into a single dialogue the official, industrial and academic arguments which at present confront each other too seldom.

A British Council of Economic Advisers

25. The establishment of a British Council of Economic Advisers has been advocated with increasing frequency in the past few years and a very strong case (para. 24a) can be made for it. Essentially it rests on the need for a focus of explicitly professional economic expertise within Whitehall independent of the regular departmental hierarchies and supplementary to the economists now diffused through the operational branches of government. Departmental economists have inevitably to focus on problems of greatest interest – and this often means immediate interest – to their own Ministries. The more they become embedded in their departments and contribute to departmental policies – highly desirable objectives in themselves – the less well-placed they are to form detached and far-ranging judgements. Inevitably too, common loyalties develop and certain professional approaches become established, which make it difficult for economists outside the reigning philosophy to make a mark. In our view a Council of Economic Advisers would be a healthy middle way between the unfettered sway of departmental expertise and the unsatisfactory institutionalised conflict of the former Treasury–DEA division.

26. We would not wish to be dogmatic about the exact form of the CEA; but essentially it would be there to study problems, often but not invariably of a longer term or more basic character, either at the request of Ministers and officials or at their own initiative. They would not be a group of 'independent wise men', but an essential part of the government machine, enjoying only such independence as might in any case come to professional civil servants in the wake of the Fulton recommendations. To underline the official status, the top three or four Government Economic Advisers might well form the majority of members, to which would be added a minority of university academics on short service assignments, either full-time or part-time. The Council would be served by a small full-time staff of economists. Conventions could be established under which the outside members would not be committed to the policy judgements contained in the published reports which, we would hope, would become a main feature of the Council's work.

27. The creation of a CEA would be a sufficient reason for setting up a SCEA. It is a sound principle, much regarded by the US Congress, when creating or institutionalising a new expertise in the Executive, at the same time to equip the legislature to match that expertise so that

Congressional or Parliamentary scrutiny of the administration can keep pace. On the other hand, even if a CEA were not established, a SCEA should still be created for the other reasons given in this paper.

SCEA and Select Committee on Expenditure

28. The need (para. 24b) for a SCEA to complement the Select Committee on Expenditure proposed by last year's Select Committee on Procedure was well explained in a memorandum (of May 6 1969) by the Procedure Committee's Specialist Adviser, Mr James Robertson, which was printed with the report. We quote paragraphs 4 and 5:

> General
> 4. The thesis is that, as in planning and controlling the way public expenditure is laid out (i.e. the way in which resources are used in the public sector or are transferred by government action to various parts of the private sector from others), so in planning and controlling the way it is financed (i.e. the way the use of resources is foregone in the private sector is transferred by government action from various parts of it to others) Parliament has to consider:
> (a) Policy.
> (b) Management.
> (c) Results.
> This means that Parliament should be in a position:
> (a) to have well-informed debates several years in advance about the policy (including economic policy) implications of financing projected public expenditure by various alternative mixes of taxation, contributions, borrowing, and charges;
> (b) to examine, in the proposed Select Committee on Economic and Financial Affairs, both the adequacy with which the material for these debates is being prepared and presented and also the management efficiency of the various government agencies and departments (such as the Revenue Departments and the Bank of England) responsible for handling taxation, government borrowing, etc.;
> (c) to scrutinise retrospectively the success with which these agencies and departments have been operating.
> 5. The debates on policy should, of course, be the same debates as those which it is proposed to arrange on the annual White Paper on Public Expenditure. Public expenditure policy and public financing policy both have to be debated as elements in economic policy.

29. The essential point here is that the Select Committee on Expenditure picks up the public expenditure review at the point at which the

growth of the public sector as a whole has been decided or assumed. From there it proceeds to an increasingly detailed examination of the progressive sub-division of that total in the light of the Government's policy priorities. This is excellent; but the starting point is itself arbitrary, or must seem so to Parliament, unless there is an opportunity to examine and debate the considerations which underlie it. In Whitehall's own deliberations, to which Parliament is at last trying to adapt its own procedures, the total for public expenditure derives from considerations of the prospective behaviour of the economy (growth, external balance, etc.) and of the fiscal and financial implications of pre-empting any particular percentage of the national economy to the public sector.

30. Indeed, historically, one of Whitehall's earliest motives for mounting the public expenditure review was to identify the implications for future taxation and budgetary policy of the programmes of public expenditure which were being developed. This enabled successive Cabinets, when they wished, to set certain limits to expenditure commitments precisely in order to reflect their strategic fiscal intentions. If Parliament is to be deprived of the whole of the financing or income side of the balance sheet (or at least to be denied the facilities of a SCEA to examine it properly), then the ability of Parliament to understand and accept the Government's thinking on the expenditure side is bound to be weakened.

31. The interaction between the two sides of the account was central to the Plowden Committee's thinking nine years ago. At the 'core of our proposals' they recommended that 'regular surveys should be made of public expenditure as a whole, over a period of years ahead, *and in relation to prospective resources; decisions involving substantial future expenditure should be taken in the light of these surveys*'. (Paragraph 12a.) It is not sensible to expect Parliament to study the surveys and their internal priorities without thinking about the reasons behind the constraints on total expenditure which must be the ultimate source of most of the problems lower down the line.

32. Moreover, unless the totality of public expenditure programmes are well aligned with the future capacity of the economy and with the willingness of governments to make the necessary fiscal and financing decisions when the time comes, the whole basis of longer-term public expenditure planning is forfeit. For then, as the Plowden Committee pointed out, 'If the economy is under continuous threat of becoming overloaded, the long-term assurances (which the Committee thought essential to stable and economical programme planning) cannot in the

event be sustained, and the Government will inevitably sooner or later be bound to call a halt' (paragraph 21). Thus, it was fundamental to the Plowden Committee's thinking that 'the other side of the survey is the prospective development of income or economic resources . . . we think that it should be possible to form worthwhile judgements about whether a certain prospective size and pattern of public expenditure is likely to stimulate or to retard the growth of gross national product, and is likely to outrun the prospective resources available to finance it' (paragraph 16).

33. So far the Government have promised Parliament no more than this: ' . . . To help judge the relationship between the rate of growth of these figures of the resource requirements of public expenditure and the total of national resources, an assessment will be given of the prospects for the growth of national production in the period ahead, drawn from studies such as the recent Economic Assessment to 1972 published as the Green Paper entitled "The Task Ahead". This assessment like that given in the Green Paper, will be in terms of a range of possibilities . . .' As paragraph 41 of the Green Paper[1] explained this is not alone enough to determine 'the acceptable level of public expenditure'. For example, the claims of consumption and investment in the private sector, the claims of the balance of payments which may be out of line at the outset and the Government's general attitude to taxation all have to be taken into account.

34. The structure of taxation – its inbuilt buoyancy, its tendency to hit disproportionately at certain sectors and all the other factors which affect public toleration of taxation – are also highly relevant since they often lie behind a government's idea of the direction and level of tax rates for which it can ask. The point needs no further labouring. There is obviously a huge and essential amount of work for the SCEA in relation to the public expenditure review alone, without in any way prejudging questions of policy.

Whitehall v. Who?

35. The argument at 24c above is, we hope, self-explanatory. The US experience certainly corroborates it. So does the successful work of the recent Select Committee on Nationalised Industries which coincided

---

[1] Green Paper (Cmnd. 4017) para. 41.

with the most decisive advances in government thinking in this area since 1945-51. The argument for such an independent interlocutor of government has often been recognised by government itself, as for example in the Treasury's encouragement and support for the publication of the quarterly *National Institute Economic Review* by the National Institute of Economic and Social Research, the appointment of the old Council on Prices, Productivity and Incomes, the later creation of NEDC with its own expert office and staff and in many other ways.

Parliament, NEDC and Accountability

36. The argument at 24d above raises a fundamental question of Parliament's constitutional role in relation to the growing network of consultation between government and interest groups at the formative stage before legislation is presented, often 'cut and dried', to Parliament. In the present age a man or an institution is frequently as powerful as the quality of the staff behind him. Information and the ability to process it is the weapon *par excellence* of modern bureaucratic and corporate warfare. Parliament would stand and would deserve to stand higher in public estimation if it were seen to participate on less unequal terms of information in the discussion of national economic policies.

Prognosis before Cure

37. The argument at 24e above draws heavily on the US analogy. Examples of major strategic developments in economic policy which received very little prior discussion in Parliament, or indeed in any disciplined environment, include:

(a) the heavy reliance on bank rate between 1951 and 1955;
(b) the Thorneycroft experiment in 1957;
(c) the enshrinement of growth as the prime goal (at least in theory) of economic policy from about 1962;
(d) the development of the growing disequilibrium in the UK's balance of payments during the 1960s, which culminated in devaluation; and
(e) the resurrection of monetary policy, with especial emphasis on the money supply, after devaluation.

38. All might have gone better if they had been first subjected to the weight of informed public discussion and analysis. At this present time,

the whole question of international monetary reform, including more active international use of exchange rates, cries out for Parliamentary examination and discussion. Then there is trade policy. And again there are questions of regional economic arrangements, such as the European Economic Community, which concern themselves with agriculture. There is the wider question of European monetary arrangements. In a different sphere there is the effectiveness of different weapons of regional policy within the UK. Few Members of Parliament have, for example, been able to scrutinise critically the theory of the Regional Employment Premium.

39. Fundamental changes are in the air in the vital area where social security and taxation meet. Yet very little public economic discussion of the real issues involved has taken place. Poverty economics is little understood at the political level. It is likely that the choice between charges, contributions, levies and taxation in financing necessary public programmes will be a major issue of political controversy over the next five or more years. Almost no preparatory work has been done to make Parliament and the public ready for this.

40. In all these areas a SCEA could play a vital role and at the same time shed great credit on itself and Parliament as the natural and proper focus of public debate at all levels on matters of public policy. Thus, much more than by the proliferation of unsystematically chosen specialist committees, a SCEA could help to reverse the long and debilitating trend away from Parliament as the chief forum of national self-determination. This would be in addition to its regular work in monitoring the quarter to quarter progress of the economy and in examining the income side of the annual public expenditure review.

Bringing in the Outsiders

41. This, indeed, is part of the thought in the argument at 24f above. The other part, namely drawing into public debate on political economy those academic and other experts who can contribute, is self-explanatory. It would be particularly useful at this time when academic economists seem to have withdrawn to a quite unusual degree from public discussion of current issues of economic policy. The correspondence columns of *The Times*, for example, are not what they once were in this particular respect.

V. Objections

42. The most familiar objections to a SCEA are:

(a) that additional Select Committees cannot be manned;

(b) that effective Select Committees detract from the attention and energy given to the floor of the House of Commons;

(c) that it is not Parliament's job to govern or to set itself up as a para-executive;

(d) that American analogies do not transplant because of the different constitution and political system of the US; and

(e) the Treasury view, namely that there is some fundamental difference of kind between publishing and discussing forward projections of public expenditure and doing the same for the income side of the account which makes it impossible to envisage the latter – the argument here seems to oscillate between a version of (ii) below, which concentrates on the danger of disclosing the Government's hand in short-term management of the economy, and the quite distinct objection that both present and future tax policy is in some way uniquely controversial and therefore not normally discussable in Select Committee. Special cases of this objection include:

(i) that the topics proposed could not be usefully discussed without trespassing into areas of policy which would be improper in itself and which would put officials in an impossible position; and

(ii) that there would normally be nothing useful that Ministers or officials could say to a Select Committee about taxation without in some way prejudicing the security of the budget speech.

43. There are no doubt other objections. But these seem to be the most obtrusive. We examine them in turn.

Manning (42 a)

44. This is clearly a matter on which Parliament will not need much advice from outside. We would only point out that our proposal does not necessarily involve a net increase in the number of Select Committees or in the average burden of Select Committee work of Members of Parliament. This holds true even after allowing for the implementation of the recommendations of the Select Committee on Procedure last year

for the creation of a new Select Committee on Expenditure. Such an Expenditure Committee would as we understand it absorb the present functions of a good many of the existing specialist Select Committees. We envisage the SCEA as fitting into a Select Committee Structure which otherwise would only include:

The Privileges Committee
The Select Committee on Procedure
The Public Accounts Committee
The Select Committee on Expenditure (as proposed by last year's Report of the Select Committee on Procedure)
(possibly) The Select Committee on Nationalised Industries.

45. We would also point out that adequate staffing is a major element in our recommendations. This, we feel, would enable the average MP to become a much more productive unit, thus increasing his output substantially while not increasing the amount of work he would have to do. More effective work, rather than more work, is surely the aim.

The Floor of the House (42 b)

46. This objection is, we feel, ill-founded, although it has some distinguished Parliamentary support. We certainly neither wish for nor fear any development in the direction of the balance of importance between the Committees and the Floors of the US Congress. That balance arises from the legislative and executive functions of certain powerful US Congressional Committees which would not be exercised by any possible Select Committee of the House of Commons.

47. Secondly, one of the central purposes of our proposals is to reflect greater credit on Parliament by enabling debates on the floor of the House to benefit from properly digested information.

48. Thirdly, we do not find that the present standing with the general public of Parliament is such that proposals for its renaissance should be regarded complacently. We do not really see how any insitution can suffer from doing and being seen to do its job better. At present the floor of the House is often at its best dealing with specific issues of individual freedom or national emergency – and at its worst dealing with the continuing questions of political, social and economic strategy. We think that the second category is of equal importance in a sophisticated modern democracy. It cannot be satisfactorily handled by the methods and the organisation of a simpler past.

49. Fourthly, we repeat that it is not a necessary part of our proposals than an individual Member should need or be expected to spend any greater part of his time in Select Committee or any lesser part on the floor of the House. It is a question, not of the volume, but of the effectiveness of the time and energy that he can devote to both. We have particularly noted and we welcome the observations on this question of Mr William Hamilton (*Hansard* 22/1/70, Cols. 759-762) in the two-day debate in January 1970, on the Select Committee's former recommendations for a Select Committee on Expenditure.

A Para-Executive (42 c)

50. A distinction is frequently made between administration and policy. While questions of administration could come before a SCEA, this would not be its primary purpose, which could best be described as the analysis of policy options. This is fundamentally different from the Executive's job of taking or implementing decisions. If the quality of their analysis justified it, Ministers and Opposition might find SCEA reports a useful supplement to the analysis of the Civil Service or the academic research bodies.

51. The main purpose of the exercise would be, however, to facilitate Parliamentary and public debate; and if the SCEA simply led governments into a fuller disclosure of the material supporting their policies – with the implications this would have for more explicit and rigorous thinking within Whitehall – the result would be amply justified. The recent White Paper on EEC membership is an outstanding example of an official document, the analysis and assumptions of which require more rigorous scrutiny than could be given in plenary sessions. Such a scrutiny emphatically does not imply that the SCEA would pronounce upon, still less decide, whether the UK should apply for membership.

52. The SCEA would, if successful, be a rival, not to the Executive, but to the Royal Commissions and numerous *ad hoc* committees (such as Richardson on the value added tax) set up to advise Ministers on specific problems. Parliamentary Committees were normally used in the first half of the nineteenth century for such work; and the resulting Blue Books, for example on factory conditions, became part of the history of the age. Royal Commissions and Parliamentary Committees continued side by side in the second half of the nineteenth century; and it was only in the twentieth century that the independent committee finally

triumphed.[1] One reason for this development was the possibility of including non-partisan experts on independent bodies of inquiry. A SCEA with an adequate expert staff would retain this advantage, while helping Parliament to recapture an essential part of a role which has since passed to other bodies.

American Transplants (42 d)

53. This objection is a very familiar one wherever and whenever it is proposed that Britain should in any way benefit from American ideas and experience. The Americans themselves are on the whole much less sensitive and much more pragmatic about transplanting British institutions across the Atlantic, a practice of which they have some extended experience. We believe that it is entirely relevant to inquire whether a particular American (or any other) institution owes its success to peculiar local conditions which could not or should not be reproduced in Britain. But we also consider it facile to assume that every successful American institution owes its success to those particular aspects of the American political system which diverge from their British counterparts.

54. It is vital, when thinking of and comparing Congressional and Parliamentary committees, to distinguish different kinds of Congressional committees. They range from those, like the House Appropriations Committee and its sub-committees, which act as para-executive departments allocating funds in the minutest detail and in frequent disregard for 'objective' criteria, to others, like the Joint Economic Committee, which have no legislative or executive functions at all. The latter achieve their influence precisely through their ability to educate Congressional, Administration, Press and public opinion to look at new problems or to look at old problems in new ways. It is the first category of Congressional committees which usually springs to the minds of most non-specialist Englishmen when the subject is raised. It is only the second – and utterly different – category which is at all relevant to the present proposals.

55. In our judgement nothing that is important in the formal and informal *modus operandi* of the Joint Economic Committee depends upon any aspect of the US Constitution and political system which

---

[1] See *The Power of Parliament* by Ronald Butt, Constable 1967 and 1969, p. 81

conflicts radically with the British system. The division of the executive and legislative powers on the American model is not a necessary condition of the existence and success of the US Joint Economic Committee. It works well because there is a need and an appetite in the US for the best attainable public discussion under the aegis of government about the conduct of economic and financial affairs. In the United Kingdom there is just as great a need.

56. We do consider that the freedom of the Joint Economic Committee to pronounce directly on controversial questions of policy is essential to its effectiveness. It is the enquiry and the largely public debate, the marshalling of information and the taking of authoritative official and private testimony which matters most, not the reported (and usually disagreed) opinions of the Committee at the end of the day.

57. It is true that such a Committee needs vigorous and dedicated chairmanship, as well as good staffing. But we see nothing in the British version of the two-party system to exclude this possibility. In short, we believe that on examination the advantages of the Joint Economic Committee could be transplanted, *mutatis mutandis*, from Washington to Westminster without falling foul of even the most stereotyped picture of Anglo–American constitutional differences.

The Treasury's Evidence (42 e)

58. The argument (or equivocation) here is essentially the one (or ones) deployed in the Treasury's evidence to the Select Committee last summer (written memorandum of June 1969, and oral testimony by Sir Douglas Allen, Permanent Secretary to the Treasury, on 2 July 1969). We find it (or them) singularly unconvincing and in marked contrast with the lucidity, vigour and constructiveness of the Treasury's evidence to the Select Committee on the question of Parliamentary participation in planning the expenditure side of the public sector balance sheet. Indeed, the contrast is so strong that we have come to doubt how far the position which the Treasury took last summer can really have represented their considered and definite conclusion on this question, which had anyway only just been formally raised in a memorandum of 6 May 1969 by the Select Committee's former distinguished Specialist Adviser, Mr James Robertson.

59. The essential argument of the Treasury's memorandum was that the income side of the account, especially where taxation policy was involved, was so different in kind from the expenditure side of the

account that what might be suitable Parliamentary procedure on the one front should not be applied by analogy to the other. This needs to be examined in some detail. But first we would recall the general arguments already set out (in paragraphs 28–34) for regarding the income and expenditure sides of the planning exercise as mutually interdependent. For example, the real meaning of increasing or decreasing the propor-tion of the national income that passes through the public sector can only be fully understood in its human and political as well as its economic dimensions when it is translated into specific implications for taxation, public charges, contributions and government borrowing. And one needs to face, to analyse and to argue about those implications on the income side in order fully to appreciate the constraints which they impose and the opportunities which they offer on the expenditure side. Historically, this was half the motive for the Plowden Committee's central proposal for forward reviews of expenditure and resources. It is scarcely conceivable that Parliament, or any other body of intelligent people, could rest content for ever with just the expenditure side of the account, merely discussing it in relation to a pre-determined overall aggregate into whose basis and implications they were not allowed effectively to inquire.

60. Nor does it seem to us that Parliament can indefinitely accept without more convincing argumentation the vivid contrast (in oral evidence given to the Committee on 12 March 1969, by Sir Richard Clarke) between what, according to officialdom, Parliament ought to know about expenditure policies and what it has no right to know about the income and resources side of the balance sheet. We quote below part of Q.182 (on page 71) and all of Q.225 (on pages 80–1):

> ... 182. (*Mr Albu*) The Committee is engaged on an inquiry on two levels. One is the methods by which Parliament can control the distribution of goverment expenditure; the other is the methods by which Parliament can control the effectiveness of government expenditure. Do you think Parlia-ment is better engaged in discussing the estimates as they are at present presented rather than the detailed functional estimates that might be presented under a different system? ...
>
> ... , (*Sir Richard Clarke*) In my view both the functions Mr Albu mentioned are necessary ones for Parliament. First, the question of the layout of the resources between the various forms of government expenditure is manifestly just the kind of basic issue with which it would seem to be vital for Parliament to be concerning itself, such as whether pensions are more important than health or defence more important than foreign aid. These kind of issues are great issues of public concern which naturally come to

Parliament. They do not require much in the way of detailed statistical information. The other question, the 'value for money' kind of question – whether the governmental machine is operating efficiently in the spending of the money – is again a matter of great importance. The right thing would seem to be the development of the Public Accounts Committee technique and various other techniques in order to get that focused in the most effective way. It is open to question whether it is now focused in the most effective way. Clearly that is a function quite cardinal to Parliament . . .

. . . 225. (*Chairman*) In your Stamp Memorial Lecture, Sir Richard, you said that the long-term expenditure has to be considered in relation to the long-term resources and thence to the long-term claims of private consumption and private investment and thus to considerations of what changes of taxation will in the long term be likely to be needed in order to enable the economy to accommodate the growing public expenditure. Are you then suggesting broadly that this will have to be limited to the Cabinet rather than to Parliament? – (*Sir Richard Clarke*) The original purpose in this matter is to relate it to government decision-taking, a Cabinet activity. What kind of things Cabinet may decide they wish to publish or present to Parliament in order to develop their arguments is for governments to decide rather than for Parliament. What it was essential for me to say was what ought to be done before these decisions were taken . . .

61. We now list the main things which the Treasury say in their memorandum about the taxation or income side of the account in the course of trying to demonstrate its fundamental difference from the expenditure side for the purposes of Parliamentary scrutiny by Select Committee:

(a) . . . as paragraph 32 of the Green Paper 'Public Expenditure: A new Presentation' (Cmnd. 4017) pointed out, 'changes in Central Government taxation are one of the main instruments for short-term regulation of the economy; there must therefore be scope for short-term flexibility and for this reason the Government cannot commit themselves in advance' (Paragraph 6).

Comment: The same is true, at the margin, of expenditure; and the Government does not 'commit' itelf on expenditure in the public expenditure reviews (see Cmnd. 2915, paragraph 63, Cmnd. 4017, paragraph 18, and Cmnd. 4234, paragraph 3–4). Structural tax changes, which seldom can and never should be introduced *ab initio* in a budget, normally have just as long a lead time as the main public expenditure programmes. There is probably rather more flexibility at the margin with taxation; but it is open to question how far tax changes ought automatically to be regarded as the sole fiscal instrument, the residual item, in the Government's short-term budgetary planning, even supposing that fiscal policy is an efficient instrument of short-term economic managment in the first place. A SCEA might, indeed, examine the empirical and practical foundations of both these conventional wisdoms of the past. Even if the distinction between expenditure and taxation as stated by the Treasury were entirely valid, it would not be an objection to a SCEA with or without Treasury assistance, investigating the resources, the fiscal and the financing implications of the Government's expenditure plans in the medium-term, abstracting from the possible fluctuations of the business cycle. This is a perfectly normal analytic device, which has in fact been used for years by the government itself.

(b) ... Put another way the essential difference is this. In order to secure a sensible and economical use of resources and avoid the waste which would be brought about by interruptions, public expenditure should be planned and broadly adhered to (Paragraph 7).

Comment: Is this supposed to be untrue of taxation policy? We do not credit the implied assumption that flexibility varies inversely with forward thought and planning. The relatinship is surely one of direct correlation.

(c) This being so, the principal fiscal instrument available to the Government for the bringing of aggregate demand into line with resources is the instrument of taxation. Taxation could therefore only be programmed as expenditure is programmed, if the Government were able accurately to predict the course of the main components of private sector demand including exports. The fact that it cannot, and that large variations can take place in such items as private investment and the balance of payments, makes it imperative to use taxation as an instrument of short-term adjustment. It is for this reason that decisions about the overall level of taxation, which essentially constitute the Chancellor's budget judgement each year can only be made for the period immediately ahead when a reasonably reliable assessment can be made about the course of aggregate demand (Paragraph 7).

Comment: Again there is an obsession with cyclical fluctuations in private sector and general economic magnitudes. The Treasury again appear to have overlooked the normal economic technique of medium-term 'use of resources' analysis. Precisely these general and private sector magnitudes are regularly projected forward five years, abstracting from business cycle fluctuations, in Whitehall itself. The Department of Economic Affairs economic assessment to 1972, 'The Task Ahead', published a year ago provides a standard example in Chapter 6 and Table 6.1 (as does the National Plan (Cmnd. 2764) in Chapter 15 and Table 15.1). We understand that the medium term assessment has now been taken over from the DEA by the Treasury's revived National Economy Group. Moreover, what the Treasury calls 'decisions about the overall level of taxation' are merely decisions about adjustments at the margin to the total of taxation. The same applies and should apply to expenditure.

(d) 8. The proposition that the overall level of taxation must depend on the particular characteristics of the conjuncture is true also of the rates of individual taxes and hence on the balance of the mix. As the Specialist Adviser remarks in paragraph 9 of his paper different taxes have different characteristics and different economic effects. The precise elements of the conjuncture may make some taxes more appropriate than others. Moreover the capacity of some taxes to withstand increases or the case for making reductions in others may vary over time: at one moment, for example, the state of demand for a taxed item may be such that to make a further increase would result in diminishing returns, though this might not be true sometime later (Paragraph 8).

Comment: Each sentence could as well be said of expenditure.

(e) . . . Finally, decisions about budget changes are decisions about distribution of burdens or reliefs. They therefore raise issues which are essentially political in character and which the Chancellor of the day will wish to decide in the total context of political, social and economic circumstances obtaining at the time rather than in advance (Paragraph 8).

Comment: Does the Treasury believe this to be untrue of expenditure? It sits oddly with what the Chief Secretary to the Treasury, Mr John Diamond, said – in our view most estimably–in the recent public expenditure debate, *Hansard*, January 22 1970, cols. 737 and 746:

> The whole point of having this kind of debate is so that any Government can be aided by the expressions of opinion in the House which, by that time, will be reinforced by a knowledge of the feelings in the community at large, so that in determining priorities in the years ahead, note can be taken of those developments, and
>
> The third advantage which I claim for what we are doing, and the most important, is the deliberate and voluntary sharing by the executive with Parliament, and hence with the community, of the process of reaching decisions affecting the living standards of us all. The proposition has only to be put in those simple terms for it to be self-evident that this eminently democratic process should occur, but the interesting thing to note is that it has not happened hitherto, and the remarkable thing is that is was thought right that it should not . . .

We do not see why issues which are 'essentially political in character' and which have to be decided 'in the total context of political, social and economic circumstances' should have to be either short-term or shrouded in prior mystery. We prefer the Chief Secretary's approach. We see no reason why it should not be applied on the resources and taxation side of the balance sheet, although we do not expect the Government to announce a specific programme of future tax changes. All that is necessary is a forward assessment of the prospective 'fiscal gap (plus or minus)', given the economic outlook, the Government's expenditure plans and the prospective yield of existing taxes at existing rates. From that baseline, a SCEA could examine alternative ways of closing the gap, as well as trading these against an adjustment of the expenditure plans (especially if charges are technically defined as 'negative expenditure').

(f) Because therefore no government can present its proposals on taxation as much as three years ahead, it would be unprofitable for any government to open itself to examination about its long-term thinking in the way that it could usefully open itself to an examination about its long-term plans in the field of expenditure (Paragraph 9).

Comment: For the reasons above, this strikes us as a *non sequitur*.

(g) Moreover in the case of taxation there is an additional reason why it should not do so. While certainty about the level of taxation may assist the private sector in taking decisions about the allocation of its resources, if the Government were to be in a position to predict—or even only to hint at—the likelihood of certain changes in taxes or its reliance on certain taxes rather than others, the effect might be entirely disruptive. If for instance the Government were to imply that in the long term their intention was to make substantial alterations in the structure of the taxation of companies uncertainty could well be created, as it was in the comparatively short period between November 1964 and April 1965 (notwithstanding the detailed outline of the corporation tax which the then Chancellor of the Exchequer gave to Parliament at the beginning of December 1964), and the impact on companies' investment plans and on the flow of investment from abroad might be seriously adverse. Or if it were to be implied in any precise form that the taxation of certain items of rapidly growing expenditure could be increased, an undesirable shifting forward of expenditure might take place; if a decrease were envisaged the effect would be to cause a postponement. In other words, a position of anything other than neutrality about the future levels of particular items of taxation is likely to have disturbing effects on investment consumption and, almost inevitably, on the dealing in stock market securities (Paragraph 9).

Comment: To the extent that this argument has any validity it applies over a negligible range of the possible agenda of a useful SCEA. For the rest the history of the US Tax Reform Bill in 1969 should dispose of any anxieties about forestalling of tax changes because of prior officially blessed discussion about them. Special considerations are nonetheless often alleged to apply to tax policy because of the need to avoid jeopardising the security of the Budget Speech (see para. 42e(ii)). Even on an entirely conventional view of the latter, the distinction is now recognised between the tax structure and tax rates. The involvement of a major tax reform in the budget security mechanism will often mean that it will have been inadequately discussed, even inside Whitehall, before it is announced to an unsuspecting House of Commons. Governments have themselves recognised the unsatisfactory nature of this by introducing the Green Paper device, notably in the case of the Regional

Employment Premium in 1967. Indeed, the Treasury make this very point in their own memorandum. The natural complement to the Green Paper is an adequately staffed Parliamentary Committee to probe it; the absence of such a body leaves the field entirely free to producer and regional pressure groups with their own access to the government machine. The whole concept of budget security deserves, however, a more rigorous analysis than it has so far received. It clearly could, despite the American experience, be destabilising to trade to have the pros and cons of alternative rates of indirect tax for different commodities discussed beforehand (even though some distortion in the shape of 'holding off' or 'advance purchases' is in any case likely when widespread changes are expected). Direct taxes are in a different category, as there is little that people can normally do to anticipate changes here. Indeed, income tax changes are in effect announced in advance already, as they are not normally implemented until the July following the budget. There might be some minor anticipation by those with fluctuating incomes if changes in rates were published before the beginning of the financial year in question; but again US experience does not suggest this would be a major consideration. Nevertheless, the desirability of avoiding a sharp breach with present procedures suggests that a SCEA should not become involved in consideration of specific tax rates, either direct or indirect. The same emphatically does not apply to the 'Budget judgement' i.e. the question of how much to remit or take back in tax in any particular year or economic situation. This is a major economic decision, which under the present dispensation is announced like a rabbit out of a hat by the Chancellor on Budget Day. Academic bodies such as the National Institute of Economic and Social Research do come out with recommendations; but these receive no Parliamentary discussion and there is no opportunity for a constructive Parliamentary dialogue about the economic outlook. In the spirit of making haste slowly, we would envisage the SCEA conducting any pre-budget exercise of its own without the aid of official witnesses. But it is worth asking whether all aspects of the budget deserve the same degree of security clampdown and whether the notion of 'Budget secrecy' has not become a cult extended to whole areas outside specific tax changes, where it is probably inappropriate. We would not, however, place our main emphasis on individual budgets at all. There are whole areas of long-term tax policy which are hardly discussed in Parliament and which we suspect are inadequately examined by government departments. The kind of information which Treasury and Revenue officials would be called upon to supply would be no different from that supplied in the past to bodies such as the Richardson Committee or the Royal Commission on Taxation; and it is hardly improper that officials should supply Parliament with information they already furnish to such non-Parliamentary bodies.

62. We doubt whether there is much that we could or need to add to make the arguments in the Treasury's memorandum look any less convincing than they already do without benefit of additional commentary. Almost every proposition listed in the paragraph above applies as much to the expenditure side of forward planning as to the income side. Hence the suggestion that these points establish a difference so fundamental that the whole basis of Parliamennaty scrutiny should be radically different is implausible to the point of self-evident untruth.

63. We now turn to the oral evidence given last summer to the Select Committee by Sir Douglas Allen, the Permanent Secretary to the Treasury. The emphasis in his evidence was different from that in the Treasury's memorandum. The written document concentrated on the difficulty of revealing to Parliament much about the income side of the annual forward planning exercise. Sir Douglas seemed mainly preoccupied with the difficulty which he felt officials would experience in discussing tax questions in any time scale before a Select Committee of any kind. The points of course overlap. But they are distinct; and in important ways they diverge.

64. In so far as the point at issue here is the general question of budget security, we have already commented on it under paragraph 61g above. Insofar as the point relates to the difficulty for officials in discussing anything so controversial as a tax change (or the absence of one), we would insist that there is a great deal of difference between discussing a controversial question and being controversial. The elucidation of controversial questions entails much painstaking assemblage of information and analysis of relationships, alternatives and so forth. With this, official help can be invaluable. In general, we think that the difficulty for officials in discussing controversial questions publicly or before MPs is greatly exaggerated. For example, we would cite the evidence given to the Select Committee last year by Sir William Armstrong, the Head of the Civil Service Department. He was asked about the deficiencies of Parliament's present procedures for the scrutiny of expenditure. He replied that it might be impertinent for him to comment on deficiencies. But he volunteered some basic facts. In several columns of uninterrupted exposition he then managed to point the way to most of the Committee's most important and creative findings and recommendations. He said nothing controversial; but he greatly illuminated a major controversy.

65. It seems to us that in the course of his evidence Sir Douglas Allen at least half acknowledged the existence of this kind of distinction.

Initially he was very cautious:

Q. 710 ... *Sir Douglas Allen*: Where however one is into the policy, and particularly the policy and political judgements that are involved in selecting one tax rather than another, we get into a field in which it is virtually impossible for officials to help a committee very much. We can parade the facts, such as they are. We can give information about the yield of taxation. We can discuss the very detailed information which is available in the reports of Revenue Departments. But we could not assist the Committee very far in discussing the reasons why one particular tax was chosen against another or what the effects would be of having put up income tax by a different amount in the budget than the Chancellor in fact proposed. So that there is a very considerable difficulty in our eyes about the role of a Select Committee of the traditional type asking questions of officials in relation to tax, which is such a sensitive subject in many ways and at many times of the year, and which is so closely wrapped up with policy judgements and what I might call value judgements which we would not be entitled to make.

66. And he concluded also on the negative tack:

... 761. *Chairman*: Of course, in phrasing my last question to you I was aware of that. There is one final point I would like to put to you because it perhaps brings to the head the point that we have been skating round. I wonder if you are in fact saying to us – I am not saying I object to it – that in the context of some of the questions we have been putting to you today the Treasury does not have a corporate view that it wants to express to anyone other than Ministers on matters of tax change and tax reform. Is this really what you are saying?

Sir Douglas Allen: I think that is a way of putting it with which I would agree, yes ...

67. But the following more positive exchanges also occurred:

Q. 713. *Mr Mackintosh*: What is the objection to the actual factual knowledge of the effect on different sections of the community of a particular tax? I do not understand this for a moment. It seems to me absolutely essential that Parliament, whatever their view of the desirability of a tax for this group of the community or for that group of the community, should know what the precise effects should be. This seems to me totally different. 'Do you think it is a good thing that these people should be taxed?' Nobody would dream of asking this of an official. They would say, 'Given a tax at such and such a rate, what would its effect be on the sector of the community A, B or C?'

Sir Douglas Allen: We would certainly do our best to assist the Committee in answering that sort of question. In many areas of questioning about the likely effects of a new or unknown tax, such answers would be fairly speculative, but we would of course be able to deal with those.

714. *Mr Mackintosh*: I think it is a total mistake if the witnesses imagine that a committee of this kind would be asking their opinion of the desirability of either an individual tax or a given 'mix' of tax. The questions would be, how they worked, what the problems of collection were, what the side effects would be. It seems to me that most Select Committees and most officials would be very clear in their own minds as to what point they could not stray beyond in this type of examination and would stop there?

Sir Douglas Allen: We may have, of course, misread the memorandum, but there was a great deal of emphasis on the 'mix' of taxes, which tends to lead one on to the discussion as to whether one 'mix' is better than another 'mix' . . .

719. *Mr Howell*: Do you feel, as someone who is obviously intimately concerned with the tax structure, that public debate and public opinion on tax in various forms is sufficiently informed? *Sir Douglas Allen*: No, I do not think it is. I think there is a very strong case for much more discussion and understanding of taxation and taxation matters in this country. My remarks are being directed exclusively to a problem which arises if officials are asked opinions about taxation which may be thought to reflect the views of the Government and lead to some kind of anticipation.

749. *Chairman*: But why should we not look at the negative income tax idea, and report on it?

Sir Douglas Allen: I am throughout indicating difficulties if you want views from officials. I am not saying that you should not look at negative income tax and report on it. I am not saying that you should not ask, if you were doing so, Treasury officials to give some information, but you could not get very much information because it takes one into an area where a great deal of detailed work is necessary and the possibilities of government action start having to be considered before the thing has much relevance . . .

68. This and a recognition of the great technical complexities involved in the analysis of the income side of the forward planning operation seem to us sufficient to establish that official evidence to a Select Committee on Economic Affairs would be both feasible and helpful without placing officials in any kind of untenable position (see para. 42e (i)). Again the American example powerfully suggests the unreality of the dilemma which is so commonly supposed to exist in Britain.

69. The one area where embarrassment could arise would be overseas financial or trade negotiations. Here common sense and case law could achieve a great deal. The basic demarcation would be between currency negotiations on which the Government was engaged, or the appropriateness of a particular parity, on the one hand, and the examination of

goals or mechanisms on the other. A SCEA would not, for example, interfere in the course of negotiations with the EEC; but it might well carry out an expert examination both of the recent White Paper and of any agreement that emerged from negotiations. The SCEA would not discuss issues such as devaluation, but it might well investigate alternative methods of international adjustment. It would not have concerned itself with the negotiations which led up to the Basle sterling area arrangements. But it might well have examined the resulting arrangements and analysed the alternative next steps, preferably well in advance, and without getting involved in negotiating tactics.

70. There are two kinds of question which could put officials in an embarrassing situation. These would relate either to confidential information or to the actual advice given to Ministers. Officials would be protected from these questions by existing conventions. Their main job would be to explain and analyse the vast mass of available information of a non-confidential kind.

71. Far more information is already disclosed in the quarterly balance of payments statistics or publications such as *Economic Trends, Financial Statistics* or *The Bank of England Bulletin* than is generally realised. This represents the fruit of a great deal of effort both by official statisticians and their informants in the private sector; but there is a danger of much of these hard-earned labours going to waste through lack of an informed dialogue about their implications. We suspect that many officials would be glad of an opportunity to exhibit and analyse data of this kind.

72. Examples might include the recent adoption of Domestic Credit Expansion, a hitherto unknown concept launched on a largely mystified public opinion. Another example relates to the bewildering variety of balance of payments concepts. These include balance of visible trade, current balance of payments, overall or basic balance – excluding or including the 'balancing' item, adjusted or not adjusted for Eurodollar borrowing, the balance on official settlements and the movement of the reserves. It would be extremely useful to have the relationship between these concepts explained in a specialised Parliamentary Forum, as well as the reasons why the emphasis has shifted over the years from one to another. At the moment such elucidation is mainly embodied in Ministerial statements such as the Budget Speech; and the key explanations are often eliminated or abbreviated, not for any political or security reason, but to lighten the load of material. There has often in the past been quite unnecessary academic and journalistic speculation about

supposed puzzles in the official economic forecasts, which were simply due to the omission of important link material in official speeches.

73. Whitehall is clearly conscious of the deficiencies of traditional methods of exposition, judging by the proliferation of analytical articles in organs such as *Economic Trends* and the publication of the economic forecasts and other data in the Fiancial Statement. While these developments are to be welcomed, it is surely dangerous that explanations of thinking behind government policy should be given in a way which is in practice removed entirely from Parliamentary scrutiny. If official advisers are able to write of their work in *Economic Trends* or *The Bank of England Bulletin*, it is surely reasonable that they should answer questions about it to a SCEA.

74. Finally, on this point, we would say that, even if it were accepted against the balance of the argument above that officials could not give evidence to a SCEA in so far as it was concerned with taxation policy and the income side of the forward planning of public expenditure and that governments should not publish any more details of their plans on the income side, this would still not destroy the case for a SCEA. It would have to work under some disadvantages. But these would be irritants rather than fatal handicaps. Given sufficient staff and tapping of independent expertise, it would be perfectly possible for a SCEA to mount extremely useful discussions and to produce valuable analyses of the behaviour of the economy, of the implications for resources and fiscal policy of the Government's expenditure plans and of the other *ad hoc* issues of economic policy suggested in paragraphs 37-40 above. After a while, officialdom might come to feel that it was better to be heard than to allow its point of view to go by default.

VI. Conclusion

75. One objection has not been considered. This is that, although the general arguments for a SCEA are well founded, it is premature to press ahead with the idea now. The thought here appears to be partly that it will take Parliament several years to digest the new public expenditure procedure (even if the House adopts the Select Committee's recommendation for a Select Committee on Expenditure and even if future governments do not renege on the annual White Paper) and partly that Whitehall itself still lacks the machinery to produce a coherent annual statement of the forward prospects for the income side of the account.

76. These arguments have some force. But we think they are out-weighed by others. On the last point Parliamentary inquiry might stimulate the necessary Whitehall machinery. On the first point, Parliamentary digestion of the public expenditure review process is likely to be retarded, rather than expedited, by suppression of discussion and information about the income side of the account, which alone gives it its full meaning.

77. The true reasons for the Government's hesitancy about a Select Committee on Economic Affairs are, we believe, the same as those which have tempted all governments in all countries at all times to minimise the amount of explaining which they have to do. They fear giving hostages to fortune. We believe it to be the function of all Parliaments in all countries at all times to combat this instinct.

78. We believe that recent progress by Parliament and the Treasury in breaking down barriers to economic understanding and information, especially in the field of public expenditure, should be construed as a mandate to complete the job so that the next Parliament shall begin the decade with completed machinery rather than with an inheritance of unassembled and incomplete parts. This, we believe, would increase the chances that the direction of subsequent change will be forward, as well as that the work of the Select Committee on Procedure will have its proper place in the history of Parliament and of democracy.

Memorandum by Samuel Brittan and Peter Jay, Economic Editors of the *Financial Times* and of *The Times* February 17, 1970, submitted to the House of Commons Select Committee on Procedure, Session 1974

Foreign Affairs

Regionalism as Geopolitics
I

Good regionalism is good geopolitics; and bad regionalism is bad geopolitics. This integration of the supposed polar opposites in the scholastic debate among foreign policy academics is well illustrated in both directions by the events of 1979.

We live in a world of sovereign nation-states of which two are pre-eminent in military power: the United States and the Soviet Union. Each is condemned by this simple fact to be constantly preoccupied with the potential and the intentions of the other. Ideological differences, though important, are subsidiary to this basic fact of extraordinary and opposed might. Given this duopoly of military power and given the reach of modern technology in communications, travel and weapons, the theatre in which the mutual preoccupation of the United States and the USSR is played out is inevitably the whole globe, minus backwaters plus near-space. The part of the drama, whether competitive or cooperative, which is enacted directly between the two protagonists is perforce limited. Like kings on the chessboard they sit almost immobile behind their pawns and subordinates, nearly incapable of direct combat, surveying the whole arena in which their own fate is progressively and indirectly decided.

The United States and the Soviet Union directly confront one another only in narrow and peculiar circumstances. This bilateral relationship can take the form of both competition in armaments and cooperation in arms limitation. Neither has much practical effect, since direct conflict is by hypothesis unjoinable, except at a catastrophic price to both parties. Yet mutual balance and joint pre-eminence are preconditions of the whole global rivalry being played out between the United States and the USSR rather than between other lesser powers or groups of powers.

So the United States and the USSR are doomed to watch one another like hawks, to negotiate constantly by day for strategic parity and to plot ceaselessly by night for strategic advantage. Since neither can or will feel fully confident unless its parity is more equal than the other side's parity, dynamic instability is inherent in the very static stability they both seek, even when their shared interest in circumscribing the scope of their mutual competition is uppermost.

But this mutual and direct preoccupation accounts for only a small fraction of the landscape on which their rivalry has to be conducted. The occasional episode apart – such as the treatment of Soviet dissidents, exchanges of disaffected or incarcerated persons, the reception of defecting artists and the negotiation of exceptional wheat purchases – the United States and the USSR meet one another, not face to face, but in the territories of third parties.

It is there that the real competition between the superpowers mainly occurs and that the occasionally significant victories and defeats mostly happen. Geopolitics is, by definition, the art and the process of managing global rivalry; and success, again by definition, consists at a minimum of consolidating the strength and cohesion of the group of nations which form the core of one's power position, while preventing the other side from extending the area of its domination and clientele. In the case of the United States, that group has been created by voluntary association and comprises the major European nations grouped in NATO, Japan and Australasia, and, at least in the economic sphere, the other advanced nations of Europe even though not specifically members of NATO – in other words, the group of nations we loosely call the West or the First World. In the case of the Soviet Union, its bloc was created initially by military power and is still held together by that means – as the Second World. The comparative strength and cohesion of each of these two worlds has always been basic to any geopolitical assessment of the situation.

In this same manner, we have come to describe the nations outside the First and Second Worlds as a Third World, in which each of the first two competes for the highest possible degree of cooperation and support – or, in the case of the Soviet Union, the maximum degree of domination. And it is in that Third World that we have seen, over and over again in the past twenty years, that success comes from fighting or competing on favourable terrain and from avoiding giving battle where conditions favour the enemy. The terrain and the conditions in question are in essence the local politics of the regions and the countries wherein the superpowers are fated to come across each other's footprints.

We do not normally think of relationships within the First World as 'regionalism'. But in fact the classic example of good regionalism proving good geopolitics was the reconstruction of Western Europe and Japan after the Second World War that brought the West into being as a coherent entity. To be sure, strategic and conventional military strength – principally American – was basic to the necessary sense of security among these nations. But at least as central was the sense of firm political and economic cooperation created in the first instance by the Marshall Plan and then by an expanded free trading system based on the principles adopted at Bretton Woods. Shared values were enlisted and then spread, and a tide of history was able to rise to the flood.

But the Third World was always a different story, lacking the heritage, the already demonstrated capacities and, to a large extent, the values of the West. And it is in this World, in particular, where the strong lesson of at least the last twenty years – and especially of the Vietnam and post-Vietnam era – is that significant advances are only achieved, beyond the immediate periphery of the United States and the Soviet Union themselves, when one or the other superpower aligns itself with the forces on the ground which have history, which is a label for all manner of strongly established trends and moods, on their side. Almost unimaginable amounts of crude military power did not prevail in Vietnam because the local tide was not setting that way. This, obviously, has nothing necessarily to do with moral right and wrong. There was nothing moral about Hanoi's ambitions, then or now; and there was a good deal of morality in the instinct of the Kennedy/Johnson generation to avoid a Munich in Southeast Asia, even if this morality was stymied in the outcome by the practical misjudgements that were also involved.

The great persistent advantage which the Soviet Union has had over the last quarter of a century has been that the chief preoccupation of so much of the Third World has been with decolonisation, an issue on which it was easy and convenient for Russia to align itself with movements of national liberation. Of course, the United States was also an anticolonial power for a few years after the Second World War – to the considerable irritation from time to time of the real colonial powers, such as Britain and France. But in what has probably turned out to be the greatest strategic blunder of the era of American power – Vietnam was more a tactical catastrophe with strategic ramifications – the United States abandoned that role before the 1940s were over and embraced instead the fatally negative role of anti-communist champion. If this be thought to be wet liberal nonsense, consider this piece of advice from the presumptive high priest of *realpolitik* in American foreign policy:

If the United States remains the trustee of every non-communist area, it will exhaust its psychological resources. No country can act wisely simultaneously in every part of the globe at every moment of time. A more pluralistic world – especially in relationships with friends – is profoundly in our long-term interest. Political multipolarity, while difficult to get used to, is the precondition for a new period of creativity . . . The new nations weigh little in the physical balance of power. But the forces unleashed in the emergence of so many new states may well affect the moral balance of the world – the convictions which form the structure of the world of tomorrow. This adds a new dimension to the problem of multipolarity. . . The American role in the new nations' efforts to build legitimate authority is in need of serious re-examination . . . The problem of political legitimacy is the key to political stability in regions containing two-thirds of the world's population . . . nor should we define the problem as how to prevent the spread of communism. Our goal should be to build a moral consensus which can make a pluralistic world creative rather than destructive. Irrelevance to one of the great revolutions of our time will mean that we will ultimately be engulfed by it – if not physically, then psychologically.[1]

Unfortunately, these eloquent precepts were largely ignored by American policy at the height of the Cold War, particularly in the era of John Foster Dulles. In his thinking, preventing the spread of communism was identified overwhelmingly with the support of shaky alliance structures and relationships that led American policy over and over into instances of 'bad regionalism'. Any attempt to maintain neutrality in what he saw as a global Manichean struggle between good and evil was denounced as immoral, and the United States was drawn into all-out and unquestioning backing of a host of individual governments that were at best authoritarian and were often at odds with their regional neighbours. The underlying aspirations of peoples and areas were put to one side in the effort to create a fictitious 'free world' that would hold off the Soviet Union – and for a long time 'Red China' as well – by military force and often by political repression.

That period of bad regionalism has continued to haunt American policy. It created a legacy for more discriminating US foreign policy makers which cannot quickly or simply be lived down. Escaping the network of friendships and alliances which the Dulles mentality created may involve what is seen as betraying friends, letting down clients,

---

[1] Henry A. Kissinger, 'Central Issues of American Foreign Policy', in Kermit Gordon, ed., *Agenda for the Nation*, Washington, DC: The Brookings Institution, 1968, pp. 599, 603 – 606.

encouraging adversaries and leading neutrals to hedge their bets, so upsetting the geopolitical balance. The trusteeship of every non-communist area may well have been the wrong or wrongly defined role in the first place; but withdrawal from such a legacy without giving the dangerous impression of unilateral geopolitical abdication is endlessly difficult, not least when the imperatives of adversary domestic politics and adversary government–press relations strengthen the probability that each move will be interpreted as lack of valour rather than as discretion.

In truth, the contemporary American geopolitician has a fate like the cheating billiard sharp's in *The Mikado*: he is doomed to play 'extravagant matches' on 'a cloth untrue, with a twisted cue and elliptical billiard balls'. The matches are extravagant because they involve inescapable geopolitical rivalry. The cloth is untrue because the competition is played out for the most part in regions and nations which act most frequently in response to aspirations and rivalries quite apart from those of the superpowers. At home the cue is twisted by the torque of congressional, press and pressure-group politics; and the balls are misshapen by the legacy of bad regionalism in the past which has populated the American side of the table with too many tottering and rebarbative regimes whose 'political legitimacy' rested too narrowly on US trusteeship of their shop-window 'non-communist' status.

For eleven years, US geopolicy has been in the hands of men who understood this dilemma and wanted to adjust for the untrue cloth and to encourage rounder balls, even if popular and press impressions tended to cast them still in the role of latter-day Dullesian cold warriors. The undeclared intellectual consensus between former Secretary of State Kissinger and President Carter's National Security Adviser, Zbigniew Brzezinski, goes well beyond the general notion of creative global pluralism as a basis for American involvement with friends and neutrals (and with adversaries who are potential neutrals).[2] The need for a higher cause than mere equilibrium and order; for a moral dimension; for the recognition that the necessary equilibrium and order have to be dynamic, not static; for appreciation of the flexibility of political

---

[2] Compare Kissinger's 1968 apothegm – 'Our goal should be to build a moral consensus which can make a pluralistic world creative'–with Zbigniew Brzezinski's 1977 peroration, 'It is our confident judgement that our collaboration (with the 'global community') can enhance the chances that the future destiny of man is to live in a world that is creatively pluralistic.'

131

multipolarity contrasted with the rigidity of military bipolarity; for relevance to the problems of the emerging two-thirds of the world; for avoiding exclusive preoccupation with US–Soviet relations; for seeking positive relations with the Third World; for acknowledgement of turmoil as a permanent condition of the world; for a new order adjusted to this turbulence and for engaging the moral sanction of the American public—all emerge as shared central themes in their conceptual work (though not always in their policy-making).

Meanwhile, however, the problems of stability and progress in the Third World have become more and more difficult. We see in operation what I have elsewhere called Jay's Law of Global Chaos.[3] Whereas the sources of turbulence in the world are growing exponentially – with more people demanding ever higher standards, more insistently, and giving expression to group or national aspirations, and with ever more destructive weaponry at hand—the sources of stability (domestic political structures, international diplomacy and institutions) can be strengthened, if at all, only arithmetically and at a slow rate. With the United States and the West seen as centres of power and privilege not adequately responsive to Third World aspirations and needs, and the Soviet Union still treated by a deplorable double standard that excuses its self-serving policies while accepting uncritically its rhetoric, there have been all too many seeds for the destructively monolithic negativism of the 'have-nots' that expressed itself, for example, in the September 1979 Havana Conference of the Nonaligned.

In the face of this situation, the philosopher's stone of US foreign policy, namely a positive cause or creed with which the West can combat the appeal of Marxism to Third World leaders looking for political legitimacy in overthrowing colonialism and establishing their own, often undemocratic, rule, was as far from being proclaimed and understood in 1977 as it ever had been. Important though the achievements of the Kissinger era were in ending the Vietnam conflict, promoting *détente* with the USSR and opening political contact with China, the fundamental questions identified by Kissinger in advance (and re-emphasised in recollection now) were as far from being answered as they had been in January 1969, when the Nixon Administration took office.[4] What new order does the United States offer the world? And what great principle or principles define legitimacy and guide American involvement?

[3] Berkeley Commencement Address, 5 April 1979.

1979 was the third year of the Carter Administration's effort to supply some answers to the questions identified by Kissinger in 1968 but thereafter almost wholly ignored in the Kissinger years. It was also the last year of the decade throughout which the problem was recognised but not solved. If good regionalism was indeed the most effective geopolitics, what exactly were to be the content and principles of good regionalism?

II

The cohesion and strength of the West remains, as we have just noted, the bedrock of US foreign policy. Inevitably, the economic power of Western Europe and its growing political independence, and the extraordinary economic performance of Japan – the very objectives of American policy in the post-war period – have created a new pattern of relationships and changed the nature of US leadership. Today that structure continues to hold together in its fundamental aspects, but there are growing strains that make the reality probably less good than the appearance. Yet the Carter Administration clearly improved its handling of these strains during 1979.

In the 1940s, the United States, with some significant British assistance, created a Western security order, linked to an even more imaginative political, military, trading and monetary order, which gave the West a structure, a stability and a prosperity the like of which it had seldom, if ever, enjoyed. In the 1950s and, less easily, in the 1960s, that order survived on the basis of an unspoken bargain – America decides and Europe complains – which reflected the realities of American external military and economic power and European internal political weakness.

As the 1960s wore on, and quite evidently in the 1970s, neither side wished to play that game any more, as America's relative economic weight diminished and Europe's political *amour propre* expanded. But

---

[4] In the first volume of his memoirs, Kissinger writes of the legacy of Acheson and Dulles that 'our doctrine of containment could never be an adequate response to the modern impact of Communist ideology, which transforms relations between states into conflicts between philosophies and poses challenges to the balance of power through domestic upheavals.' Henry Kissinger, *White House Years*, Boston: Little Brown and Company, 1979, p. 62. Closer still to the heart of the matter, he writes, 'no nation could face or even define its choices without a moral compass that set a course through the ambiguities of reality and thus made sacrifices meaningful.' *Ibid.*, p. 55.

there was no clear agreement on what alternative or more symmetrical game the two sides of the Atlantic should play. American governments found Europeans eager to participate in the prestige of making big decisions, but by no means equally anxious to share the political responsibility for these decisions. The neutron bomb affair of 1978 was a reminder of this, with the United States repeatedly soliciting European endorsement of the weapon while repeatedly being told to make its own decision. The long drawn out mating dance of the theatre nuclear force modernisation negotiations, though ultimately successful, repeated the lesson in 1979. Moreover, Europe's own need for a unifying purpose continued to push it, not in the direction of sharing America's global burdens, but rather into a spirit alternatively of assertive rivalry with its former benefactor and studied preoccupation with parochial concerns. This was perhaps natural at this stage of Europe's search for identity, but not for that reason a mature role or one that was comfortable for the United States.

On the surface, Western leaders strove manfully and successfully to keep the show on the road. At Guadeloupe in January and in Tokyo in June, President Carter met the other Western heads of government. He secured their support for SALT, and they secured a pledge from him on US oil imports, which had been a natural and justified point of criticism of American policy. A multilateral trade agreement was finally signed in April. The decision, albeit a fragile and difficult one, to modernise theatre nuclear forces was finally wrung out of the European allies in mid December as the culmination of prolonged and skilful diplomacy by the Administration. President Carter's standing in Europe also benefited dramatically from his handling of the Iranian crisis at the end of the year; and Europeans persuaded themselves that some of the earlier misgivings about his leadership, about the application of human rights to the Soviet Union and, even after November 1978, about his willingness to grapple firmly with inflation had been premature or exaggerated. Nor, so long as such committed Atlanticists as French President Giscard d'Estaing and West German Chancellor Schmidt lead their two countries, is any overtly dangerous move to weaken the Atlantic Alliance going to be made from Europe.

But, under the surface, the Alliance's foundations – and the foundations not only of NATO, but of that whole political, economic, financial and military order for the West – are being eaten away bit by bit. The catalyst of this corrosion is in part the philosophical vacuum in the West diagnosed by Kissinger eleven years ago and still unfilled.[5] But there are more positive forces impelling Western Europe to neglect its primary interest in the political cohesion and economic openness of the Western order as a whole and to give instead the lion's share of its energies to its search for identity. The shrill, though usually private, celebration of every supposed failure of American leadership in some cases betrayed a narrow preoccupation with US–West European rivalry as though it were a zero-sum game, in which any gain for one player is a loss for the other. Yet the gap between giddy aspiration and mature responsibility – willing to wound, but afraid to strike – is wide enough to obscure inconsistences, for example between simultaneously peddling reckless doubts about American willingness to use nuclear weapons in the defence of Europe and absolute insistence that any weapons deployed to correct the supposed Euro-strategic imbalance must be American-owned, American-produced and, above all, American-operated – and, of course, American-financed.

Even more dangerous in the long run, however, are the threats to the openness and efficiency of the Western economic order that derive from creeping autarky, mercantilism and protectionism in industrial and commercial policies. To be sure, the signing of the multilateral trade agreement consummated a modest formal advance and certainly avoided catastrophic reverses for liberal trade; and Britain's abolition of almost all exchange controls in October was a bonus. But the basic political momentum of corporate and labour pressure, rendered respectable by the patina of 'European' symbolism, is gradually propelling government at both community and national levels into heavier and heavier involvement in uncommercial and illiberal projects, particularly where American enterprise still has a competitive edge – though this does not inhibit simultaneous criticism of the US payments deficit and weak dollar. Aviation, defence procurement, telecommunications and other high-technology industries are the most prominent examples.

---

[5] 'In the bipolar world of the forties and fifties, order could be equated with military security. . . In the sixties, security, while still important, has not been enough. Every crisis from Berlin to Czechoslovakia has seen the call for "strengthening NATO" confined to military dispositions. Within months a malaise has become obvious again because the overriding need for a common political conception has not been recognized. The challenge of the seventies will be to forge unity with political measures. . . "Burden-sharing" will not supply that impetus. Countries do not assume burdens because it is fair, only because it is necessary. . . Even with the best will, the present structure encourages American unilateralism and European irresponsibility.' Henry Kissinger, *Agenda for the Nation*, pp. 597–599.

This is not just a matter of the natural development of new industries in response to market opportunities and profitable investment in more sophisticated technologies. The European industries are as entitled as any other to hope for such developments. What damages the open fabric of the Western economic system is the deliberate fostering of such industries in defiance of commercial principles by preferential government procurement policies, uncommercial funding of investment by government corporations, public financial support of unprofitable projects and general administrative favouritism. The faults are by no means all on one side; but from the point of view of US foreign policy, which has to give a high place to the health and cohesion of the West, the actual and far greater potential growth of economic friction over autarkic industrial policies, both real and imagined, is a profound danger.

General economic conditions are likely to deteriorate in the 1980s. The new undervaluation of the US dollar against West European currencies will begin to reverse the dynamic of trade and investment that underpinned European economic recovery in the 1950s and 1960s. So the political pressure in Europe, allying traditional fears of unemployment with the new search for expressions of Europe's aspirant political identity, will tend to impel demagogues, socialist and eventually democratic leaders seeking electoral support down the road of economic nationalism. A new, directly elected European Parliament, seeking a cause with which to occupy the huge vacuum of its explicit impotence combined with its implicit legitimacy, also offers an ideal forum. The potential of this for political friction within the Atlantic community, and so for dissipation of the cohesion on which the West's military strength ultimately depends, hardly needs to be rehearsed. The gradual and inevitable decay of the folk memories of the 1930s has reminded us that even the simple, but basic, lessons of collective security and economic liberalism, which were taught so painfully then, can have little more than a generational half-life. If economic adversity and political weakness lead to a renaissance, albeit in a new and more sophisticated form, of the economics of Mussolini, that should surprise only those in the United States and elsewhere who believed that Europe could and would become a 'born-again' America simply by institutional elaboration and legal construction. If the United States and Japan prove to be just as bad under similar economic pressure, that will make the crisis of the West as a whole worse.

Nationalism, punctuated by intervals of lucidity which last as long as the memory of the last disaster that nationalism wrought, has always been and is likely always to remain Europe's most natural political dynamic, despite all the wailing and hand-wringing of liberal and socialist philosophers. The scale of global politics now requires that nationalism, to be effective, must be the nationalism of a whole subcontinent. The nationalism of the traditional powers has waned in importance with the passing of a Euro-centric world and the rise of the superpowers. It is wholly characteristic that in these circumstances Europeans should find the will to submerge the old rivalries in a new and geographically grander nationalism.

That, once born, a new Europe will neither behave like the United States nor serve American purposes nor give priority to Western strength and economic interdependence is a prospect that American foreign policy-makers should perhaps have evaluated in the 1950s and which they now will have to confront in the 1980s and 1990s. It will become increasingly difficult for enlightened American leaders to contain comparably divisive protectionist and isolationist pressures in the United States when it can be pointed out that America's partners in the Western scheme of things are no longer even pretending to play by the rules of the immediate post-war era. The path of good regionalism may become extremely hard to define, quite apart from becoming worse domestic politics in the United States. More than a decade after his diagnosis, Kissinger might agree that his prescription for Europe as 'a counter-weight that would discipline our occasional impetuosity and, by supplying historical perspective, modify our penchant for abstract and "final" solutions' owed more to hope than to experience.[6]

These are long-term concerns, and they were not noticeably aggravated in 1979. Indeed, this past year ended on a better note of mutual respect and comity than the last several years have. But the fact remains that the mutual involvement of the United States and Western Europe is taken for granted rather than nurtured, while the original sources of that cohesion in the concepts and institutions of the immediate post-war period are being neglected. The continuing, indeed increasingly powerful, threat of the Soviet Union still breathes life into NATO; but even in military matters there are dangerous tendencies: on the Left to neutralism, on the Right to independent European defence capabilities. At present they are small straws in the wind, though it has taken a major diplomatic effort to haul the ambiguous concept of Euro-strategic

[6] *Op. cit.*, p. 599

137

balance back from the implication that European powers need to be able to do nuclear damage to the Soviet Union comparable to that which the Soviet Union can do to them. Such a programme would be the heresy, naked and unashamed, of 'decoupling' the United States from Europe. The eventual theatre nuclear force modernisation also denied the neutralists what could have been a dramatic success; but it was not a total victory and they remain in the field, especially in the smaller countries, ready to seize every new pretext for appeasing the Soviet Union and disparaging American purposes and will. This brings us back yet again to the need to identify and reaffirm what the West stands for, what its global interests are, what responsibilities and mutual obligations it imposes on its members and what the relationship should be between the imperatives of Western health and those of European identity.

If US foreign policy toward the West European region faces a grumbling crisis far more serious than the cheerful enumeration of summits, formal agreements and affable declarations can fully disguise, there is very little the United States can do about it. Washington can seek discreetly to strengthen benign forces in Europe, to discourage malign ones, to avoid reacting or, worse, over-reacting to 'European irresponsibility' with 'American unilateralism'; it can continue to shoulder without protest the political odium for hard decisions while offering as much show of consultation and participation as Europe seems to want from time to time; it can minimise by leadership and cooperation in economic and monetary affairs the economic slump of the 1980s; and it can deter the Soviet Union from exploiting the inevitable tensions and incoherence with siren calls for the neutralisation and demilitarisation of Europe. But it is likely that the lessons of the 1930s will be gradually forgotten, the institutions of the 1940s will be allowed to decay and the characteristically nationalist impulses of European history will once again flourish – until the consequences of this folly force people yet again to relearn the essential facts of peace and prosperity.

III

It was above all in the Third World that the Carter Administration gave new emphasis to the desire to associate the United States with the forces of change in the world. And the strongest manifestation of this emphasis has for the past three years been its human rights policy. The articulation of both principles may have been more apt to cause alarm among the wrong kind of friends abroad and the opposition at home than to enchant potential supporters who wondered what the Administration meant. But this reflected a perennial dilemma of those who embark upon new policies. The benefits of any such changes in posture are bound to be reflected only in general terms, for the most part.

But over the last three years there can be little doubt that the Carter Administration has succeeded in changing the image of the United States that had been created during the Cold War and accentuated by the *realpolitik* of the Kissinger years. No longer is the United States regarded as indifferent to issues of human rights, and the record in this area during 1979 was a good one.

In Africa and Latin America, in particular, the year was remarkable for the number of modest steps taken in the direction of less tyrannical, or more constitutional, or even more democratic, governance. Moreover, this was achieved, if not by the United States, then either with American encouragement or at least without US opposition and therefore without the United States being made to look like the champion of shameful oppressors. While the examples certainly do not all fit any general formula, still less reflect the working out of a master plan, nonetheless the catalogue is worth emphasising at a time when it is fashionable to see the United States suffering ubiquitous geopolitical defeat.

In Africa, the fall of Ugandan President Idi Amin could not but be regarded as beneficial to human rights; and the United States showed wisdom in leaving Tanzanian President Julius Nyerere in no doubt of its benign neutrality during the Ugandan-Tanzanian war that led to Amin's downfall. Nigeria began a return to civilian rule with its first national elections since 1964. The particularly odious Central African Emperor Bokassa was overthrown, albeit at the instigation of a French-managed coup which substituted a somewhat unconvincing stooge as successor, one David Dacko. Earlier in the year, Macias, the tyrant of Equatorial Guinea, had been overthrown.

But it was in Latin America that the most significant changes in the direction of more democratic rule took place. An amateur in Latin American matters can only speculate on the degree to which these changes owed at least a psychological debt to the continuing progress since 1975 of democracy in Spain, still to some extent the cultural mother country for much of Latin America. During 1979, Spain held its first elections under its new fully democratic constitution, and a comparatively strong single-party government was elected. Whether or not its example exerted a significant influence on Latin America, the events of 1979 seem to demonstrate a new surge in democratic feeling in that area.

Among the notable events there was the restoration of constitutional government in Ecuador in April. A similar return to constitutional government in Bolivia in August was briefly aborted by an ensuing military coup, but in the end a new civilian president was able to take office in November. Neither of these changes could be attributed directly to US influence, although the efforts that top American representatives made to indicate their approval were important symbolic actions. Far more directly relevant to US policy was the expulsion of Somoza from Nicaragua and his replacement by a new Sandinista regime.

The United States was deeply involved in Nicaragua, and its policy there could hardly be counted an unqualified success, since the United States would undoubtedly have preferred a moderate and constitutional successor government. US moves for a regional military force designed to ensure fair elections were rejected by the Organization of American States, and in the final stages any moderate regime could only have been installed by some form of covert action, which indeed appeared to be advocated by such critics as Henry Kissinger but was categorically rejected by an Administration deeply conscious of the adverse repercussions throughout the region of past covert action in Chile and elsewhere.

But the Carter Administration broke new ground in not only disassociating itself from a client dictator of long standing but actively working for his removal. And by the end of the year the Administration had laid out a policy of seeking to work with the Sandinista government, especially through economic aid. In this course it was in tune with the predominant sentiment of the Latin American region as a whole, which had strongly supported the overthrow of Somoza. At an earlier time, the United States had applied the hard-line policies of the Dulles era to the advent of Castro to power in Cuba, and harsh American pressures contributed to Castro's present pro-Soviet posture, with all its damage to US interests not only in the Caribbean but in Africa and elsewhere. Plainly the Carter Administration is determined to avoid repeating this classic example of bad regionalism.

Evidence of democratic advance in Asia was harder to find in 1979. Apart from the extraordinary and baffling surges of activity on Beijing's Democracy Wall, whose potential seemed at first significant and later less so, the main event was a setback. Pakistan's President Zia ul-Haq

aborted his country's planned return to a democratic form of government and reimposed draconian constraints on political activity.

In neither of these situations did the United States have any significant
influence. The real test case of American policy occurred in South Korea,
a classic case of an American client dictator, Park Chung Hee. His turn
to martial law in 1972 and subsequent repressions had been unques-
tioningly accepted by the Nixon and Ford Administrations. Under the
Carter Administration, the human rights policy was applied through
constant urgings for the release of opposition leaders and others.

Thus, when Park was assassinated in November 1979 by his own
central intelligence chief, the United States was at least in the position of
not being inextricably associated with his fate, as happened in Iran. At
the end of 1979 it was far from clear that a new constitution and new
elections would be achieved, but Secretary Vance had been quick to seize
the opportunity to throw US influence behind liberalisation.

Similarly, the human rights posture of the Carter Administration has
led it to disassociate itself from the martial law rule of another client
dictator, Ferdinand Marcos in the Philippines, who survived 1979 but is
plainly increasingly under pressure for change. Neither there nor in
Korea can the United States wholly avoid the past legacy of unquestioning support, but the new American posture should serve to permit the
United States to retain strong, and geopolitically important, relationships with both countries should a democratic opposition find its
way to power in either.

It is easy to be sceptical about the significance of those democratic
straws in the political wind. Few of them directly reflected US policy.
Hard-nosed *realpolitik* critics will contrast them unfavourably with the
muscularity of the Soviet arms build-up and crude intervention in
Afghanistan. Moreover, democracy and human rights can never by
themselves be an adequate counter to Marxism as a comprehensive
banner under which to fight the geopolitical battle for hearts, minds and
friendly governments, especially in the emerging nations. Nonetheless, a
start has been made, as previous administrations never managed to do;
and the American people have been reconnected to US foreign policy.

Despite Cuban President Castro's rhetoric and Khomeini's abuse, a
grudging recognition that the President of the United States is a man
with honourable intentions towards other countries (which do not
consist in supporting the *status quo* however oppressive) has gained
ground. Inevitably those who have developed a vested interest in the old
order, under which America was expected to take care of its friends with

no questions asked, have been noisily unhappy and have prated of weakness. But the price of opposition was inherent in embracing a framework for change and in any strategy of withdrawing from the foreign policy cul-de-sac of Dulles and, despite his advance warnings against it, of Kissinger: namely, reflex trusteeship of 'every noncommunist area'.

Strength and toughness have their place, as does the ability discreetly to aid well-disposed internal political forces in key countries whose geopolitical orientation hangs in the balance. All of these are necessary conditions; but none is a sufficient condition. A successful superpower must be able to display overt principles which are, in Kissinger's words, 'relevant to one of the great revolutions of our time' if it is to catch the regional tides that lead on to geopolitical success.

IV

Perhaps the clearest test of the Carter Administration's policy of seeking to identify the United States with regional aspirations and attitudes has been in southern Africa. No set of problems more vividly illustrates the contrast between good regionalism and the results that might have flowed from a continued overriding emphasis on the Soviet threat.

Under the Carter policies, US geopolitical interests have been much better served over the last three years than those who only read the headlines may suppose. The perception in 1978 was that the Soviet Union, in the shape of ten foot tall Cuban puppets, was sweeping through the continent unopposed by a weak and soft-headed US Administration, which naively believed that the triumph of civil rights in the American South could be exported as a universal bromide for indigenous African struggles. Britain's Labour Government, also suspected of soft sympathies for black Marxists, was believed to have led Carter's McGovernite foreign policy makers into a shameful geopolitical betrayal or misjudgement in southern Africa. The reality was different.

Over the past several years, US policy in fact lost a country and gained a continent. Indeed, that may in one way be too cautious a judgement. The country which the United States was supposed to have 'lost' was Ethiopia. Yet, the disposition to see the Soviet Union's political transfer in 1978 from Somalia to Ethiopia as a coup for communist world aims is evidence chiefly of a determination to discern deep cunning and unerring efficiency in one's adversary, and only blundering incompetence in one's own side. The facts were that the USSR forfeited in Somalia a thousand miles of Indian Ocean littoral, a strategically located potential sea base, a quiescent interior and an admirable jumping-off point for interference in the Red Sea and the Arabian peninsula. And in plunging into Ethiopia at the cost of one of the largest and most expensive airlifts in history, the USSR reaped in return a heavy and not easily reversible involvement in an internal political quagmire.

In 1979, however, the hidden and ubiquitous hand of the Soviet Union went largely undetected even by the most imaginative analysts. This was not, by any means, because the Soviet Union is in any way benign or without ambitions in Africa which threaten geopolitical equilibrium. It most certainly has such ambitions. But they had for the moment been outsmarted, principally by UN Ambassador Andrew Young's astute perception of the appeal to Africa of mature political and economic relations with the West. Andrew Young's personal credibility in representing a new and different American attitude to Africa undoubtedly contributed importantly to the speed with which good regionalism in Africa succeeded in fostering America's geopolitical interests there.

In order for a healthy and constructive relationship between newly independent Africa and the West to develop, a lot of ghosts had first to be laid: ethnic Europeans on either side of the Atlantic as the natural 'kith and kin' of white racists in southern Africa; imperialist America wishing to impose capitalism and to exploit Africa's resources; superpower America making African peoples and states pawns in its struggle with Russia for world hegemony; hypocritical Britain talking independence, but still hankering after neo-colonial opportunities and retaining huge economic interests in apartheid-ridden South Africa. Steadily and gradually, the Carter Administration did begin to gain credence for the idea that there was a new US policy in Africa; that the Organization of African Unity principle of African solutions to African problems was respected; that the United States was not just in the business of playing cynical geopolitics and that it wanted mature and good relations with any country that was willing to reciprocate.

The two most important demonstrations of that policy were in the negotiations over Namibia and Zimbabwe/Rhodesia, which are perhaps the purest examples of good regionalism being good geopolitics just where glib opinion sees the clearest clash between the two. As stated at the outset, big gains are made in US –Soviet competition outside Eastern Europe and the Western hemisphere only by the superpower that successfully catches the locally prevailing political winds. In Africa that wind has for twenty years been black nationalism, but the leaders of the surrounding black front-line states do not relish prolonged chaotic warfare on their doorsteps, nor eventual Soviet domination.

Lord Carrington, the British Foreign Secretary, brought negotiations for internationally recognisable independence to final success during the year with outstanding skill and firmness. But much of that skill – and much of President Carter's as well – had to be used in resisting the determination of the Right in Britain and the United States to snatch defeat from the jaws of victory. If the United States had committed itself to massive defence of white interests in southern Africa, as the Right urged, it would have ended by fighting with its back to the sea, facing North, condemned by the entire world, on political terrain where it was bound in the end to lose. The Soviet Union would have had its pretext for expansion in southern Africa in the name of support for legitimate African nationalist liberation movements. For the time being it has been denied that geopolitical prize precisely by a Western strategy which harnessed the interest of African politicians and the principles of post-colonial African politics to a settlement in Rhodesia which was also consistent with broad Western interests. Despite South Africa's resistance, the success in Zimbabwe/Rhodesia could yet persuade Pretoria to give a similar formula a chance in Namibia.

V

How, then, do the principles of good and bad regionalism relate to the Middle East, now by far the most acute area of competition between the Soviet Union and the United States and the West? There, during 1979, the overthrow of the Shah was beyond question a major geopolitical setback for the United States, and the extreme anti-Americanism of the new regime of Ayatollah Khomeini was underscored by the hostage crisis that began in November and was still unresolved at the end of the year. Meanwhile the Soviet Union, confronted in Afghanistan with a growing insurrection against the Marxist government it had helped to install in early 1978, moved in December to carry out a military coup and then to a full-fledged invasion of Afghanistan by Soviet forces.

It is the fashion in many quarters to see these events as the result of an alleged decline in the military power and prestige of the United States in

144

the area and the growth of Soviet military power, coupled with Soviet influence on local Marxist regimes. While no one can argue that these factors were wholly irrelevant, the significant reality was quite otherwise. What happened in Iran, as it related to the United States, was overwhelmingly the result of bad regional policies in the past. And in the case of the Soviet takeover of Afghanistan, a takeover always within the military capabilities of the USSR for the last thirty years, the Soviet Union may once again have gained a country but lost a region — provided that the United States and the West work in concert with the genuine anti-Soviet feelings in the area which the Soviet invasion may now have brought into flame. Good regionalism remains at the heart of the terribly serious problems the United States now faces in the area, both in the need to carry forward the peace process between Israel and the Arab nations and in the need to work with and through those and other nations in countering the new Soviet presence in the area.

There was nothing in 1979, and probably not in either of the two preceding years, that the Administration could sensibly have done to prevent the fall of the Shah. This was, if only in hindsight, the inevitable harvest of a quarter of a century of creating and fostering as a bastion of Western influence a regime which was not merely irrelevant to one of the great revolutions of our times (to use Kissinger's measure), but also, and even more to the point, not durable. When doom came, albeit at an unforeseeable moment, it was idle to blame the Administration for not being able to prevent it, or for looking uncomfortable as the grisly events of the Shah's departure, the Ayatollah Khomeini's return and subsequent barbarities unfolded. The essential trick by then was to adjust to the inevitable while limiting the geopolitical damage, not only by discouraging any temptation the Soviet Union might feel to exploit the opportunity, but also by reassuring friendly regimes in the area that might otherwise feel insecure.

In theory, the Administration seems to have read the situation aright and to have set out to accommodate its policy to the Iranian revolution, while containing its side effects. The Administration also moved rapidly to act on its correct perception that Saudi Arabia needed prompt reassurance. Unfortunately, perhaps because events moved so fast, bad geopolitics for a while took over from good regionalism with predictably unfavourable results. The Administration seems to have assumed, in sending Secretary of Defence Harold Brown and his party to Saudi Arabia in February and in offering demonstrations of US military support, that the Saudis' principal anxiety would also be geopolitical, and that they would be prepared to participate, at this stage, in new and broader military relationships.

The Saudis appear not to have seen it that way at all. They saw Iran as illustrating the danger for their own feudal regime of Arab radicalism and of anti-American Islamic fundamentalism. They perceived the remedy for this as lying in the resolution of the unifying issue from which Arab radicalism and Islamic anti-Americanism drew their cohesion, namely the problem of Palestine. At the very least, the Saudis felt the need to align themselves with prevailing moderate Arab opinion, which anyway coincided with their perception of the manifest rights of the question, especially over Jerusalem. To be suddenly and flamboyantly embraced by the United States in a demonstration of crudely geopolitical purposes cloaked in a military mantle was the last thing the Saudis felt they needed at such a moment.

Worse still, a vicious circle was created over the implementation of Camp David. Good regionalism in the Near East, as well as the criticially important geopolitical reassurance of Saudi Arabia, demanded essentially that the second Camp David 'shoe' should be made to drop in the course of 1979 – i.e. that a negotiated agreement on Palestinian autonomy be established which could realistically lead, whatever may have been said on paper, to a Palestinian homeland within a few years and to internationally backed guarantees of Israel's security. Yet Saudi alarm at US handling of the Iranian aftermath – despite successful US moves to restabilise the jeopardised balance between North and South Yemen – made it much harder to secure moderate Arab support for the process and increased the formidable pressures on Egyptian President Sadat at a most critical time for him, though he survived them with notable fortitude.

Some may doubt whether the 'second shoe' could ever have been made to drop. But 1979 probably began with the best prospect that there had been for decades for starting that process. At Camp David President Carter and his principal advisers sincerely believed in and thought they had accomplished the makings of a comprehensive settlement, albeit in two parts. Moderate Arabs would have liked to have believed this, but were not sure and could not afford to take forthcoming positions until they were sure. And the chances of confounding the sceptics and of outmanoeuvering the cynics and outright opponents of a comprehensive settlement depended on attracting the early support of the moderate Arabs for the Camp David process.

This was indeed a daunting task and had from the start the seeds of failure through cumulative and mutually reinforcing hesitation and scepticism. But Israel was at least formally committed by the Camp David agreements to embark upon negotiations. President Carter, Secretary of State Vance and National Security Adviser Brzezinski were jointly and severally more sympathetic to righting the legitimate Palestinian grievances than any of their predecessors since the war. Egypt was deeply committed to the process. The Palestinians themselves had even shown some weak signs of being willing to compromise over the more extreme and rheotrical demands of the Palestine Liberation Organization's charter, if they could actually believe that Israel could be induced to make real concessions. Begin seemed strongly placed, if he would, to lead his countrymen to take some calculated risks, just as de Gaulle had been the right man to persuade France to surrender Algeria. Elections in the United States were eighteen months away – time enough to tackle the issue on its merits. Even so, the obstacles were formidable.

The critical battles for suspension of moderate Arab hostility seem to have been lost early in the year. By the autumn Ambassador at Large Robert Strauss conceded in his characteristically blunt fashion that the negotiations for Palestinian autonomy were 'stalemated'. Thus the United States was left without a credible policy for tackling the region's central problem as perceived by most of the people who live and govern in the area. This regional fiasco was also a geopolitical setback because despite the temporary advantage of the Egypt–Israel peace, the US position in the area had come to rest far too heavily on the survival of Sadat. The Soviet Union was left free, whenever SALT was ratified or abandoned, to ride the inevitable tide of Arab wrath against Israel and the United States.

At the end of the year the game was not over. President Carter's personal commitment and energy remained a wild card of great potential force, and the true self-interest of the moderate Arabs and of Israel still favoured successful autonomy negotiations. The Iranian revolution remains a huge complication; but, handled in the right way, it is also a powerful reminder of the broader instability and unpredictability of the area and therefore the prudence of pushing forward with the one and only initiative which in thirty years has offered a tangible prospect of a peaceful settlement of the Arab–Israel conflict.

Unfortunately, the Iranian revolution itself took an especially nasty turn in November, when Iranian militants took hostage the staff of the American Embassy in Tehran, with the approval of Iran's leadership under the Ayatollah Khomeini. The extreme anti-Americanism in Iran was the direct result of past American policies – a legacy once again of bad regionalism.

In its handling of the crisis, the Administration earned some fierce criticism in the early days from its most hawkish domestic opponents; but as the crisis wore on respect for the President's measured response increased, especially in the eyes of the American people and foreign governments. Even the most savage early critics of Administration weakness and vacillation muted their criticisms, though it was also clear that others were restraining themselves until it could no longer be said that their attacks were endangering American lives and weakening the American President at a time of national emergency.

Perhaps the clearest lesson of the on-going Iranian crisis is the great difficulty of trying to practise good regionalism in the wake of two decades of bad regionalism. Those two decades of excessive reliance on the Shah and his politically unrealistic programmes had led to a situation from which no strategist would have chosen to start out. But at least the Administration seems to have kept its eye on the two essential issues: first, that under no circumstances must the United States be seen to contemplate concessions, justified or not, in response to the taking of hostages; and second, that the United States should not be provoked into emotionally dictated military actions that could only lead the Iranian regime to unpredictable reactions and that would, as events have already demonstrated, be overwhelmingly likely to cast the United States in the role of villain in the eyes of Muslim sentiment throughout the area.

Now, of course, the situation in the whole Middle East has been drastically altered by the Soviet invasion of Afghanistan. To see this as the result of some new correlation of superpower military forces in the area is, to repeat, a false reading of both history and present circumstances. The Soviet Union has always had it in its physical power to take over Afghanistan. Whether its present actions succeed in any wider purpose must depend upon the effectiveness of the measures already under way to penalise the Soviet Union directly through economic and political measures, and above all – in terms of the Middle East – on the capacity of the United States and other Western countries to work with the anti-Soviet feeling that prevails there today in taking effective counter-measures within the area.

Unquestionably, an element in those counter-measures must be the strengthening of American military capacity to act in support of threatened Middle Eastern nations, starting with renewed arms supplies to Pakistan. Already these nations, as well as nations in Africa, have shown themselves much more ready than in the recent past to provide at least limited military facilities for US forces. And there are those who urge that the United States seek to create some new alliance structure in the Middle East that would bring together formally the moderate Arab nations, perhaps even with Israel.

But surely the whole history of Soviet–Western competition in the Middle East in the last twenty-five years argues for a much more sophisticated and cautious approach. The fates of the Baghdad Pact and later of CENTO – not to mention past Soviet efforts to create their own alliances – testify to the ineffectiveness of formal structures. Indeed, any attempt to depict the struggle in the area as one between the Soviet Union and the United States is bound to be counter-productive. It is, in fact, one between the Soviet Union and the independent nations of the Middle East, and it is on the basis of their often divergent attitudes and interests that any fabric of security cooperation must be created.

In short, if the United States should now turn to a policy of naked power that neglects the political realities of the area, it will lose. The essence of sound policy, even in the face of this new and unprecedented crisis, remains the practice of good regionalism. And one of the key elements in this must remain the achievement of early progress toward the resolution of the Palestinian issue, thus laying the foundations for a lasting Arab–Israeli peace. Only if this bone in the throat of leading Arab nations is removed can the United States hope in the long run to see the area as a whole free itself of the threat of extended Soviet influence or control.

VI

The aims of US policy toward the Soviet Union at the start of the year were to maintain *détente*, to reach an agreement on a strategic arms limitation treaty (SALT II) and get it ratified, and to discourage Soviet adventurism around the world. All three were gravely jeopardised by the Soviet intervention in Afghanistan at the end of the year, an action which may now necessitate a complete reappraisal of US-Soviet relations. But the 1979 record still deserves to be studied in full and on its merits.

Détente was already in some jeopardy at the outset of the year from the unexpected announcement in December 1978 of the decision to recognise Peking; from increasingly hawkish reactions in the United

States to the Soviet arms build-up; the pattern of Russian machinations in Africa and the northern tier of the Middle East; the killing of US Ambassador Dubs in Kabul in February; and the remorseless pressure of Hanoi on the rest of Indochina. The SALT II agreement looked attainable; but it and its ratification were always vulnerable to unforeseen developments – such as the loss of intelligence bases in Iran, and the 'discovery' in September of a Soviet brigade in Cuba, never mind crude aggression against a neighbouring state. As for discouraging Russian adventurism, the Administration faced the perennial problem defined by Kissinger of navigating between dangerous confrontation and equally dangerous passivity.

Dealt this hand – and before the invasion of Afghanistan threatened to bring the roof down – the Administration on the whole did surprisingly well in preserving its basic bilateral objectives and avoiding, sometimes only just, the main hazards which events at home and abroad threw in front of it. The abruptly announced decision to recognise China apparently put back the signing of the SALT treaty by several months; but *détente* was not at that time significantly derailed, once it was made clear that the United States was not fully playing the China card. The SALT II treaty was signed, though not ratified. Overreaction to the Soviet brigade in Cuba was avoided, though not without some initial Lear-like threats of unspecified retaliation on the President's part. Indeed, the most visible action of the Russian leadership in the latter part of the year was ostensibly pacific, namely Soviet President Brezhnev's offer to withdraw some Soviet forces and theatre nuclear weapons from the European zone, if NATO would agree to forego modernisation of its theatre nuclear weapons. Whatever the motive – and there were certainly those who saw this as a cynical and transparent manoeuvre to prevent NATO from plugging an important gap in its defences preparatory to renewed Soviet politico-military pressure on Western Europe – it was consistent with the spirit of *détente*.

But if the fundamentals of US–Soviet relations were preserved, this was achieved at a cost to a number of subsidiary policy aims. The full impact of the restoration of diplomatic ties with China, which could have had important dividends for American self-confidence and global standing, was blurred, not only by the need to reassure the Soviet Union that no change in US–Soviet relations was intended but, above all, by the feeling that perhaps China had played the American card as a preliminary to its 'punitive' adventure against Vietnam in February. Even so, Russian behaviour in Africa, the Middle East, the Persian Gulf and even in Indochina after the Chinese invasion of Vietnam seemed for most of 1979 remarkable chiefly for its restraint, at least judged by the standards of the acute alarm that was being expressed in normally responsible quarters early in the year.

The blurring of the impact of normalised relations with China was not the only price in 1979. Neither the Administration nc³ the Russians showed much skill in translating their restraint in mutual dealings to advantage in building a stronger constituency for *détente* within the United States. What should have been seen as a cool Administration keeping its head when all about were losing theirs – and securing Soviet restraint and cooperation by skilful exploitation of Moscow's anxiety for SALT ratification – was too easily replaced by the more excitingly sensational picture of a weak American leadership nonplussed and outplayed by ineluctable Russian cunning. As a result, the Cold War constituency in the United States gained ground – well before the Afghanistan intervention gave it its biggest windfall in years. Substantial defence expenditure commitments, some of them not then well thought through, had to be made. These came on top of both the substantial reversal already made by the Carter Administration of the previous decline in US defense budget shares in GNP and of successful US leadership of reluctant NATO partners in the same direction in 1977 and 1978. Even Kissinger judged it politic to cast his great influence as the most skilful architect of *détente* on the side of alarm in a spine-chilling address in Brussels in September, which cast doubt on the security of the American guarantee in light of the Soviet military build-up.

This failure to strengthen domestic support for *détente* had many causes: hand to mouth public relations disguised rather than emphasised the unifying rationale of US policy toward the Soviet Union; the theme of President Carter's Annapolis speech of June 1978, advocating sensibly modulated cooperation and competition, was not sufficiently repeated; an insufficiently suppressed urge to demonstrate spasmodic toughness found trivial, rather than substantial, outlets (e.g., the strange affairs of the non-absconding wife of the absconding Russian ballet dancer, and the White House's 'tough' reaction, which later had to be reversed, to the Soviet brigade in Cuba). Other more seriously fumbled gestures – the dispatch of unarmed fighters to Saudi Arabia; the widely advertised refusal of landing rights for US military aircraft in Spain; the Turks' consent to such landings only if the Soviets did not object; the dithering of US aircraft carriers in and out of the Indian Ocean – too

151

easily captured attention which should have been directed to the consistency of the Administration's essential handling of the Soviet Union.

Last, there was the unquestionable reality of the Russian arms build-up, the only really substantial element – pre-Afghanistan – in the whole litany of Soviet misdeeeds. But here again the effort should have been made to communicate convincingly the validity and continuing success of the Administration's initiatives in rousing the NATO allies to an appropriate response, both in total defence spending with more cost-effective procurement procedures, and in facing up to the need to modernise NATO's theatre nuclear forces. The first tended to get lost in the auction for Senate SALT votes, with higher percentage figures for the growth in defence spending being hawked round by all parties without much precision about what they would buy and why. Even the modernisation of theatre nuclear forces seemed for a while to have been unnecessarily hazarded by the premature commitment to a land-based solution. This could hardly have been better calculated to maximise the political risks of the European allies ducking their responsibilities. But at the crucial NATO meeting in Brussels on 15 December 1979 an affirmative decision was finally achieved. It remains vulnerable to a change of the political coalition in Italy, to the fragility of Belgian and Dutch policy and to West Germany's determination not to be alone in accepting deployment of new nuclear weapons directly threatening Soviet territory.

But for 1979, the actual achievement was real and important, demonstrating that a sensitive and cooperative US response to anxieties originally expressed in Europe can lead the Alliance to face its responsibilities without America alone having to bear the odium of thrusting a controversial decision down complaining European throats. The message to the Soviets should have been clear: NATO is capable of a coherent response to a threatening Russian arms build-up; the United States has not lost control of its allies; *détente* is still a high Alliance priority; and arms control is desired but will not be negotiated from a position of Western inferiority.

It is too soon to judge how far this interpretation of the progress of US—Soviet *détente* in 1979 as it seemed at the time may have to be revised in the light of the Soviet intervention in Afghanistan and its consequences. If the Soviet Union should proceed not only to take over Afghanistan for keeps but to threaten other nations in the area from a new Afghan base, or if the Russians should breach the ceilings set in the now-shelved SALT

II agreements, then indeed the West may have to gird itself, militarily and economically, for a long period of much more ruthless direct competition from the Soviet Empire, though the shared global interest in preventing a nuclear holocaust will remain as valid as ever.

But if the Soviet Union clearly confines its actions to Afghanistan and encounters difficulties both there and in the rest of the Middle East, so that it finally realises the mistake it has made, then the basic principles discussed can continue to apply, though in a more watchful spirit.

Détente must never be confused with appeasement. A decision to abandon any search for *détente* should not be made instantly on the morrow of a shocking event. Nonetheless, the need to compete effectively in the rest of the world – beyond the direct military balance and the immediate border areas of the superpowers – will be at least as great as ever.

VII

The broad theme underlying this review of US foreign policy in 1979 has been that geopolitical success and failure depend on regional success and failure, which in turn depend on how the superpowers relate to locally prevailing political winds. The West and, in particular, the United States as its leader, has operated under two general handicaps: the legacy of bad regionalism engendered by a simplistic geopolitical strategy from Truman to Nixon; and the lack of a positive political philosophy with which to combat the appeal of Marxism and the stigma of colonialism and imperialism in the ideologically uncommitted parts of the developing world.

As a result, a serious crisis of confidence in American power has begun to develop. The old strategy of overt and covert support for every non-communist regime, however unsavoury, no longer worked; nor did its characteristic methods and weapons. This was partly because those methods and weapons had come to be too widely rejected in the United States, and even more because 'friendly' regimes inevitably built up so much opposition locally that they either collapsed or had to be propped up by even more naked American sponsorship. If one asks why the Soviet Union, whose own regime and whose client regimes are even less savoury, can successfully carry its sponsorship to any lengths with comparative political impunity, the answers must be in part sheer ruthlessness uninhibited by a free political democracy at home, in part the philosophical edge that Marxism has enjoyed throughout much of the world in the immediate post-colonial age.

The attempt to move US foreign policy toward a new strategy has been enormously difficult, partly because human rights and democracy are not by themselves sufficiently relevant to the concerns of most of the world's new nations, and partly because dropping the least savoury of the old clients causes instant tremors of alarm among America's friends while encouraging their opponents. Moreover, once the credibility of a superpower is called into question, it can suffer for a while an almost catastrophic loss of effective influence.

Some critics have argued that the United States should go back to the old strategy, building up its military strength and bloodying more noses. But they cite no evidence that that strategy would now be immune from the weaknesses which defeated it before. A sophisticated and fully coordinated programme of action that restored a sustainable political equilibrium in the Middle East could indeed restore confidence in American power, to say nothing of American will. But a ham-handed emphasis on delusive military 'solutions', however 'tough', would do more harm than good.

The real problem is deeper: to manage global turbulence in such a way as to prevent a major geopolitical upset for long enough to enable the more promising new strategy to be understood and to earn some dividends. Some encouraging signs, especially in Africa and Latin America, have already been cited. But the size of the task is still vividly illustrated in the state of the North–South dialogue. One of the true disappointments of US foreign policy was symbolised during the September 1979 Havana Conference of Nonaligned States. For all the stage-management and hypocrisy, the plain fact was that the nearest approximation of a moral consensus at this gathering was on the Soviet side. It does little good to point out how unjust this is, how bogus, how little account it took of the real achievements of the Carter Administration in promoting diplomacy based on just those principles Kissinger had advocated in 1968, i.e., relevance; morality; creativity; pluralism; and legitimacy. Geopolitics is about winning. As measured – however imperfectly – by Havana, the moral balance of the world has not tilted to the champion of freedom, democracy, human rights and all that – not yet.

Had the Soviet invasion of Afghanistan preceded Havana, however, things would probably have fallen out differently. In early January 1980, the defeat of Cuba's candidacy for a Security Council seat above all and the overwhelming vote of the General Assembly to condemn the Soviet invasion of Afghanistan showed a sharp rise in anti-Soviet feelings – though again it would be a mistake to interpret the switch as pro-American. The issue in the General Assembly was rightly presented by American representatives and others, not in US–Soviet terms, but as a threat posed by the Soviet Union to the independence of all nations.

Thus the massive condemnation of Soviet behaviour was much more than a generalised expression of that 'world opinion' so often derided by tough-minded 'realists'; it may not get Soviet forces out of Afghanistan, but it will plague the Soviet Union for a long time to come all over the world, and in concrete and power-related ways. And the vote would scarcely have been so decisive if the United States, under the Carter Administration, had not been conducting itself in the past three years at the United Nations in the spirit of Andrew Young rather than Patrick Moynihan, or if the Administration had not, in its whole conduct, given the convincing lie to Soviet charges that old-style US manipulation contributed to the Afghanistan situation.

But there is much more still to do. The attitudes reflected in Havana still persist, and at their root lies not only the fact that many of the governments of the so-called nonaligned world came to power as a result of struggles against Western powers or their client regimes, but also the persistent neglect of the economic dimension in US global policies. The substance of Western trade and aid policies for developing countries has been better than their reputation among both donors and beneficiaries – and far better than anything the Soviet Union has had to offer. But there has been no imaginative effort – Kissinger's speech at the UN Seventh Special Session in 1975 apart – to weld this into an overall political strategy for winning friends and shedding the ideological handicaps which the West has incurred from the colonial era and Marxist propaganda.

Despite the good intentions and different approach of the Carter Administration, no real progress was made on this front in 1979. Indeed, domestic attitudes in the United States tended to sour against Third World countries, with prominent commentators arguing with new impatience that no American interest was served by cultivating good relations with them. This again underlined the difficulty of a strategy which can only yield dividends over a decade or more.

There is scope indeed for an imaginative approach. It must start from the indivisibility of the globe, from the need for nations to coexist peacefully on it; from the threat to that posed by extreme economic inequality and absolute poverty; and from the enlightened self-interest of the developed countries in tackling poverty and extreme inequality in ways that are politically acceptable to the beneficiaries. In this spirit the more affluent countries could together offer to underwrite the minimal, bottom-line, balance-of-payments needs, based on an expertly assessed rolling development programme, of each developing country or group of such countries. Then each would be invited individually to sign up with the donor consortium. Once this was done there would be much less reason for the developing countries to confront the developed as a hostile bloc talking ideological abstractions, and much more scope for reasoned negotiation about alternative forms of development assistance through trade and aid, since the bottom line would no longer be an issue.

But even an imaginative world economic policy would not by itself plug the philosophical gap in the West's armour. The answer, if one is to be found, will not lie in some instant new 'ism'. The ability of the Western countries to overcome their social, economic, energy and environmental problems and to demonstrate that free societies can be stable, just and successful will indeed be very important. That may involve quite radical changes away from the centralisation of power in large and remote public and private bureaucracies. But, to be philosophically successful, the West will also have to identify more clearly with the general and specific goals of the Third World. It will have to offer a world political and economic order that makes small countries feel secure, poor countries confident of development, aggressive countries fearful of retribution, and all countries properly independent within their necessary interdependence. The order must offer better prospects than disorder.

Many of these concepts already underlay the post-war order built round the UN Charter and organisation, international law, an open world economy and world development institutions. The American contribution to them has been pre-eminent. But too often the United States has allowed that initiative to be taken away from it by its perceived failure to demonstrate sustained fidelity to them or by excesses perpetrated implausibly in its name. The Carter Administration has done much in its US role, if not in the North–South dialogue, to re-establish the American willingness to play by the rules of a system of international law and collective deliberation, most notably in its handling of the Iranian seizure of American hostages late in 1979. But the threads of a particular action have not been woven together into a generally understood Carter doctrine or strategy to capture the imagination and respect of a suspicious, cynical and unstable world. That will be a worthy task for a new year, a new decade and, perhaps, a new presidential term.

Foreign Affairs, 1979

An Arranged Marriage and an
Affair of the Heart

As the representative of my country you may expect me to say a word or two about the relations between our two countries. They are so warm and special that there is hardly any need to dwell upon them. The most important thing about them is that they are the property of the British and American people and that it would be the greatest impertinence for mere governments to seek to control or exploit them. They are something everyone of us knows and feels in his or her heart, and need no lengthy analysis or demonstration. But I do sometimes meet people who say: Now that Britain has joined the Common Market with the countries of the continent of Western Europe, does not that mean that it attaches less importance to the special friendship with America?

This error is sometimes opposed to the cynical view that in Europe Britain is some kind of Trojan horse introduced into the Common Market for the purpose of subverting its true destiny to the greater convenience of the United States. This has always seemed to me a mischievously negative way of expressing what is a much more constructive role. As I see it, Britain's involvement in the European Community is, in many ways, like a Christian marriage: entered into 'reverently, discreetly, soberly and in the eyes of God' or at least the next best thing, a referendum – 'duly considering the causes for which it was ordained'. It has been our plain duty and intention to cleave unto our partners for better, for worse, for richer for poorer, in sickness and in health.

Where the analogy does not do quite so well is when it comes to the bit about forsaking all others. Our relationship with the United States, after all, has many of the characteristics of a long-standing extra-marital affair. It arises entirely from natural affection. It is embodied in no contract. It has required no lawyer or priest to solemnise it or commit either of us to improbable feats of fidelity. It will last as long as mutual attraction sustains it; and it has, on occasions, to be discreet, as, for example, at such very private assignations as we have together this morning. Now cynics may say marriage has not always been found to be the strongest bond. They may argue that the real test of primacy is to be

158

found in the answer to the question: With which partner do you first discuss your relationship with the other? There may even be those so downright shameless as to assert that more men discuss their wives with their girlfriends than discuss their girlfriends with their wives. This monstrous speculation, of course, strikes at the roots of all decency and should be dismissed entirely from your minds.

For myself, I see no need for talk of mutual exclusiveness. This is not a zero-sum game. The real fact of life is that we in Western Europe and you in the United States are all on the same stage; the stage of the Western world as a whole. It is on the stage of the democratic industrial nations that the great issues of the contemporary world as they affect us have to be played. It is on this stage that we shall individually succeed or fail in mastering the crisis of the defects in the political economies of nearly all the countries of the West. It is on this stage that the trading countries of the world will succeed or fail in living together in free exchange through the throes of this difficult era, while we are trying to conquer a fundamental economic malaise. It is on the same stage that we shall either find or fail to find the basis for durable co-existence and *dètente* between East and West. And it is upon this stage that we shall find or fail to find the generosity, the imagination and the realism to reconcile the richer and the poorer nations – the North and the South – in their cohabitation of one planet. Within the Western community there are many and various criss-crossing relationships. You have them. We have them. There is Britain's relationship with the rest of the European Community. There is our relationship with you. There is your relationship with Germany, with France and Italy and so on. All of these interwoven lines are part of the fabric of the West; and every warp, weft and woof of this material contributes to the strength of the whole. Whether one emphasises the Common Market or NATO or the trilateral relationship or the Anglo-American connection or the old Commonwealth or the OECD itself, one is talking about part or all of the same primary association of the members of the Western community. One does not need to arrange those parts in precedence; and if one felt the need to do so, one would be embarking upon a dangerous road leading to the weakening of the whole. Nonetheless, the whole depends on the cohesion and strength of the parts; and scarcely a day goes by without my being conscious of the job which we in Britain can do and have to do in ensuring that the whole is indeed greater than the sum of the parts.

Address to the Spring Quarter Commencement Convocation of Ohio State University on Friday 9 June 1978

Britain's New Realism

Perhaps I may first say a word or two of a personal kind about my impressions of Anglo-American relations seen from the, for me, very new vantage point of an ambassador's office and about the new era beginning in my own country. I was first of all very fortunate to be marvellously briefed in London by the Foreign and Commonwealth Office and by many other government departments, by trade union leaders and private corporations and by my eight immediate predecessors at 3100 Mass. Never I would think in the history of diplomacy was so much taught by so many to so few in so short a time. This experience, which had me travelling from Brussels to Belfast as well as up and down miles of corridors and dozens of elevators, left me with an abiding impression of the extraordinary breadth and diversity of the interface between our two countries. I began to believe that there was no one in Britain, no matter what he was doing, who did not feel a burning need to be kept closely in touch with his opposite numbers in the United States or who did not expect the Ambassador to see to it that all obstacles were removed from his path. While this is doubtless an exaggeration and while I at times felt somewhat daunted at having such a flood of intercommunication flowing through my study, I was deeply impressed at the richness, closeness and enthusiasm of the interest and friendship felt in Britain for the American people and for so many aspects of American life and activities.

Diplomacy, I began to realise — at least where it concerned that multi-lane highway between the US and Britain — was no longer a matter of the measured exchange of elegant pleasantries and occasional exquisite indignation between stately chancelleries, but rather an integral part of the hurly-burly of everyday life across increasingly invisible international frontiers. People in all walks of life in Britain are fascinated uniquely with what is going on in the US, with how it may affect them, with the opportunities it may afford them, with new ideas that may benefit them and, above all else, with the living proof which America represents that against all odds and all reasonable expectations problems can be solved and free societies can survive and prosper.

Secondly, I was exceptionally lucky to arrive twenty-four hours before an important round of talks between our Foreign Secretary David Owen and Secretary of State Cy Vance about our joint policy in Rhodesia. Apart from being a rare, instructive and impressive opportunity to see the top foreign policy-making echelons of the Administration – both in the State Department and in the White House – in operation right from the word 'go', it seemed to be an object lesson in how business should be done. Indeed, I began to wonder, if all international relations were like this, how there could be so many problems in the world. Of course, it helps when the business is being done between old and close friends and allies who see eye to eye on all the main issues. But I was very struck by the speed and ease of communication, by the automatic assumption of mutual confidence and shared values and by the open willingness on both sides to modify previous thoughts quickly and cheerfully in response to sound points raised on the other side. I realise, of course, that things cannot always be quite so harmonious; but I do like to think that in relations between the US and Britain we at least always start from third base because we do not have to spend time overcoming differences of values, language and intellectual frameworks. Where we disagree at least we understand how and why we disagree. Take even the vexed question of Concorde's landing rights at New York. We have spent a lot of money with our partners in France building this plane. We naturally want to operate it on the premier transatlantic route for which it was designed. We believe that we are entitled to do so under international agreements and American law. You understand that. But the Port of New York Authority interprets its responsibilities as requiring it to oppose landing rights at Kennedy airport; and it is defending its right to do so in the courts. There is very strong feeling on the part of some of the inhabitants of the airport area; and there are elections coming up in New York City and State. We understand all that, as we understand that the Federal executive cannot dictate either to the courts or to state and municipal authorities under your Constitution. The matter is being pursued by a due – though some would say unduly slow – process of law in accordance with the ideals of the rule of law and an independent judiciary which we like to think of as one of our most successful exports. We know that we shall get fair play and that Concorde will be allowed to prove itself in New York.

We take this view because we are a mature and grown-up democracy who confidently believe in the ideals which both you and we profess. A few years ago we might not have been quite so calm. From Suez to the inflation crisis of the mid seventies we went through a very bad twenty years, which might well have sapped the self-confidence of any but the most blindly proud people. The name of the game was growth, and we were no good at it, though not notably worse than the US, which could, however, better afford to rest on its laurels. Confidence in the standards observed in public life took some bad knocks; and party politics sometimes spilled over outside its proper domain. We could not make up our minds conclusively what was our proper role in Western Europe; and we sometimes found it easier to paper over our manifest shortcomings with wall-to-wall excuses, eked out with the absurd reassurances that, even if the twentieth century just was not quite our scene, this was of little consequence for a nation that had done so well in other centuries and had given the world Magna Carta, thatched cottages and cricket.

But the two years from the summer of 1973 to the summer of 1975 were a true catharsis. We went to the brink, looked over and frankly did not fancy the drop. A new realism began to spread through the country. British trade union leaders put together the toughest and most successfully policed two years of pay restraint that we have seen, even though this went with the first sustained fall in real living standards in post-war memory. The Chancellor sat on the money supply, which followed a course of steady disinflation that Professor Milton Friedman himself might have charted. The budget deficit was brought under control and was consistently smaller, in relation to the size of our economy, than those of the US and West Germany. The stock market has now recovered more than all the ground it lost from the early days of 1973 and looks set fair soon to achieve new all-time peaks, though it will take a little longer, no doubt, to make up the ravages of mid-decade inflation as well. Inflation is now coming steadily down. The balance of payments, helped by the fruits of the North Sea and the Chancellor's dogged refusal to let home spending rip, is moving briskly into a large prospective surplus. Britain's reserves are now rising so rapidly as to be almost an embarrassment. The pound is steady and foreign investors are increasingly looking towards Britain, a land without Eurocommunists, grave political uncertainties or astronomic labour and other costs, as one of the most attractive outlets in Western Europe for industrial and commercial expansion.

But the change goes much deeper than these favourable cyclical trends. Being cyclical some of them will doubtless turn unfavourable at some future point; and I would not wish to base a case purely on those kinds of shifting statistical sands. The new realism reflects a change of heart which is:

(a) in part a product of the experience of the early to middle 1970s;

(b) in part a product of a new generation in all parts of our national life who never knew the era of Empire and great-power status and so have no hankerings to go back to an irrecoverable past, who caught the American preference for success over the most elegantly justified failure, and who have begun to show how realism allied to imagination and inventivenenss can begin to transform the old stereotype of the necessary relations between capital and labour;

(c) and in part the product of a new leadership in our national life which prefers facts to fancies and which is determined to give priority to policies that strengthen the nation over a decade rather than to postures which may grace tomorrow's headlines. As the Prime Minister put it to me as we walked the white cliffs overlooking the English Channel the weekend he took over the government, he saw his role as being that of Moses, to lead the people away from Egypt into the desert in the direction of the promised land even if it were never given to him to see it. That struck me then and strikes me now as the language of realism and statesmanship, and we already begin to see its fruits.

This change of heart has not only been apparent in Britain's domestic affairs, it has been exemplified also in our dealings with the world. The decision of the British people in 1975 to confirm their membership of the Common Market was decisive, laying to rest a long and unsettling debate about the form of our involvement in Continental affairs. This has given new and practical significance to Winston Churchill's old saw about Britain's unique position at the natural intersection of European, Commonwealth and Atlantic relationships. That role is no longer based on a real or illusory status as a global power, though Britain's long experience in international affairs and the Labour Party's traditional belief in a principled foreign policy, based on the ideals of universal human rights and self-determination, are together proving an invaluable heritage in today's conditions. Thus we have seen this year steadfast and prompt British support for President Carter's stand on human rights, unprecedented Anglo-American cooperation in Southern Africa, important developments in political cooperation in Western Europe under the

163

British Presidency and a constructive contribution in the Paris North-South Dialogue, where all three axes of our world relationships come together. Without any lingering pretensions beyond our means we have settled down in a sensible pursuit of our reasonable interests and ideals whenever our history and our skills enable us to aim at practical achievement.

But, of course, we are not going to overcome the problems of decades – indeed, so far as our poor growth performance is concerned of over one hundred years – in a brief span of years. It is a long hard hike through that desert. We shall certainly go through a very rough period this autumn and winter as we adjust to the return of free bargaining over pay. Re-entry is always a scorching experience; and when you are dealing with the free decisions of twenty-three million independent-minded working people you cannot expect to fine-tune the process with all the accuracy of a NASA computer. Yet, even here, we already see favourable signs: car-workers who are not willing to be led into industrial confrontation which they believe unjustifiable and unprofit-able; the Government Airports Authority which is resisting strong pressure to set a dangerous early precedent; and other encouraging straws in the wind. I am sorry about the inconvenience to the travelling public in the case of the Heathrow dispute. I can think of no greater misery than to spend hours stuck on the ground in an airliner waiting to take off. But there is something even more important at stake, and I believe that most travellers know that.

I give you fair warning, Mr President, that we are back in business in Britain, not because we have solved all our deeper problems – we are only starting on the most urgent – but because we have recovered our self-confidence and our self-respect, because we are no longer divided on the fundamentals of economic realism, because decency and trust are beginning to return in our public life, above all else and quite simply, we are fed-up to the back teeth with failing and introspection and we are coldly determined that over the *next* twenty years we are going to succeed. And that I believe will be the best foundation for the continua-tion and reinforcement of that special friendship and mutual enjoyment with the US which is, as David Owen put it to me on television earlier this year, the most important relationship we have.

Speech at the National Press Club, Washington on 7 September 1977

The Four Multipliers
of Strife

I say to you, and I say to you plainly, our world is in trouble. To illustrate why let me propose to you a paradox and then seek to unravel it. In 1941, in what must surely have been the most awesome and audacious act of statesmanship this century, the two great leaders of the English-speaking world, Franklin Roosevelt and Winston Churchill, devised and signed what became known as the Atlantic Charter. This extraordinary document was produced in the darkest days of the most calamitous war in history. Almost the whole globe was engulfed in the conflict. No one but a man of the blindest ignorance or the most indomitable will could have expected victory against an implacable, malevolent and overwhelmingly powerful foe. Every nerve, every sinew, every waking hour and every resource of intelligence and character were at full stretch to confront the immediate peril. Yet, somehow, with a tiny fraction of the resources, of the technology, of the knowledge, of the time and of the energy which we now have, the President and the Prime Minister charted the shape of a post-war world which would replace, not only the chaos and destruction of even a victorious war, but also the political upheavals and the economic convulsions which had so disfigured the previous twenty years. Later to be embodied in the United Nations, in the twin Bretton Woods institutions of the World Bank and the International Monetary Fund, in the General Agreement on Tariffs and Trade, in the Marshall Aid Scheme and its embodiment in the Organisation for European Economic Cooperation (later the OECD) and finally in the North Atlantic Treaty and its Organisation, the principles of Universality, of the rule of International Law, of non-aggression, of openness in trade, of stability in money and of mutual assistance in economic development and adjustment, cemented by a concrete and visible commitment to collective security, gave us in the West thirty of the most extraordinary years of sustained prosperity, stability and peace that Europe and perhaps the world as a whole had ever seen.

Now that fabric is fraying; and everywhere the world order that flowed from the Atlantic Charter is threatened again with political turbulence and economic failure. Tensions are rising in Asia, the Middle East, Africa and South America. Nuclear weapons proliferate. Local conflicts spread. The peace is kept less and less often for shorter and shorter periods. In Western Europe people fear the aggrandisement of Russian conventional forces and theatre nuclear weapons. In our Western economies inflation accelerates from cycle to cycle, while unemployment tends to rise. The twin follies of economic nationalism, namely protectionism and autarky, are propagated and flourish, as sure a sign of moral and intellectual disintegration as cannibalism, of which indeed they are the economic equivalent. Cheap and convenient energy and other basic resources become scarcer. Currencies ricochet up and down like hammers on a piano. Meanwhile most of the world's people in the poorer countries grow impatient and desperate, as they prowl, lean, hungry and understandably snappish, round the walls of the enchanted garden of industrial affluence.

These are our problems; and yet they pale by comparison with the challenge which confronted those two statesmen back in 1941. Even so, with all our resources and no insupportable conflict on our hands, we somehow cannot find the wisdom, the imagination, the cohesion and the will merely to maintain and extend that fabric or order and progress which was woven in the daunting days of the 1940s. Why? It should be so much easier; and yet somehow it seems so much more difficult. That is my paradox. I promised, however, to explain it; and I will.

Let us go straight to the roots. I give you four fundamental multipliers of strife.

(a) We have added as many people to the world's population since 1941 as were added in the whole of the previous tens of millions of years of human history.

(b) We have encouraged each one of those people to believe that he is entitled to and can enjoy a material standard of living beyond anything even dreamt of by his forefathers, though our resources of land and materials and energy exhibit no prospect of such exponential growth, if indeed of any growth at all.

(c) We have so politicised the world's notions of the means to economic self-advancement that we have encouraged each of those people to believe that the way to achieve the higher standards to which he is entitled is essentially to seize them and to seize them now.

(d) We have massively extended the availablility and efficiency of the means of mutual destruction from the hand-gun upwards. Multiply these four together – (a) times (b) times (c) times (d) – more people pursuing higher standards more insistently with greater menaces – and you have indeed an explosive increase in the potential for conflict.

And what do we have to put in the path of this juggernaut of chaos? Nothing but our old-fashioned skills of political leadership and diplomatic persuasion, in the cause of better mutual understanding and the devising of ever more elaborate human institutions, which in turn more and more strike our increasingly educated and independent-minded people as alien, remote and unacceptable. Even supposing, which would be a bold assumption indeed, that our political and diplomatic ingenuity is increasing, one must still doubt whether it could increase at more than an arithmetic rate. Yet the sources of turbulence grow geometrically and exponentially.

The conclusion seems to be obvious. Nature, as we are reminded by Malthus, that early great British economist, has its remedies for a plague of humanity as for a plague of locusts. When they have destroyed their habitat, they destroy one another or are destroyed by famine or disease. But for us, as humans, these are not remedies, but only the ultimate failure. You may say to me, well what are all the leaders and diplomats in Washington and the other capitals of the world doing about it? – and I tell you in all candour that they are holding their fingers in the dyke from day to day and from hour to hour. Governments in free societies live within the tolerances and understanding of their people; and real progress comes not from their programmes and policies, but from the ideas which the truly great thinkers in the land produce, so changing the whole frame of references within which the politicians practise their necessary art of the possible. These were what enabled Roosevelt and Churchill to lift themselves above the immediate storm and to define the far horizon, though doubtless the storm of war itself granted the greater freedom of initiative and decision than peace-time leaders often enjoy. But I say to you now in your groves and your ivory towers that it is on your campuses and in your studies that the war for peace will be won or lost. There are no New Albions left to discover, unless perhaps in space; and the only Spanish Main to plunder is our own vulnerable wealth. The ingenuity of the mind is the last shot in our locker.

Address by the British Ambassador at the Charter Anniversary Exercises at the University of California, Berkeley, 5 April 1979

Europe's Ostrich and
America's Eagle

The liberty, security and prosperity of every man, woman and child in Western Europe depend, and have for a third of a century depended, essentially on the health and strength of 'the West'. Its health and strength in turn depend and have depended first and foremost on cohesive relations between Western Europe and the United States.

A European living in America perhaps tends naturally to worry more than others, even Americans living in Europe, about that relationship. But there are solid, and long-term, reasons for anxiety which transcend an impressive catalogue of recent, but ephemeral, successes (the edge has been taken off even those successes, at least for some Americans, in the wake of the Russian invasion of Afghanistan).

A recent tour through London, Brussels, Bonn and Paris reinforced three disturbing impressions about European attitudes to the relationship with the United States:

First, that America's wish to be involved indefinitely in the security of Western Europe is taken for granted as a self-evident American interest rather than recognised as something to be worked for and earned as an overriding European interest.

Second, that Europeans are complacent about the relationship and their contribution to it.

Third, that, in so far as strains and stresses are acknowledged, the fault is exclusively seen to lie or to have lain in Washington whether because of an overbearing American insistence on a dominant role, as allegedly evinced by Mr Henry Kissinger, or because of a converse lack of strong American leadership, as supposedly exhibited by President Carter.

To explore and develop these themes is emphatically not intended as a bill of indictment against Western European attitudes and behaviour for its own sake, nor as a comparative judgement that one side of the Atlantic is more to blame than the other for the problem in the relationship. It is intended only as food for thought for Europeans, who may be tempted to neglect what they owe to the relationship in their preoccupation with what it owes to them and with their own regional destiny.

Before Afghanistan, Washington and the main European capitals were at government-to-government level feeling rather pleased with one another; and relations were certainly more cordial than during either the earlier years of the Carter administration or the turbulent discordances of the Kissinger era. The successful outcomes of both the multilateral trade negotiations and the NATO theatre nuclear force modernisation talks engendered enormous relief – failure in either case would have been very harmful to the relationshp – and better mutual feelings.

Admittedly, the European response to the plight of the American hostages in Iran was differently seen on either side of the Atlantic. To the Europeans themselves it seemed that they had given first priority to showing solidarity with the Americans even where they were nervous about the particular actions taken or contemplated by Washington.

To the Americans (especially the public, but also government officials in private) the European response seemed half-hearted and inhibited by special interests and fears. Solidarity was achieved at the United Nations by the end of the year; but there was a lingering American feeling that the Europeans looked on this too narrowly as a purely American problem in which they were concerned only as friends rather than as huge consumers of Gulf oil with a vital interest in the political stability of the region.

The cooling last year of President Carter's rhetoric on human rights was welcomed in Europe as evidence of a more mature approach to the liberation of Soviet dissidents along lines long favoured by the Europeans themselves and as less threatening to *détente*.

The recovery of President Carter's domestic and international prestige during the Iran hostages crisis, at least for the time being, considerably improved relations between Washington and the West European capitals. The first, albeit belated, signs that America was beginning to face up realistically to the need to curtail its appetite for imported oil by allowing the price mechanism to begin to work again in the American market, coupled with the first tentative evidence that President Carter's Tokyo pledge would be kept and that American oil imports might have peaked, also dulled the edge of the Europeans' most legitimate grievance against the United States. This honeymoon has soon soured in the wake of the Soviet invasion of Afghanistan. French mischief and German incoherence left the Americans feeling that when the going gets tough their allies get going. Britain's sponsorship of France's neutrality formula for Afghanistan may help the *entente* and ease some of the recent strains between Britain and the EEC. But from Washington it also looks like another classic example of the temptation discussed below: damaging the cohesion and the interests of the West for the sake of a Euro-gesture.

But all these things were essentially ripples on the surface of the post-war history of American–West European relations. If the questions are asked which way is the tide setting and what will the quality of those relations be at the end of the 1980s, then altogether deeper forces have to be examined.

A Western order, liberal and universal

The shape and cohesion of the West were created in the 1940s out of the lessons of the 1930s, reinforced by the new threat of Soviet power. Among those lessons were:

(a) that unbridled nationalism is the world's most dangerous force;
(b) that the world needs a framework of law and institutions under which disputes can be conciliated in the full light of world opinion and within which pacific nations can feel secure while belligerent ones will be effectively deterred from seeking to acquire territory by force;
(c) that, failing conciliation and deterrence under law, collective security is the best defence against an aggressor;
(d) that economic nationalism – protectionism, autarky, mercantilism – not only damages prosperity, but also reinforces political nationalism and engenders friction between nations;
(c) that an anarchic monetary system tends to promote economic nationalism through competitive beggar-thy-neighbour exchange rate practices and a scramble for reserves;
(f) that it is more profitable politically and economically for rich and surplus countries to meet the capital needs of the poor and deficit countries than to try to force reparations out of defeated enemies irrespective of their economic condition – and so, by extension, it is better to support also the development of, rather than to exploit, the world's backward regions.

These lessons informed a new international philosophy, based on the principles of the rule of international law and the sovereignty of the nation state under it, of the conciliation of disputes, of collective security, of liberal trade and payments, of cooperative global management, of a flexible and stable currency system and of capital aid for post-war reconstruction and for new development. The spirit of this philosophy was liberal, universal and optimistic, emphasising the freest possible interplay of people under a minimal system of rules necessary for this interplay to be orderly and creative rather than anarchic and destructive.

In the same spirit the nationalist concept of the primacy of the nation – and its power, glory and wealth – within which the individual marches as a mere foot-soldier in a disciplined army whose purposes are higher than and frequently in conflict with his own was to be discouraged. Also rejected was the purely pragmatic balance-of-power approach to international relations – anarchy moderated by fear.

These new principles were embodied in the characteristic institutions which defined the post-war political and economic order: the United Nations and its agencies; the World Court; the Bretton Woods twins – the International Monetary Fund and the World Bank; the General Agreement on Tariffs and Trade; the Marshall Plan and the Organisation for European Economic Cooperation (later the Organisation for Economic Cooperation and Development); and the North Atlantic Treaty Organisation.

There is, of course, a certain artificiality about this lumping together of global institutions with regional institutions and calling the resulting set-up a Western order. Yet the philosophy which inspired both was the same; it flowed from the Atlantic Charter devised by Winston Churchill and Franklin Roosevelt in 1941 as a proclamation of the better world that would be built after the War.

The emphasis did indeed shift in the late 1940s from the purely idealistic and universalist aspirations of the global institutions to the need for specific regional security and economic arrangements, as the Soviet threat to Europe emerged from the smoke of Hitler's final defeat. The Marshall Plan and NATO thereafter gave the 'West' more concrete form, though the GATT and the IMF remained just as important elements in the economic order under which North America and Western Europe – and later Japan – lived.

This order gave substance to America's continuing involvement in Western Europe. Given the extent to which this American involvement is now taken for granted in Europe – as if it were the naturally prevailing wind to which European doors and windows can be opened to as great or as little extent as Europeans choose – it is important to remind ourselves that this involvement only came about as the result of a prolonged and evenly balanced political fight in the United States before Pearl Harbour, and that its continuation has been closely linked to the concepts of collective security and a liberal economic order in the post-War world.

The American isolationists were finally defeated in the early 1940s by enlightened east-coast leadership and Japanese folly. They stayed defeated after the War by a combination of Soviet folly and the same internationalist outlook among the prevailing political establishment in Washington.

But they were never exterminated; and they can always draw sustenance from economic adversity, blaming 'foreign competition' and 'unfair trade sponsored by foreign governments' and exploiting 'unfriendly' political behaviour by allies and others. In short, America's involvement in Europe, like every other American policy, rests on a balance of political forces within the United States that is neither God-given nor immutable.

. . . but resting on the Soviet threat

Winston Churchill and Franklin Roosevelt finally won the battle for America's commitment to Europe in 1941 (with some help from Ed Murrow and the Japanese) on the argument that freedom is indivisible and that America's vital interests and security were threatened by the far-away events in Europe. The continuation of that belief now rests on the Soviet global threat.

When in the wake of the Soviet invasion of Afghanistan, Americans read in their newspapers that the editor of *Die Zeit* has said: 'Europe must not become a zone of tension if tension prevails in other regions . . . The West cannot win in Berlin the battle it lost in Afghanistan', they wonder what happened to eternal vigilance and to the indivisibility of liberty and, indeed, whether what is sauce for the European ostrich may not also be sauce for the American eagle. Must America become a zone of tension if tension prevails in Europe; can America win in Nebraska the battle it might lose in Berlin?

The views of one editor, however respected, can be dismissed. But reports of the representative attitudes of European allied governments in this crisis play more seriously into the hands of American isolationists:

> Beneath a surface solidarity of strong words and symbolic gestures supporting the tough US response to the Soviet invasion of Afghanistan, most European allies remain reluctant to isolate the Soviet Union by cutting off Soviet access to Western trade and technology . . . a majority of the allies do not want seriously to interrupt their trade with the Soviets and Eastern Europe or to jeopardise the East–West dialogue they still believe to be vital to Western Europe's economic future . . .
>
> Beyond economic considerations, there are also important foreign policy differences between the European allies and the US . . . The French and West Germans are trying to steer a more independent course between the two superpowers. They see the Soviet invasion of Afghanistan not so much as an East–West confrontation threatening Europe as an opportunity to steal influence from the Soviet Union in the third World. They want to work through the Common Market rather than NATO to strengthen economic and diplomatic ties with Egypt, Turkey, Pakistan, the oil-rich Gulf nations and other Third-World countries.*

The point, for Americans, is not the notion of emphasising the Soviet Union – versus the World rather than the purely East–West dimension of the aggression against Afghanistan. That, indeed, had been the centre point of President Carter's own counter-strategy from the first day. It is the notion that the European Common Market rather than NATO can steal a march, not so much on the Soviet Union, as on the United States by making new Third World friends (and incidentally ones who have repeatedly criticised Carter for being too weak, not too hawkish, about Soviet designs) while isolating themselves from the risks of renewed Cold War tensions.

This aftermath of Afghanistan is but an example of the wider thesis here, namely that the cohesion of the West as the primary foundation of our prosperity, liberties and security is threatened, in part, by broad political and economic developments toward European unity. Since many on both sides of the Atlantic still see a more unified Europe as an antidote to nationalism, as a reinforcement of democratic and liberal economic principles and as a better partner for the United States in its global role, this needs some explanation.

* *Washington Post*, 15 January 1980, from Leonard Downie Jr, London.

A genius for nationalism

Historically, the inspiration of the ideal of European unity was, indeed, as an antidote to the nationalism of the old Europe of France, Germany, Italy, Britain and others. The economic philosophy of the Treaty of Rome was ostensibly liberal in the classic sense. American support for the movement rested heavily on the belief that a United States of Europe could be cloned from the United States of America, created in its own image to share its values and its burdens: the twin-pillars of Atlantic cooperation.

But things do not always work out the way they are intended. Circumstances and innate characteristics commonly prove stronger than structures, designs and dreams. The whole political history of Europe from the collapse of Christendom to Hitler's war has been an exercise in the most sustained and unbridled nationalism the world has known.

Despite the contrary theorising of every significant political philosopher from Plato to Plamenatz (excepting only some minor nineteenth-century Germans and, perhaps, Hegel), the nation – its needs, power, glory and wealth – has consistently predominated in political priorities over both the individual and the international community. Nationalism is, indeed, Europe's characteristic political genius, now alas exported to every corner of the globe.

The idea of European unity as a submerging of the dangerous national identities of the past made idealistic sense so long as we lived in the past – in a world where Europe was for all practical purposes the world and where, therefore, France, Britain and Germany were great powers. In the world of the superpowers and global geopolitics it was out of date. The by-now mini-powers of a Balkanised Europe under Russian and American tutelage were effectively impotent to create the havoc at which they had excelled in a Eurocentric world.

There was no longer a need to unite Europe in order to take the old European nations. On the contrary, it was only by creating a united Europe, or at least a superstate in Western Europe, that the old nationalist soul could expect to operate in the big new global league. If the ghosts of Frederick the Great, Queen Elizabeth, Napoleon and Hitler in politics, or of Colbert, Joe Chamberlain, Schacht and Mussolini in economics were ever to be freed in the world of the late twentieth century, it could only be by forging a state of the size and with the resources of Western Europe as a whole.

The fact that nobody involved saw themselves as laying the foundations of the next European Reich gives no guarantee against the house they built being inhabited by other spirits than those of the original architects. How far this has happened and is likely to happen, we shall now inquire.

So far the jury is still out. In trade matters the European community has on the whole acted consistently with the GATT and, therefore, with the health of the West and its economic principles. The delays and compromises entailed by the need for a common EEC position in trade negotiations – and the endless aggravation to the United States of being able to get clear answers neither from Brussels nor from national capitals, each referring them to the other – have been at least balanced by the pressure which community membership has put on Europe's natural protectionists to liberalise.

Less satisfactory has been the embryonic development of industrial policies in the European community. The essentially illiberal notion that it is a European interest to encourage the development, even where this runs counter to commercial logic, of European-owned industries, especially in the glamorous high-technology areas, has gained ground; and this ancient relic of economic nationalism has enjoyed a new patina of respectability from gaining a 'European' gloss.

Fortunately, Brussels has so far made little real progress in getting specific industrial policies off the ground; but its use of autarkic rhetoric, which treats a foreign-owned plant generating employment, added value, income and government revenues in Europe as not being a legitimate, indeed welcome, part of the European economy, has made it easier for national governments to succumb to the perennial political temptation to favour unsound enterprises with public money, government contracts and informal protection.

The United States is by no means innocent of such practices, especially in defence contracting and traditionally protected areas like shipping. But the growth and practice of a new ideology of industrial autarky in Europe – in aerospace, computers, defence production and other high technology sectors – weaken the liberal forces in America and give ammunition to the political and labour lobbies for 'Buy American' programmes.

Little need be said about agriculture. So far the chief sufferers from the scandal of the EEC's Common Agricultural Policy (CAP) have not been the United States but low-cost producers in the rest of the world. But it is already clear to the best experts in the Brussels commission that during the 1980s the EEC's subsidised surpluses are going to spread from dairy produce into other agricultural products which will be directly competitive with American exports.

Rival currency blocks?

In monetary matters Europe's contribution to preserving and adapting a coherent, cooperative and stable system based on the IMF has been small and frequently distorted by narrow national temptations and by distracting political gestures. Frequently it has seemed to say to the United States that it should accommodate Europe's mercantilist desire for export-boosting surpluses (to say nothing of OPEC and Japanese surpluses and the solvency of the developing world) while at the same time expanding the American economy and keeping the dollar strong.

The fact that no conceivable set of American policies could reconcile these irreconcilables underlines the partiality of the European outlook, which is similarly betrayed in the parallel conviction that it ought to be possible for them simultaneously to run huge balance-of-payments surpluses by maintaining advantageous exchange rates, but without accumulating unwanted dollars in their reserves – and that, if that is not possible, is because the United States is doing something wrong.

This is not to excuse the real failures of American policy to control inflation or to curb oil consumption. But the characteristic 'damned-if-you-do, damned-if-you-don't' attempts by Europeans to blame America for the incoherence of their own aims long predated the big American inflation and the energy crisis.

This old-fashioned desire to eat one's cake and have it – and to blame nanny, if one cannot – owes little to the growth of European self-consciousness as such. But the development of a European Monetary System (EMS), with or without aspiration to an eventual EEC currency block and even a single currency, undoubtedly does.

To be sure, there is a minimalist version of the case for the EMS which sets the aims no higher than rather greater stability in foreign exchange markets for the member currencies. The issue then is merely a practical one of whether, in real life, central banks are over time likely to achieve more or less stability than free floating; and history by no means confirms that intervention tends to be more stabilising than destabilising or that the authorities can at all reliably distinguish speculative pressures from structural shifts.

But clearly an element in most governments' adherence to the EMS was the 'European' gesture it made, with the implication that, as American economic power and dollar domination diminished, Europe would complement, if not replace, the dollar with some kind of currency entity of its own. The main argument against giving Europe a single currency – that this would suppress the most effective mechanism of adjustment between the various European economies, thereby condemning them to accelerated economic divergence and the EEC to increasing political strains – is not germane directly to the issue of American–West European relations.

But the willingness to take a step in the direction of rival currency blocks, interacting not by agreed rules and cooperative deliberation, but by anarchic competition, is symptomatic of Europe's growing disregard of the prerequisites of the harmony and strength of the West, especially where the opportunity is seen to make a 'European' gesture, even one which is actually damaging to the real interests of Europe itself. To be sure this deeper corrosion of the bonds of the West does not prevent good day-to-day cooperation across the Atlantic in bodies like the Group of Five and between central banks, although even that has been partly purchased at the price of an unwise American acceptance of responsibility, without power, for the dollar's external value and of a prospectively deep American recession in 1980–81.

Decoupling

The EEC as such has no formal role in defence. But here European self-consciousness and desire for identity are affecting a most vital link in Western cohesion. Perhaps the most revealing and disturbing recent example was the concept of a Euro-strategic nuclear balance and the controversy surrounding it; and its significance is not diminished by the success for the time being of NATO in papering over the cracks by its decision last December to deploy modernised theatre nuclear forces in parts of Europe.

The original *simpliste* notion – memorably propounded by Mr Helmut Schmidt in his Alastair Buchan lecture in 1977 – was that the limitation of intercontinental nuclear weaponry under SALT would or could lead to a situation in which Western Europe was threatened by Soviet intermediate range ballistic missles (such as the SS20) without Europe deploying any comparable counter-threat to the Russians. This was a beguilingly confused notion.

It also glossed blandly over the obvious fact that, on the assumption of intercontinental stalemate or disarmament and of inter-regional nuclear symmetry, the Soviet Union would be assymetrically threatened by the United States. For NATO's theatre nuclear deployment in Europe, involving American-controlled threat to Russian territory, would be matched by no comparable Russian threat against American territory.

The primary confusion, however, is in the concept of a European counter-threat to the Russian SS20s. Either it means a counter-threat (by NATO) based on European soil; or it means a counter-threat (by Europe) based anywhere convenient. The first is innocent, but internally fallacious. The second is coherent, but sinister.

The first is innocent in the sense that it relates to a pan-Western, that is, NATO, response to a presumed threat to some members of the alliance. But it is fallacious in the sense that the existence of a Russian threat (by the SS20s) to European territory implies the need for an effective deterrent, but not necessarily for that deterrent to be based on European soil. The back of the moon, the sea or indeed the existing American inter-continental ballistic missile (ICBM) force, even constrained by SALT, might turn out to be good or better solutions.

The insistence at the outset as a matter of principle on the deployment of missiles on the ground in Europe betrayed the fact that to some degree the second and sinister meaning was intended. This was confirmed by the repeated harking, though in semi-hushed voices, in Europe on the possible unreliability of the American nuclear guarantee. This could hardly be relevant to a European counter-threat in the innocent sense, since any NATO deployment was almost bound – as turned out to be the case – to be American controlled and therefore just as open to the suspicion of unreliability as the American ICBM force.

These thoughts were intelligible only if an unstated premise was that Europe, in the sense of West European governments acting independently of NATO and of the United States, needed to be able to deter Soviet SS20 attack by being seen to be able to order a nuclear retaliation against Russia capable of inflicting unacceptable damage. However much or little either doubts about the American guarantee or simple aspiration for another European status symbol – this time independent nuclear capability – may have contributed to this unstated premise, it amounts to – indeed is – 'decoupling' (that is European defence separate from NATO) naked and unalloyed.

That, in turn, would drive a massive nail into the coffin of Western political cohesion and hand to the American isolationists – Mansfield-ism is quiescent, not extinguished – their biggest opportunity in years. The fact that responsible European leaders ran a mile from any such interpretation as soon as it was surfaced, insisting that any new deployment of European theatre nuclear forces must – despite American 'unreliability' – be American owned, produced and controlled (and, needless to say, financed), could not altogether disguise the fact that they had advanced a concept and entertained audible doubts about the United States which made sense only if they were harbouring, at least in their political subconscious, the sinister interpretation of their own words.

There is one logically possible non-sinister interpretation of the European insistence on the deployment of theatre nuclear forces in Europe, namely that it was intended as an American hostage which would trigger otherwise uncertain White House action if Europe were attacked by the Soviet Union. This too is absurd, as hardware can scarcely be an effective hostage when, by the 'unreliability' assumption, a quarter of a million American troops on the ground are not.

Carter was tactful

This systematic European ambivalence, willing to wound but afraid to strike, tempted by the glamour of status and gestures but shy of the responsibilities and burdens of real power, has been visible in other defence issues, as for example, the neutron bomb fiasco (political, not military). The difference between responsibility and frivolity could not have been more precisely illustrated than by America's repeated invita-tion to the key European leaders between September 1977 and March 1978, to say whether or not they wanted and would support production and deployment of a weapon which could, in practice, be used only in Europe's defence, and their endlessly reiterated refusal to be drawn beyond stating, privately as well as publicly, that the decision was entirely for America to make. The contrast was further underlined by the speed with which the European leaders rushed to denounce the Amer-ican decision as soon as it was made and President Carter's stern refusal ever to tell the real story of how the allies had behaved.

The roots of this European political pre-maturity lie in two incom-plete transitions: first, from American protégé to American partner; and, second, from multiple nationality to concerted identity. The old relationship, whereby it was understood that America decides and Europe complains, well suited as it was to the economic and military strength of the United States and to the political weakness of European governments, is no longer desired on either side of the Atlantic; but no new equilibrium, symmetrical or not, has replaced it.

The making of a bogey

There is no doubt about the shape of the new model for which the early American enthusiasts for European unity were looking: a United States of Europe created in the image of the United States of America, sharing its outlook and its burdens in keeping a turbulent world safe for democracy and capitalism. That this has not happened and is not likely to happen derives not just or even mainly from the incompletion of European unity, but more profoundly from the improbability of any new European identity, once launched, ever taking that form.

Indeed, of all the misconceptions about 'Europe' the blindest has been that 'it will never happen' – which may fairly be called the 'Geoffrey Rippon argument' from his monotonous repetitions of it in rebuttal of all possible projections of the political and economic consequences (*sic*) of British membership of the EEC. It is happening and will happen more and more. The questions have always been whether or not it will take a benign form and, in the present context, what its impact will be on the basic foundation of West European security and prosperity, namely the political, economic and military order of the West.

The creation of a great new political entity is an enormous undertaking; and the essential chemistry cannot be provided by constitutional lawyers, foreign policy experts and economic technicians. At some point the new identity has to capture the loyalty and imagination of the people; and this comes not from rational calculations of economic advantage and international harmony, but from fear of, or rivalry with, some threatening or competing outside force. In the absence of such a common enemy the old loyalties – and loyalty to even smaller sub-nationalities – prevail in the emotions of the people.

Russia was never a plausible candidate for this role. The threat it presented was military, whereas 'Europe' in the early phases of its evolution was bound to be an economic institution. The military threat was too massive to be seriously countered by 'Europe'; and, anyway, America through NATO was already handling that problem.

It was indeed America itself which was bound to be and became the focus of 'European' rivalry: its economic strength, its dominant industries, its international corporations, its pervasive culture, its political leadership, its assumption of the global burdens of the former colonial powers and its currency. All of this offended European *amour propre*.

There was and remains, to be sure, no real European appetite to assume the burdens of global policeman, reserve currency, and underpinner of everybody else's economic prosperity. But it boosted and boosts European morale to spotlight American errors, to savour its failures, to exploit its market, to resent its overseas investments, to have a critic's ringside seat at its global tribulations, to mock its culture, to deride its leaders and to bewail the 'weakness' of its currency.

As the original inspirations of European unity – German fear of its own heritage, everybody's fear of Germany, the small countries' fear of the big ones, France's need to have someone else pay for its lunatic agricultural system, the left's fear of a fascist renaissance, the right's fear of indigenous communism – began to fade, a common external bogey was needed to quicken the pulse and inspire continuing efforts for unity. From that perspective the United States of America served well; and from that perspective it was easy to lose sight of the West as a wider collaborative venture in whose health 'Europe' had a very practical vested interest.

It was therapeutic, as well as just fun, to play Monday-morning quarter-back during the Vietnam war, after Camp David, through the Iranian revolution and in the face of the Russian invasion of Afghanistan. It would have been tough and divisive to ask ourselves whether the European nations could actually contribute to the successful resolution of these problems, including the protection of their own shared interest in, for example, the security of oil supplies.

Europeans may legitimately argue that Vietnam was a bad mistake; that it would have been nice if Camp David had nailed down agreeement on a Palestinian homeland as well as guarantees of Israel's security; that uncritical support of the Shah in the early 1970s – and perhaps ever since 1953 – was dangerous; that the invasion of Afghanistan should be presented as an East-South, not an East-West problem. But the ceaseless gleeful enunciation of these critiques is no substitute for a serious European foreign policy or for a practical contribution to achieving the West's legitimate aims. This becomes embarrassing as well as futile when the charges miss the target anyway.

President Carter's foreign policy crystallises the lessons of Vietnam, too much so for the taste of many in America. He has more sincerely desired and worked harder and more successfully for Palestinian rights than any American or European leader. He carried coolness towards the Shah to the point of being accused of betraying a vital friend. He did, as already stated, present the Afghanistan invasion as an East–South – or Russia v The World – problem from the very first day and with repeated emphasis.

So Europe has repeatedly shown in the past decade that, while it does not like being a mere American protectorate, it is by no means ready or willing to become a real partner even in the defence of Europe, let alone in America's wider global responsibilities involving crucial West European interests.

But it has also been falling repeatedly between the two stools of the old national capitals and the new Brussels supra-capital. That this is so, even in matters of clear community competence, is merely aggravating to Americans. That it is so also bedevils political and security issues and measurably impairs the usefulness of the allies as allies and as friends.

The American government understands perfectly well the sources of this weakness: the transitional stage of European unity; the simultaneous indispensability and impossibility of German leadership whose military, geographical and economic dominance is outweighed by its fearsome history and divided soul; the perverse imperatives of French dignity; the ambivalence of British sentiment and the failure of its economy; and the internal weaknesses and preoccupations of Italy and the smaller countries. But to understand is not always to like; and the American government is not ever America.

Only predigest

For the health of the West much could even now be done to develop a more effective cooperation at foreign-minister and political-director levels between America and the three leading West European nations, somewhat analogous to what has long existed, with Japan added, in economic and financial affairs in the Group of Five. The sensitivities of the other EEC countries are, of course, even greater in the political domain; but in the handling of current crises and in the development of shared strategic perceptions and future plans it is not acceptable that the etiquette of EEC political cooperation should stand in the way of effective concert of the West.

This would not by itself cure the deep-seated weaknesses of European political leadership or prevent altogether the temptation to substitute a Euro-gesture for a serious policy. But it would, over time, make stronger collective leadership easier, and frivolous or ignorant sloganising less likely. This is not at all to say that the European nations are not entitled to independent points of view, but rather that there are more and less constructive ways of presenting them to America and the world, depending on how far the global implications for the West of what is said and done are fully taken into account and predigested with America.

This could mitigate the frequent American feeling, mentioned already, that they are damned if they do and damned if they don't; damned if they stand up to the Russians for aggravating the Cold War and damned if they pursue *détente* for conspiring to promote an American–Russian world condominium; damned if they make specific proposals for dictating to their allies and damned, if they first seek the allies' opinions, for not showing leadership; and damned if the dollar is strong for embarrassing the weaker European currencies and damned if it is weak for causing alleged problems to the managers of the surplus currencies.

Nothing of this kind will remedy the narrowest form of Euro-mentality, which it is distressing to encounter even occasionally at senior levels in the European diplomatic services, that seemingly sees the fortunes of Europe and America balanced on a see-saw, a zero-sum game in which every and any loss to the other is a gain to the one and in which, therefore, every American folly or misfortune, real or imagined, is a signal for rejoicing.

Nor, at the other extreme from the ridiculous to the very serious will it cure the divergent political dynamics of Western cohesion on the one hand and European unity on the other.

As so often Mr Kissinger spotted it first (in his book *Agenda for the Nation*) and said it best:

Atlantic relations, for all their seeming normalcy, thus faced a profound crisis ... In the 1960s security, while still important, has not been enough (to define a Western order). Every crisis from Berlin to Czechoslovakia has seen the call for 'strengthening NATO' confined to military dispositions. Within months a malaise has become obvious again because the overriding need for a common political conception has not been recognised. The challenge of the 1970s will be to forge unity with political measures ... 'Burden-sharing' will not supply that impetus. Countries do not assume burdens because it is fair, only because it is necessary. While there are strong arguments for Atlantic partnership and European unity, enabling Europe to play a global role is not one of them ... Even with the best will, the present structure encourages American unilateralism and European irresponsiblity.

And in the first volume of his memoirs, *The White House Years*, he has confirmed and refined the judgement after his eight years in office:

> In the late 1960s the Atlantic alliances stood in a state of disarray that was more painful for following a period of extraordinary success ... Only a federal Europe, it was believed (by American foreign policy-makers in the 1960s), could end Europe's wars, provide an effective counterweight to the USSR, bind Germany indissolubly to the West, constitute an equal partner for the US and share with us the burdens and obligations of world leadership ... American advocates of European unity sometimes embrace it more passionately then their colleagues in Europe. A few thoughtful Europeans, however, questioned whether it was all quite so simple; they doubted whether 'burden-sharing' (the jargon phrase) would solve the problem of identity or of national purpose. Europe, they felt, needed a political purpose of its own and not simply a technical assignment in a joint enterprise.

But even Mr Kissinger seems to have assumed that, when Europe found this 'political purpose of its own', it would fit into his 'common political conception' on the basis of which effective Atlantic 'unity' would be forged. The challenge of the 1970s has, in the event, merely become the challenge of the 1980s; and the lesson of the 1970s is that Europe's own 'political purpose' is its own existence, its identity and its prestige, all of which necessarily feed in part on a keen sense of rivalry with the United States. It is therefore unlikely to play the role assigned to it by Mr Kissinger and other pro-Western optimists who favour European unity.

The next European Reich

This is where we are. But where may the 1980s now take us? The central danger is that the old spirit of European nationalism will enter anew into the body of the EEC and take it in the all too familiar directions, first of economic nationalism (autarky, mercantilism, protectionism), then of political centralism and ultimately of military self-assertion, eroding and in the end destroying the bonds and so the benefits of the West.

This may seem alarmist and improbable. But imagine, as is realistic, a decade of the worst economic adversity for half a century – high unemployment, costly and unreliable energy supplies, high and accelerating inflation, currency instability, flagging investment and productivity, labour frustration and unrest.

Second, reflect on the huge power vacuum constituted by the directly elected European parliament. Its formal powers are narrowly constrained. But its implicit legitimacy, as the only body that can claim to speak for the people of the EEC as a whole, is almost limitless. Once again it is not the rule-making of constitutional lawyers and the old national parliaments which will define the future role of the European parliament, but the inherent biochemistry of the political seed which has been planted.

As the economic going gets rougher, political unrest will grow; and the characteristic politics of depression – demands for protection from foreign competition, for government works, contracts and subsidies, for central economic planning backed by *dirigiste* powers and for an autarkic 'industrial policy' – will develop. Any politician of moderate ambition, normal sensitivities and exceptional forensic gifts will see his chance.

The European parliament will become the natural forum, not merely for challenging in such a crisis the inadequacy of the division of responsibilities between the national capitals and Brussels, but also for launching massively supported demands for sweeping new powers at the centre – vested no doubt in the parliament and so, of course, in the very leaders of this campaign – to implement a great New Deal for Europe.

The nostrums and the panaceas will not solve the economic problems. But they will have achieved the transference of effective power to the centre; and the control of foreign and military policies will soon follow.

Unhappily, this grab for power is unlikely to have the happy sequel it enjoyed in Britain after the seventeenth century and in America after the election of Roosevelt. The continental tradition in politics is not deeply democratic, tending rather to the extremes of demagoguery and authoritarianism. Even Hitler started by getting himself elected. Once power has been concentrated in the name of democracy and of the need for decisive action in the economic crisis, the democratic vehicle tends to be found to be inconvenient and soon to be abandoned not far from the scene of the crime.

Thus can the next European Reich evolve out of the innocent dreams and economic gadgetry of the early Euro-idealists. This will seem ridiculously far-fetched to those who believe that the last few decades of continental history can be indefinitely extrapolated in a straight line and who believe that the commanding political ascendancy enjoyed by men like President Giscard and Helmut Schmidt at the end of 1979 is a reliable predictor, not merely of their success in the elections they face respectively in 1981 and 1980, but also of their continued rule for years to come.

Likewise anyone who believes – if anyone does – that the economic conditions of the 1980s will be no worse than the 1970s, will deny the premise of such a speculation. Others may accept the premise and argue that its consequences will be, not a concentration of power at the centre under some Euro-demagogic banner but, on the contrary, the disintegration of the EEC into its old component nationalisms, whose residual claims on popular loyalties will prove stronger in such a crisis than popular confidence in any New Euro-Deal. This is conceivable, though hardly less damaging to the cohesion of the West, with which we are here concerned.

Even if the process posited here stops well short of the political culmination suggested and even if the old national capitals prove to be as important agents of the flight into economic nationalism as the existing or transformed Brussels apparatus, the impact on transatlantic relations can only be corrosive. The always volatile balance of political forces in America will react to these events and to the industrial and political pressure which they generate at the grass roots for an equally 'robust' (that is, nationalist) American economic response. Isolationists and protectionists will win again the battle they lost to Roosevelt and Churchill in 1941.

Every aspect of economic interchange will become a matter of government interest and therefore of political controversy and in the sourest possible atmosphere. Security and foreign policy cooperation will be bound to suffer in consequence; and then the American reaction will become a further pretext for 'go-it-alone' European policies.

To be sure this will be bad for the United States; but America can and will survive – if necessary, alone. Europe, also on its own having forfeited the NATO shield, will confront the Soviet Union, free at last to choose to be red or dead. This is where neglect of the West, of Europe's overriding dependence on its health and cohesion and of the need constantly to nurture its roots and to abide by its unifying principles, ultimately leads.

All of this is a warning, not a prediction, as it is a caution, not an indictment. It is addressed to fellow Europeans; and therefore it does not dwell on the many beams and motes in the American eye. The time for swapping mutual abuse and self-justifications is past. Self-examination and mutual obligation will need higher priority if we are not to find that what we so blithely take for granted and abuse today has been lost a decade from now.

The ideal of European unity and its pursuit do not need to lead in so baneful a direction. If European leaders, diplomats and bureaucrats will keep in mind that it is and should be a subsidiary reinforcement of our primary membership of the West and that therefore its behaviour and development must be consistent with the essential principles of collective security, liberal economics and political pluralism on which the West is built, then good may flow from it. But, if in its search for momentum and greater popular appeal it becomes an end in itself, a zero-sum game alternative to the American connection, a vehicle for the rebirth of nationalism in Europe on a superpower scale, a fetish which distracts our attention from the inescapable realities of our security and prosperity, then the curse of European history – death and destruction for the sake of vain glory – will be upon us again.

The Economist, 8 March 1980

The News

The chapter which follows (in four parts) embodies the original statement of what has come be known as the Birt-Jay thesis. In fact it originally appeared as four separate articles. All but the first were joint articles with John Birt, written in 1975. The first was written by John Birt alone, as an article in The Times *on 28 February, entitled 'Can Television News Break the Understanding-Barrier?', although it was fully discussed with the author at the time and embodied ideas which had jointly evolved during their collaboration from 1972 on the early days of* Weekend World. *It was in the first paragraph of that article, as can be seen, that the celebrated phrase 'bias against understanding' (his emphasis) was first used. The authorship of this phrase is unquestionably John Birt's. The associated phrase 'mission to explain' was coined much later in a different context by the present author, namely at a public meeting at Croydon on 24 September 1980 convened by the Independent Broadcasting Authority to discuss the possible advent of breakfast television. While the author certainly saw it as an extension of the earlier phrase – the one a diagnosis, the other a recommended cure – it was never used in the debates in the 1970s; and John Birt bears no responsibility for it or its deficiencies.*

Can Television News Break the Understanding-Barrier?

There is a bias in television journalism. It is not against any particular party or point of view – it is a bias against *understanding*. And this bias aggravates the difficulties which our society suffers in solving its problems and reconciling its differences.

To understand how this comes about it is useful to classify the different types of journalism which are practised on television. The degree in which an item is put into context is a convenient criterion for establishing three broad categories: news, feature and issue journalism.

Take, for example, the deaths of twenty-one people in the Birmingham explosions. A journalist's first job is to explain to his audience the

191

immediate circumstances – where the bombings took place, the warning given, how the victims died and so on. From this he can widen the coverage to set the explosions into the context of the bombing campaign and can look at what new security measures might be introduced.

He could widen the context still further by putting the bombing campaign in the perspective of the Northern Ireland conflict. He could examine how the bombing fits into the strategy of the Provisional IRA and try to assess how the escalation of the IRA campaign would be likely to change British government policy and what the consequences of any changes might be. This would necessarily involve an understanding of the real (and not just the apparent) thinking of the protagonists at Westminister, in Ulster and in the Republic.

The problem for the television journalists and producers is to decide in how wide or how narrow a context to set each item or programme for which they are responsible. I believe that deficient emphasis on this concept, both by programme makers and by the broadcasting author-ities in their planning of programmes, has contributed to the present bias against understanding. We can see how things go wrong if we examine the different forms of television journalism one by one.

Present television news programmes cover a large number of stories, often more than twenty items in a span of about half an hour. As a result the focus in any one story is extremely narrow. But unfortunately the most important stories of the moment, for example, stories about the economy or Northern Ireland or the EEC or the Middle East or oil, suffer from such a narrow treatment.

Our economic problems, for instance, manifest themselves in a wide variety of symptoms – deteriorating balance of payments, a sinking pound, rising unemployment, accelerating inflation and so on. The news, devoting two minutes on successive nights to the latest unemploy-ment figures or the state of the stock market, with no time to put the story in context, gives the viewer no sense of how any of these problems relate to each other. It is more likely to leave him confused and uneasy.

Feature journalism tends to concentrate on one aspect or one instance of a major problem rather than on that problem as a whole. Feature journalists tend to make a film about a particular instance of famine rather than about the world food problem. They expose the dangers of particular nuclear reactors rather than examine what the government's energy policy is or could be.

Programmes like, for example, *This Week* and *Midweek* often perform a valuable job in seeking out our and other societies' specific sores. But feature journalists often fail to keep clear in their minds the link between the sore they have highlighted and the wider issue it illustrates. For example, making a film about homeless people is not an adequate way of approaching the problems created by our housing shortage. Nor is a film profile of a Catholic or Protestant family in Belfast likely to be by itself a useful starting point on the road to understanding what is happening in Northern Ireland. Television feature journalism continually suffers because producers do not take the trouble to think their ideas through and thereby to discover the tenuousness of the link between, say, one unemployed man and the real causes of unemployment. Consequently an illuminating, though possibly diverting programme is made.

The constant emphasis placed on societies' sores by television journalists, with little or no attempt to seek out the root causes or discuss the ways by which the sore might be removed, may even be dangerous. It may contribute to the alienation felt by the victim of societies' inadequacies and imperfections. They can be forgiven for sharing in the assumption apparently made by many feature journalists that a sore easily highlighted should be a sore easily removed. Bad feature journalism encourages the victims (and most of us are victims of something or other) not to relate their problems to those of society as a whole and to conceal from ourselves how often one man's grievance is another man's right.

Issue journalism aims to go beyond the context provided by the feature journalist to look at such subjects as the related components of our economic problems or what our housing policy should be. Trying to get to grips with the often bewildering complexity of modern problems such as these is a formidable task, even without trying to put the result on television; and the failure rate is high. The realities one is seeking are abstract – macro-economic mechanisms, political philosophies, international strategies – and cannot be directly televised like a battle zone or a demonstration.

This kind of journalism has many hazards. Attempting to answer a question like 'what are the causes of inflation?' is intellectually very taxing and issue journalists in television often lack the knowledge to settle on the right framework for asking such a question. For example, they may focus on pay control in such a way as to imply that it is the only possible cure for inflation. If the other variables of and constraints on the economy are not explained the complex causes of inflation will not be understood. And, moreover, politically dangerous myths will be created.

Before programmes like *Weekend World* and *The Money Programme* developed production techniques for dealing with complicated issues, the journalistic tool almost always chosen for dealing with issues, especially abstract issues, was the studio discussion. Rarely has a technique been so abused.

Three industrialists discussing illiquidity or three party spokesmen quarrelling over inflation or three Ulstermen exchanging rhetoric about power-sharing will not succeed in fifteen minutes in communicating anything other than confusion. These discussions are generally set up to examine disagreements, rather than areas of agreement; and they place an unnaturally high premium on the resourcefulness under pressure of the participants. They encourage interviewees to abandon any attempt to discuss issues in a fresh and sophisticated manner. ('Could you please explain how the Liberal Party would deal with inflation, but briefly please, Mr Pardoe.') They scarcely ever promote understanding of complicated problems and are little more than an entertaining way of feeding the viewer's already existing prejudices.

But even when that small proportion of issue journalism which does not rely solely on studio discussion is successful, it faces a further obstacle. It runs the risk of being boring. A well-made report on a famine will be more watchable than a report on the world food problem. A programme on living conditions in slums will be more diverting than a report on housing policy.

The main consequence of this is that most television journalists and those who schedule programmes prefer story to issue journalism. In television as a whole there are few issue-oriented programmes. And ironically most of these are scheduled far less favourably than the very news and feature stories which issue journalism seeks to put into perspective.

I believe that the various forms and techniques of television journalism – news, programmes, feature reports, the presentation and discussion of issues – can all too easily conspire together to create a bias against their audience's understanding of the society in which it lives. And this is particularly dangerous at the moment because of the crisis through which the country is presently passing.

This is not the place to discuss the precise nature of that crisis. But suppose there is something in the view held by growing numbers of politicians and economists that, if we can find no effective method of restraining general levels of pay (at the moment through the Social Contract), then it will not be possible much longer for us to reconcile four central features of our society: parliamentary democracy; full employment; stable prices; and free collective bargaining. The country might soon have to decide which to forgo.

Such a choice would impose extraordinary strains on the political process. For this reason, if for no other, television and the press must ensure that the options available are fully and sensibly debated. At the moment television is not likely to mount such a debate. But, worse still, television could itself inhibit the resolution of the crisis by dramatising each symptom of crisis while ignoring the general equilibrium on which real understanding of causes and cures depends.

The bomb, the sit-in, the strike, the demonstration, all provide a staple diet for the news editor and the feature journalist. There is a danger that the pressure brought to bear on politicians by the incoherent highlighting of societies' sores by television will lead politicians (ever aware that their personal future and that of their party are decided by the ballot box) to deal with the symptoms of crisis rather than to take a longer time to search out fundamental causes and to deal with them.

There is an even greater danger awaiting politicians if they surmount this hurdle and do succeed in searching out the causes of our crisis. They may be inhibited from taking the necessary action because of the outrage they fear it would provoke. This age-old problem of democracy is aggravated because the media in their present forms instinctively fasten on the snags and drawbacks in any proposed new policy. It normally communicates these more effectively than the policy as a whole or, indeed, the overall problem to be solved. And any measure which has any chance of resolving our present crisis is likely to have painful and unpopular side-effects.

I believe that a fundamental re-examination of the present organisation of television news and current affairs is necessary if we are to correct the bias against understanding which the present system produces. We should redesign television news programmes so that they devote much more time than they presently do to the main stories of the day; and so that these stories are put in the fullest possible context in the time available. Feature programmes must be organised so that they are more aware of the need to find a relevant focus. And the broadcasting organisations should ensure that there are more programmes which deal with issues than there are at the moment.

Mr Callaghan recently asked whether or not parliamentary democracy can survive attempts to solve our crisis. How well television appreciates what is at stake is all-important.

The Times Friday 28 February 1975

Television Journalism:
Without Pride of Ancestry

To hear people talking about the facts you would think that they lay about like the pieces of gold ore in the Yukon days waiting to be picked up – arduously, it is true, but still definitely and visibly – by strenuous prospectors whose subsequent problem was only to get them to market. Such a view is evidently and dangerously naive. There are no such facts. Or if there are, they are meaningless and entirely ineffective; they might in fact just was well not be lying about at all until the prospector puts them into relation with other facts: presents them, in other words.

Claud Cockburn, *I Claud*. . . . .

In a previous article (*The Times*, 28 February 1975), it was argued that television news and current affairs fail at their primary job of informing their audience about the circumstances which most shape the world in which they live. It was suggested that this bias against understanding may aggravate the difficulties which a modern society suffers in trying to solve its problems.

We shall attempt in this article to diagnose the deficiencies of the system; and we will suggest how television news and current affairs – for most people their main source of information – could be organised better to overcome some of these deficiencies.

We believe that the system of television journalism was never designed according to a set of coherent and generally understood principles into which individual programmes fit. Rather, it is a misbeggoten child of two ill-assorted parents, neither of which is well-adapted to the needs of

196

news analysis. One parent is the newspaper office, typically the local paper's news-room. The other is the film business, more specifically the documentary film.

The news-room model

The archetype of a news gathering operation, the outlines of which can still be found in almost all contemporary journalism (both print and broadcast), is the news-room of a provincial paper. Hardened all-rounders sit at an all-purpose news desk looking for 'stories'. Their chief quarries are the rest of the media and certain routine sources – government departments, law courts, news agencies, stringers and so on.

Having spotted a possible story, the news desk dispatches a reporter to 'cover' it. He garners all the 'facts' he can and files this story. Another hardened group of all-rounders called 'copy-tasters', sample this material filed by reporters and pick out what strikes them as new, interesting or entertaining for inclusion in the paper.

Thus, the spotting, getting, writing and placing of stories – a process taking, typically, only a few hours – are the work of three or four different people, none of whom is expected to have any continuing, deep or specialist knowledge of the background to a story.

What, in theory, is this machine for? The purpose of journalism, print and broadcast, is first to gather information about what is happening in the world; and secondly – since a man may know everything and yet understand nothing – to place this information, where necessary, in sufficient context for a reader or viewer to perceive its significance. That is the theory. But is the conveyor-belt system outlined above capable in practice of realising these aims?

First, let us look at the collecting of information. Plainly, journalists select for printing only an infinitesimal portion of what happens in the world. So how do they decide what to cover? They are guided by a set of values which has grown up over many years and which is called 'news-sense'. It is not easy to define; but it is clear that dramatic or unusual happenings are given prominence – for example, a plane crash, a murder or the growing of an outsize marrow. And it was long ago discovered that the more such stories are presented in terms of personalities, the more diverting they are to the reader.

These values cause few problems when they are applied to simple stories of human interest – a single yachtsman sailing around the world or the private lives of the upper classes. But these criteria for establishing what constitutes a news story are inadequate, even dangerous, when they are applied, as they are, to the social, political, economic and international forces which most determine our lives.

Thus, the symptoms of our economic ills – a deteriorating balance of payments, an accelerating rate of inflation and so on – are reported as separate stories, each a collection of discrete 'facts'. So also with the treatment of poverty, the evolution of political alignments and Dr Kissinger's foreign policy. The latest anecdotes are collected by a reporter, much as the latest Test score would be; and wherever possible, the stories are presented in terms of personalities and in the most dramtic and often misleading way.

So we identify the first mismatch between the media and their material – of system to task. The reality is a seamless garment of interacting and developing processes while journalism is organised to collect innumerable nuggets of self-contained fact, to report an atomised world of a million tiny tales.

Why, then, do we have this wrong concept of journalism and news priorities? Essentially, it is because of a cultural lag in the qualifications and background of the broad mass of reporters, news editors and the like. If the archetype is the cub reporter who, having left school at sixteen, wins his spurs covering crime at Gateshead, it is not to be expected that the profession will be well adapted to explaining a world of continuing economic malaise and increasing social stress. This is the second mismatch – of manpower to task.

Thus the organisation and the values of the archetypal local newspaper office tend to produce stories which feature Mr Benn and Sir Keith Joseph in struggles for power rather than attempts to understand the ideas they espouse. They produce stories about Vietnamese orphans rather than trying to understand the nature of the conflict in Indo-China and the worldwide consequences of its ending. They produce stories about Budgets which lead on the price of beer rather than, say, the possibility that a twenty-five year commitment to full employment as the sovereign criterion of economic strategy has been suspended or given up. It is, then, these news values which produce some of the results outlined in the previous article.

Traditionalists will disagree with the diagnosis so far. They will say that it fails to take account of the natural distinction between, on the one hand, news and, on the other hand, news analysis (some features and some editorials in newspapers and occasional current affairs programmes on television). Our contention is that this distinction, at least as a primary basis of news organisation, is the basic misconception, the reigning error. It is a distinction without any proper difference.

Intelligent – in the sense of understanding, not of intellectual – news means continuous news analysis. This requires many qualified – that is, knowledgeable and educated – journalists, sometimes working in teams and continuously blending inquiry and analysis, so that the needs of understanding direct the inquiry, and the fruits of inquiry inform the analysis. To try to separate news from analysis, when dealing with the complex continuing and abstract issues which dominate the news, is to make the news unintelligible and often to make the analysis uninformed, amateur and unduly opinionated

The movie model

The other model on which television has drawn, the movie film business, has contributed to a form of feature journalism which also draws attention and effort away from the analysis of issues. This is the other element in the bias against understanding described in the previous article.

Current affairs, as distinct from television news, is organised differently and has its own archetypes. The production team, consisting of researchers, directors and producers, is likely to have a mixed range of experience. But current affairs programmes tend to be dominated by the sort of graduate producer-director whose professional heritage and ethos stem ultimately from the traditions of the film business.

In the past ten years or so, an influential body of opinion has emerged, centred on directors, which believes that film is the most appropriate, indeed the only true, vehicle for television journalism. In consequence, the documentaries made by the main current affairs programmes are far more polished and ambitious than were the short 'filmed news reports' that such programmes featured ten or so years ago. But the tendency is for such programmes now to work to film imperatives rather than to journalistic concepts, to see stories as an excuse for making 'a film', rather than to see film as simply an aid to presenting a story or explaining an issue, especially when the issue involves abstractions like social causes and effects or geo-political ideas. For the directors' lobby an ideal programme is one which has exciting locations and lively situations with animated talkers in between. Any proposed project is likely to be assessed by how it measures up to these critieria

What is lacking from many current affairs programmes is a journalistic, rather than a film, criterion for deciding which stories to cover, and
how to cover them. The current affairs programmes are not part of a
system which is continually covering the major stories (as the news-
room is); and they generally do not have subject specialists on their
teams. So, when they decide to cover some story which seems, from a
general reading of the newspapers, to be important (like one of Northern
Ireland's recurring crises or the prospect of a Rhodesian settlement),
they try to apply their movie formula rather than to make an attempt at
news analysis. And the result is those familiar programmes featuring a
week in the life of a prominent Northern Ireland politician (with lots of
verité footage) or a situation report from Rhodesia which ignores totally
the fact that the crucial pressure for a settlement is coming from outside
the country.

These criticisms of current affairs programmes should not be taken as
a criticism of the idea of feature journalism as such. If the issue journalist
– as we have called him – is to function at all, he needs to know the
answers to carefully posed questions that can only be answered by
first-hand investigation. He needs to know in detail, for example, what
is the real Israel or PLO attitude to the West Bank in order to appreciate
what may happen in the Middle East. Likewise, the issue journalist
needs to know about the difficulties of extracting North Sea oil if he is to
answer the complicated question of how North Sea oil will affect
Britain's prosperity. But the staffing and organisation of most current
affairs programmes ensures that more often than not the wrong
narrowly defined question is posed.

Inevitably the documentary film ethos comes to contaminate not only
the choice and the treatment of stories but also those members of the
team on whom the directors rely for their journalistic input – the
researchers and the reporters.

Typically, a current affairs programme team, usually comprising only
ten or so researchers and reporters, relies heavily on newspapers and
specialist magazines, which are scoured for stories that fit into the
formulae favoured by their particular programme.

Most researchers on current affairs programmes specialising in narrowly focused feature stories of this type are not trained or indeed
qualified to relate a problem like homelessness to our overall housing
problem. Thus what economists know as the fallacy of composition –
the notion that the macrocosm is the microcosm writ large – becomes

the major premise of feature journalism.

Just as the researcher is the director's assistant, working to film imperatives, so that reporter is the director's star. The reporter is generally – because of his probable Fleet Street experience – rigorous within the limits laid down by the format; but he does not try to extend a story outside them. The reporter recognises that 'concerned' interviews with victims of the system and 'grabbing' interviews with the guilty landlord or council official are more likely to establish him as a 'personality' interviewer than some painstaking and abstract analysis of housing economics which is outside his experience and capabilities.

There are honourable exceptions – both programmes and individuals – to these current affairs (and, indeed, newspaper) norms. There are programmes which are not constrained by film imperatives; but the ethos discussed above is the dominant influence in current affairs television. The emphasis on particular features of problems, rather than on the often deep-lying causes and total context of these problems, yields the consequences outlined in the previous article.

The Times, 30 September 1975

Television Journalism: With Hope of Posterity

The aim of a reformed television service – while much of our diagnosis applies to print and broadcasting, the suggestions here are confined to television because, probably alone, it still commands the resources necessary to undertake radical reforms – should be to provide viewers with timely and accurate information and with the maximum feasible understanding of the important (and diverting) events which happen in the world about them. It must also deal thoroughly with the differing interpretations and arguments to which those events give rise.

We emphasise this last point in order to correct the misunderstanding of our thesis which appeared in remarks by the Director-General of the

BBC, Sir Charles Curran, at the Royal Television Society Convention ten days ago.

He suggested that in some way our suggestions excluded 'full and free flow of fact and argument to the audience'. We would die in the same last ditch with him to uphold that principle, wishing only to add intelligent (in the sense of 'helpful understanding') to 'full and free', an aim which Sir Charles himself fully endorsed in his address at the Cambridge Convention.

As Sir Michael Swann, the Chairman of the BBC, put it last March – in a prepared address to a Leeds University seminar on broadcasting, in which he went to some lengths to commend our thesis as it appeared in an early draft – 'the need for greater public understanding of the intractable problems which beset us is so pressing that no effort is too great'. We look forward to the day when Sir Michael's and Sir Charles's statements of principle will be translated into the necessary practical reforms.

In an ideal service provided by one of the popular channels – BBC 1 or ITV – most of the available apparatus of programme slots, production personnel and journalists should be organised as an integrated operation, run by a unified news-and-current affairs department, with clearly defined and inter-related roles and functions. Within this framework there should and would be full experiment by individual programme directors.

Programmes

This department's job would be to provide a backbone of programmes which would provide a service of news analysis – on a daily, weekly and monthly basis.

Daily: We advocate that news, as presently defined to exclude news analysis, be restricted to brief news bulletins which would simply carry the bald news-breaks: floods, bombings, White Papers, economic statistics, deaths, major statements by politicians and so on.

The main vehicle of daily television journalism would be an hour-long 'flagship' programme scheduled from Monday to Friday five days a week between say, ten and eleven o'clock in the evening, replacing the traditional nine or ten o'clock news programmes. This programme would first carry the news headlines and would then concentrate on the major news stories of the day (probably no more than about five or six). It would place these stories in the fullest context possible in the time available. As the premier programme of the news-and-current-affairs department, it would have first call on the department's pooled journalistic resources.

Weekly: at the end of the week there should be an hour-long programme which would take the main one, two or three stories of the previous week and put them into perspective. This would inevitably go over some of the ground covered by the daily analysis programme; but it is important to pull running stories together at some length so that they can be properly understood.

Monthly: once a month there should be a ninety-minute programme in peak hour which would tackle the basic continuing themes of our times: e.g. the relationship between the developed and the undeveloped world; what are the root causes of inflation; what Britain's housing policy should be.

This backbone of news analysis would be supplemented by a range of feature programmes, also under the auspices of the unified department, which would examine particular and carefully posed questions. Many of these would have been thrown up by the process of news analysis (a process which tends to generate more questions than answers): e.g. what are the driving forces in Israel's relationship with America; how is the Third World hit by the increased cost of oil; what can we learn from the German inflation of the twenties?

Staffing

The whole of the staff of the unified news-and-current affairs department would be organised in two parallel echelons under the head of the department. One echelon would consist of programme editors and those, like producers, exercising the editors' delegated responsibility. The other would consist of journalists. They would be organised into subject teams headed by subject editors, such as a political editor, a foreign editor, an industrial editor and so on.

The journalists would be responsible for supplying journalistic input to all programmes in the news-and-current affairs department, though producers would be entirely free to draw also on outside talent. Probably half its resources would be expended on the nightly ten o'clock programme. Under the editor the programme producers would have full responsibility for their own individual programmes. But they would have available to them – and it is assumed they would work continuously with – the editors of the various journalistic subject teams to discuss programme items and to arrange their preparation and presentation. Thus, on the nightly programme when, say, a trade union leader makes a major speech on incomes policy, there should certainly *not* be contributions, prepared in isolation and edited end-to-end, from an industrial correspondent, an economics correspondent and a political correspondent. Rather the aim would be to generate a new style of journalism.

The programme would take its raw material from the information gathered by reporters and film crews about the circumstances surrounding the speech and reactions to it. Secondly, it would draw on the interpretations of the various specialist journalists. This material should then be synthesised into a rounded treatment of the story for television, analysing the union leader's speech and placing it in full a context as possible. Differing viewpoints on the issues raised by the strictly journalistic analysis should be brought out and, where appropriate, debated by protagonists.

Who will do it?

This prescription for a revised news-and-current affairs service could, it appears to us, be put into operation more easily on BBC 1 than in ITV, because in the BBC all news-and-current affairs programmes come, at some point, under common management. This is not the case in ITV, where the federal system enables individual companies to pursue their own programme philosophies, and where the freedom of an individual current affairs programme to define its own role is thought to be more important than an overall strategy into which individual programmes fit. Moreover, the BBC, being capable in principle of a strategic command decision, is on the face of things better able to undertake a radical change, which will offend many entrenched interests, than is independent television with its convention of unanimous consent.

The ITV companies did, of course, form ITN to cover on their behalf national and international news. We would propose that, if ITV felt the need to respond to our diagnosis, a new organisation could be formed to provide the backbone of news, news analysis and supplementary features as outlined above. (Whether or not ITN as now constituted would wish to or could grow into this wider role and whether the programme companies would welcome it are questions outside the scope of this article.) This new organisation would have the same relationship to the ITV companies which ITN presently has; but the companies could still be free, of course, to make whatever feature programmes they felt were necessary to supplement this system of news and news analysis (programmes, perhaps, which would focus on the circumstances affecting minorities within the mass audience that the above system is designed to serve – programmes for minorities defined by region, age, culture and so on).

If this proposal is thought to be too radical, we would advocate that ITN be at least infused with more resources and extended in scope so that it can provide the nightly hour-long programme of news and news analysis. We would also suggest that the IBA should then encourage ITV's main current affairs programmes to fit as nearly as possible into the conscious pattern of news analysis outlined above. In particular, the half-hour film–current affairs programmes should be encouraged to break free from their present constraints of running time and technique.

We urgently need profound change in television journalism – even in journalism as such. The purpose of our proposals is to adapt the resources and organisation available for news analysis in the contemporary world. This means breaking with the two main antecedents of television journalism, namely, traditional newspaper news operations and documentary film-making. It means building a new structure of programmes, a new concept of programme-making and a new organisation of properly qualified producers and journalists, custom-designed for the purpose. In this way the pervasive bias against understanding, which is now the chief disfigurement of contemporary journalism in all media, can be corrected at least in television, and an exciting and essential new service to the public can be provided.

The Times, 1 October 1975

How Television News Can Hold
the Mass Audience

Last year in three articles in *The Times* (28 February, 30 September, 1 October 1977) we offered a critique of television news and current affairs journalism. This was that there is at present a bias against understanding in television journalism in that the typically atomized presentation of events and issues systematically misrepresents the world and its difficulties, thereby making it more difficult than it otherwise would be for society to solve its problems.

We traced this malady to television journalism's twin antecedents, the classic newspaper office and the film industry. We proposed a remedy built around the premises, that there is no such thing as a pure 'fact', that value-judgements are out of place and that the staple of television journalism, as of all serious journalism, must be intelligent news analysis.

To these ends we suggested merging news and current affairs organisations so that a coherent structure of programmes can be designed to handle systemically the events and issues of the day, of the week and of the month. The 'flag-ship' of this fleet of programmes would be an hour-long nightly news programme at about ten o'clock. Its task would be to supplement a brief news bulletin with a treatment of the four to six main events and issues of the day at about four or five times the length now given to the typical news item. All the programmes would be informed by an overriding editorial principle that explaining the background and context of events is at least as valid and necessary a part of reporting as relating and filming the latest incidents.

We suggested secondly that these programmes, though independently edited, should be serviced at the discretion of the programme editors by a central pool of reporters and specialists. This would ensure that the highest quality and the widest range of journalistic skills and specialities would be available. Thereby it would also become possible for the first time to develop proper recruitment, training and career planning for high quality journalists.

Fears of smaller audiences

Certain fears have been expressed about the consequences of putting these proposals into effect. These fears are essentially of three kinds:

That the system of programmes we propose would attract smaller audiences than the present system of news and current affairs programmes; that the factual purity and impartiality of news and current affairs would be contaminated by editorial opinion; that the present independence of the individual television journalist would be forfeit to central monolithic editorial designs.

The complaint that the new journalism would alienate audiences is serious. For the proposals are not intended as experiments on third or fourth channels. They are concerned with how news and current affairs programmes should be conceived, organised, scheduled and presented on the main television channels now.

There is, in fact, no warrant for the assumption that the reorganised programmes – no substantial increase in the quantity of news and current affairs programmes is proposed – would be less popular than the present diet. Indeed, what evidence there is about the likely popularity of the proposed system points the other way.

As Austin Mitchell demonstrated in *The Political Quarterly* of April/June 1973, there has been a gradual fall in the audiences of the main current affairs programmes during the past decade or so. This is the period in which the modern style of programme has come to dominate both main channels.

There is also evidence that the trend towards more emphasis on events and pictures in the news, as distinct from current affairs, has at least coincided with a gradual decline in audience interest. Between 1969 and 1975 the total audience for the leading news programmes on both main channels declined by almost a fifth. *News at Ten*, which starts later than the BBC News (though not to the extent we advocate), has consistently had the edge over the BBC News throughout the period, although it, too, has suffered a decline.

The programme makers have interpreted the decline in the size of their audiences as evidence that the viewers' interest in the world about them is declining. They have concluded that the public's preference for straight entertainment is gaining ground and that therefore the right response is to make news and current affairs programmes even more slick, fast, personalised, pictorial and down-to-earth than they have been.

The treatment of major events

This now appears to be a classic example of the wrong diagnosis leading to positive aggravation of the complaint. (The failure of what was originally conceived as the ultimate manifestation of this trend – the *Tonight* programme – to attract the size of audience it wanted should cause such theorists to pause for thought, though some will no doubt prefer to blame the crew rather than the design of the ship.)

The evidence does not argue that the best way for news and current affairs programmes to increase, or even to hold their present audiences is to carry on regardless or to proceed even farther along their present path. On the contrary, the evidence suggests that it is not the public's taste which is becoming more frivolous, but that of the programme makers.

It could be that it is the shallowness and fragmentation of the television treatment of major events and issues which is driving the audiences away. In an age of more and more education, combined with more exciting events and more pressing problems, it would be odd if popular curiosity were becoming shallower.

While eighty to ninety percent of any viewer's television appetite may well be for entertainment or for programmes about his particular interests, the remaining ten to twenty percent is for knowing what is happening – and why – in the world around him. That part of his appetite naturally demands lucid, intelligible information and explanation, not more entertainment disguised as 'popular' (i.e. trivial) stabs at haphazardly chosen stories of the moment.

The treatment which evokes the excited, 'Oh, I see', of dawning understanding is invariably appreciated. Not so the wall-to-wall incident reports which evoke the impatient, 'Oh, Lord, not more violence/bad news/gloomy figures/natural disasters', of yawning apathy.

In short, understanding can be popular with the viewer. Television executives who doubt it do so either because they confuse intelligent news presentation with news for the intelligentsia, or because at bottom they believe the public to be irredeemably stupid.

The proper job of television journalists is not to try to reach a mass audience by making entertainment programmes nominally pegged to news events or the contemporary scene. The job is to try to achieve what the great popularisers have always achieved: namely, to cut through the jargon and the technical details and to reach towards clarity of exposition of the important development and issues so that the citizen may have a chance to perceive the choices available to the society and to the world in which he or she lives.

Why television news is in danger of becoming an anti-social force

The second set of objections to our proposals for merging television news and current affairs organisations derive from misconceptions of what is meant by placing events and issues 'in context'.

The first of these, and also the one which embodies the biggest misconception, is that the new journalism would dilute fact with opinion, thereby transgressing the fundamental principles of all journalism in general and those of the BBC Charter and the IBA Act in particular. It is the most difficult misconception to explain because it is deeply embedded in conventional ideas of journalism.

Tradition has it that it is the job of reporters to collect 'facts' and of commentators to make 'comments'. 'Comment is free but facts are sacred'; and so the covenant is handed down, the two must never be mixed.

It is alleged that 'news analysis', which seeks to explain events, would encroach on the role of the reporter, blur the distinction between 'fact' and 'comment' and thereby break a hallowed tradition.

This tradition, which sounds on the face of it eminently sensible, is confused; and we are in need of a latter-day C. P. Scott to restate it with greater precision. If he had said 'Prescription is free but description is sacred', he would at least have avoided the central ambiguity of what exactly 'comment' means.

Does 'comment' here mean 'comment as value judgement': how things *ought* to be (poverty should/should not be stamped out; murderers should/should not be hanged?). If it does, then there is no argument. All are agreed that the job of the television journalist should not be to prescribe how things ought to be.

But there is another possible meaning of the word comment: 'comment as interpretation' (poverty is/is not avoidable; hanging is/is not a deterrent). Traditional attempts to distinguish between 'fact' and 'comment' in this sense are misguided. There is no such thing as a pure 'fact' to be separated from 'comment'. Consequently, the concept of purely factual reporting ('TUC agrees to pay deal'), which supposedly by-passes all problems of interpretation, is an empty myth at all levels of journalism.

For a start, it begs the question why a journalist decides to describe one event rather than another. When a journalist chooses to report the latest balance of payments figures instead of what his aunt gave him for Christmas, he does so because he judges that it is more important for society to learn about the one than the other or, at least, that more people will be interested. But in order to make a judgement about *what* is important or interesting, a journalist must assume, however unconsciously, the reasons why they are more important, or more interesting.

He may think the balance of payments figures are important and interesting because he believes them to be a measure of our economic welfare. But what is welfare? How does he know the figures are a measure of it? Does everyone agree they are? Is there a consensus about their significance, and what exactly is it?

The journalist may think he avoids these difficult and contentious questions, if he is aware of them, by reporting the figures baldly (though even to report the figures and to display them prominently in part determines their position on society's agenda).

If he really were content simply to report the figures and nothing else, that might convince some, though not us, that he had not stepped over the traditional theorists' dividing line between fact and interpretation. But few journalists are content to report the bald figures. If they were, they would just publish a table of figures.

Actually, the typical reporter generally tries to connect the figures with other events: statements by government ministers; other and previous announcements of economic statistics (of unemployment, for example); calls for changes in government policy; and, of course, future prospects.

Indeed, the problem goes even deeper than the question of selecting stories. It is embedded in the very relationship between language and reality. Even if selection were random or could be based purely on market analysis of reader viewer interest, the journalist would still face the difficulty that every sentence and every word carries connotations which go beyond what he can see, hear, touch, smell and feel. Interpretation is implicit in any use of language at all to describe the world.

So, the concept of purely factual reporting is already into difficult terrain, far from home. How does the journalist decide whom to report and how to report him? How does he connect one set of figures with another? How does he decide whether or not to seek the differing views of experts in universities or specialist institutions about the significance of the figures? How does he decide whether or not to label the trade figures as good or bad news, one of which value judgements he generally feels the need to make? Which question-begging vocabulary does he use to describe what he sees?

In practice, decisions about whom and what to report are deceptively easy for him because he can rely on the reflex news 'sense' which is bred into all journalists, with all the events that have been reported in the past put into some sort of order. Equally facile are decisions about how to report the chosen events. Whether they like it or not and whether they admit it or not, journalists also have a model in the backs of their minds of how society works, of what the important questions facing it are and of who is charged with answering them; and it is against this unseen apparatus of assumptions and opinions that journalists judge the news-worthiness and significance of any news event.

In other words, all journalists interpret; they stamp all over, and always have, the imagined line between so-called 'fact' and 'interpretation'. Interpretation is present, whether or not it is admitted, in even the baldest news story because the selection, compression, simplication and shorthand labels that such stories require.

The real issue between us and our critics, therefore, is not whether 'fact' should be contaminated with 'comment', but whether or not the inescapability of interpretation is acknowledged. Because it is not acknowledged, the model of society with which most journalists work is primitively constructed and fails to take into account the differing views throughout the whole of society about how our political, economic and social systems do and might work.

The result of this is, ironically, that traditional journalists are forced along the very path they fear to tread. Most current broadcast journalism is partial – it favours the views of one group at the expense of those of another. This is because, lacking a clear sense of its obligation to society as a whole, most journalism lives under the shadow of the state and the other main repositories of power in our society: the political parties; business; the trade unions; and so on. It might almost be called 'corporate journalism'.

Much reporting is simply passing on what head offices do, say and feel is important. In consequence, head office value judgements – e.g. the labelling of groups and individuals as 'militant', 'extremist' or 'moderate' – dominate journalism; and often the reporters themselves use such labels as if they were clinical terms.

In sum, the attempt to drive a wedge between fact and interpretation has led most journalists to adopt simplistic, restrictive and highly prejudical news values.

The important difference to be noted in journalism is quite different from the chimerical fact/interpretation distinction. It is between more and less intelligent impartial treatment of issues and events. People quite simply want to know why things are happening, and when that is uncertain or controversial, why they may have happened and what sorts of reasons are being given for their having happened.

In the Northern Ireland conflict, for example, the forces include those interests represented by the British and Irish Governments, the Republican and the loyalist paramilitary groups, the Northern Ireland political parties, and so on. It is the job of the journalist continually to redefine the nature and the significance of the ever-changing forces in play and to show in what way a new happening is a sign that the underlying forces are in some measure changing.

This is no easy matter. For example, even a journalist with specialist knowledge of economics and foreign affairs may spend many months trying to understand the considerations that must be taken into account before he can set out a framework into which can be put the arguments about, say, whether or not membership of the EEC is desirable for Britain.

The conscientious journalist must talk to experts – to government, trade unionists, specialist institutions and universities as well as to politicians and to pressure groups in this and other countries – in order to ascertain first what the most germane areas of inquiry may be and second, what is common ground and what is not within these specific areas. The journalist will begin to understand what has been researched and what is not agreed about, say, the short-term economic consequences of our membership of the EEC or about the arguments for and against customs unions. Such understanding of the arguments will allow him thereafter to see how some new circumstance (e.g. the French grape-grower riots) fits into this picture or, if it does not, how the picture should be changed to accommodate it.

This approach could in principle be accommodated within the present system if the task of defining all these forces in play fell to the journalists working to weekly deadlines (on current affairs programmes), with the task of working out the implications of some new circumstances falling to those working to daily deadlines (on news programmes). But at the moment the practitioners in news and current affairs reject even this approach as unnecessary because they assume understanding is easy.

News journalists argue that the present news programmes already 'dripfeed' understanding of complicated situations over a long period of time. 'Capsule analysis', they say, can be and is attached to the reporting of incidents in Northern Ireland or pronouncements from the Bank of England, or whatever, so as adequately to set such 'difficult matters' in their context.

This belief greatly underrates the complexity of the world in which we live. If an event bears on the great issues of the moment, its implications will be too complicated to assess in the one or two-minute spot which the news would presently allocate to the task. The very term 'capsule analysis' betrays the thinking of the archetypal news journalist – that news consists of exceptional and self-contained events which take place against a static and familiar background (which can be instantly re-encapsulated) rather than as a momentary and partial manifestation of a continuous, though ever-changing, flux.

The failure of most current affairs – as distinct from news – journalism is not so much that it fails to appreciate that the path to understanding is difficult (though it does). More seriously, it has failed to develop a vehicle which is capable of being driven along that path. The studio discussion, for example, with spokesmen representing some or all of the forces-in-play tends, in most of its manifestations, to be ramshackle. It is simply not up to the task, although occasionally it can be a useful reporting device to advertise the mood, attitudes and emotional interplay – whether of solidarity or hostility – within a particular group. Current affairs journalism also relies heavily on the documentary or film report. It too often, though not always, fails to promote understanding. It does so, not because it is ramshackle, but because there is a fundamental fallacy embodied in the methodology of the typical film report.

That fallacy, known to economists as 'the fallacy of composition', is the belief that the big picture is the sum of its component parts, in other words, that it is the handy example writ large. For example, it tends to assume that if every homeless family finds itself homeless because it cannot find the price of a house, then homelessness is caused by lack of money. It supposes that the forces acting between the galaxies are the same as the forces acting between sub-atomic particles, only bigger and that, if each soldier in rival armies is fighting out of patriotism, then patriotism is the cause of war. Every thinking person recognises this fallacy; and yet almost every television journalist who tries to tackle a macro-problem – unemployment, war, social injustice, famine, even natural disasters – walks head-first into the trap.

It is done, of course, in the name of bringing the abstract down to earth and the complicated home to so-called ordinary simple people (recall the fears for the mass audience), as well as to keep the job within the limited competence of the all-purpose lone reporter. But ordinary, simple people are not simpletons; and even if they were, they would not benefit from false accounts of the world about them.

The big picture is just as much part of the real world as the personal tragedy, the general as much as the particular, the abstract as much as the concrete. Both have to be reported and explained; and neither can stand proxy for the other by simply multiplying or dividing the scale, a feat television journalism attempts each day. We need astrophysics and atomic physics (and much else besides) to describe the physical world. So, be properly suspicious when next you are invited on a bus tour of the inside of the atom in order to understand the cosmos.

There is no easy path to understanding. The conscientious journalist, having climbed the mountain, should of course make it much easier for those who follow. But we should be suspicious of those who offer a low and painless road to the top. For it seldom, if ever, exists.

There is a last ditch objection to our case. You may be right in your critique of television journalism, it is said; but nothing can be done about it. Television is an unsuitable medium for the exploration of difficult or abstract issues and complex macro-problems. It is only suited to the telling of simple, easily explained and dramatic tales.

It is better to arouse interest in a serious subject, so the argument goes, by covering in an entertaining fashion some particular aspect of it. This encourages the viewer to turn to newspapers and to specialist journals where he can find, if he wants, the deeper and considered analysis on which he can reflect at his leisure. In a phrase, the medium is stupid even if the producers and viewers are not.

This defeatism is unwarranted. Television's ability to match picture to sound often makes difficult ideas easier to follow than they are in print. Moreover, the possibilty of illustrating the abstract with tangible examples of what in practice these abstractions can mean, makes programmes on subjects like public spending or energy policy actually more digestible than their exact equivalents in print would be. Outside mainstream journalism a programme like *Horizon* has shown consistently that difficult scientific ideas and their implications can be made intelligible on television to the layman.

In sum, most journalists, including television journalists, work to obsolete and muddled concepts which need to be replaced by the values of a new journalism – values which will make the journalist's task more demanding but more rewarding both for him and for the public he serves.

The third set of objections to our proposals are made by television journalists working in the present system of news and current affairs programmes who believe that certain features of our proposed system are not in themselves desirable and, moreover, would pose a threat to what they do.

The first such objection is that the primacy of the on-the-spot reporter should not be modified. It is maintained that at the core of all journalism there is only the impartial lone reporter, who covers an event or a situation and reports things as he sees them, generally to be printed or shown in unadulterated (though sometimes abbreviated) form.

The weakness of this tradition based on the self-centred event and the lone reporter is that in a situation where there are complex political, economic and social forces in play, the journalist tends to report only the most tangible manifestations of these forces. This generally means the most dramatic, and often the most violent, manifestations. Industrial disputes are reported at the picket-line, wars at the front, and so on.

But events elsewhere and policies formed, perhaps in secret, many thousands of miles away, may be as decisive as the local terrain. Consider the Angolan war. The principle applies to most of the stories which dominate news and current affairs programmes; disputes within British Leyland; the developing politics of the EEC; public spending cuts; and the debate about the degree of power which should be devolved to Scotland.

Such stories can seldom be tied down by one reporter employing the traditional techniques. Filmed reports from a hotel roof or from a dusty desert road, on occasions supplemented by an on-the-spot interview with protagonists, just do not tell the tale.

Far from wishing, as has been suggested, to see the network of reporters which has been built up over the years by news and current affairs programmes done away with, we want their numbers to be increased in order that more, not less, information may be available and so that, from a vigorous interplay between reporters, editors and specialists, more understanding news values will grow up to govern the collection and the presentation of this information.

The second objection in this category is that an integrated system would do away with some of the present-day current affairs programmes – particularly those making documentary films – which attempt to provide social, human or cultural perspectives about some major or minor news situation. Certainly, television – though not as part of the integrated system proposed – should continue to make such programmes.

This, however, should probably not be done to the present extent, nor at the expense, as at present, of what should be the main tasks of television journalism – news collection and analysis. Of course, many of the particular skills of the television journalists working at the moment on current affairs programmes would be needed in an integrated system – for example, those skills possessed by reporters with experience of the particular form of news collection known as investigative journalism.

The third objection to our proposals by defenders of present practice is that an integrated system of news and current affairs programmes would become monolothic and that this would lead to a set of constricting values determining 'the line' which journalists are to take when covering a particular story. Some critics go farther and fear that an integrated system of programmes could fall into the wrong hands and be used for sinister purposes.

To allay these fears it is necessary to recall the basic purposes of an integrated system. The bias in the present system against understanding the forces which most determine our lives arises not only because important stories are covered in such a way as to make understanding difficult or impossible, but also because, with little or no coordination between programmes, there is no guarantee that a particular story will be covered systemically or even at all.

In some weeks programmes seem to be about the concerns of the time and the stories of the week. In other weeks they bear little relationship to them. At the moment it is a hit-and-miss system. It should not be.

Under the integrated system in a given period of time, say a year, a running story like the management of the British economy would be covered on several occasions in different ways at different levels of inquiry. The monthly programmes, for example, would be concerned with comparatively fundamental issues like 'What do economists have to tell us about the root causes of inflation?' while one of the weekly programmes would from time to time ask shorter questions like 'What does Mr Healey's budget tell us about Mr Healey's current ideas on the root cause of inflation?'

In an integrated system programme teams involved in longer-term inquiries would be able to draw on the experience of the teams involved with the day-to-day reporting of these stories. Likewise, the day-to-day operation of news gathering and analysis would be informed by the greater insight acquired by programmes with longer term and wider perspectives.

Take the analogy of newspapers. The present system of television news and current affairs programmes is the equivalent of having our present daily newspapers split into their constituent parts with each page or section edited and published as a separate newspaper. It is as though one newspaper took the role of the front page, another of the feature page, another the sports page and so on.

Plainly, newspapers may benefit from a high degree of day-to-day editorial devolution; but this extreme would prevent the useful interplay which should, and occasionally does, take place between those involved in carrying out the different functions of a newspaper. Under an integrated system of programmes for television the natural and proper 'Unit of service' is the service provided by a channel (BBC 1, BBC 2 or ITV) and not by the individual programme. As with newspapers, of course, the more competing and independent services there are, the better it is.

Although the advantages of an integrated system of news and news analysis are apparent, the danger of a central 'line' – emanating either from the head of the news and current affairs organisation or from the common pool of journalists – is nonetheless real. This is why, while individual programmes should be assigned roles centrally, programme editors must have complete freedom to choose stories, programme teams and the in- or out-of-house journalistic expertise to be used.

Provided that this vital feature of an integrated system is preserved, programmes with a clearly defined mission to demonstrate the forces in play in the stories they cover would, in practice, be found to require less supervision by the broadcasting authorities and bureaucracies than the present random approach. In consequence, an integrated system should result in less rather than more danger of journalists working to a centrally controlled 'line'. Subtle controls would be more difficult to enforce; and less subtle controls, which are possible in any system, would be as obvious as they always are.

In sum, the new journalism would not devalue the reporter, go over the heads of the audience or thrust opinions improperly down viewers' throats. Much is at stake if we do not move towards this new journalism. If television does not provide a cool exposition of the complicated and deep-rooted problems which face our society and our world, if it does not provide a forum in which the nation can discuss the various proposed solutions to them, and if instead it simply provides a hot diet of the manifestations of these problems, then it may reasonably be said that television journalism has become an obstacle, rather than an aid, to understanding and so has become anti-social.

The Times, 2 September 1976

Electronic Publishing

It is a great privilege for me to be invited to deliver this important lecture at this year's Edinburgh Television Festival. I want to use the opportunity to offer a contribution to tackling a problem which is, I believe, increasingly disturbing in the current debate about the future of what we used loosely to call television and radio broadcasting and should now more compendiously call electronic publishing.

The problem, as I see it, can be best summed up as a lack of perspective – both chronological and moral – in our perception of what is going on and of what we believe is about to go on. To put it more baldly, we give the impression of being constantly startled, unnerved and nonplussed by each successive revelation of the technological changes which are expanding the capabilities of electronic publishing so rapidly. We do not know what is going to happen next and we are certainly not sure what to think about what is already happening.

It is not just that the mysteries and magic of the changing technology itself bemuse and amaze us. Nor is it just that existing institutions find themselves stupefied by the financial, commercial, managerial and creative questions thrown up by each new successive change in the technological possibilities. More profoundly, as citizens and as a society we too easily give the impression of people who feel that they are falling off the edge of a cosy, stable and familiar 'flat earth' into a fathomless abyss of unrecognisable and frightening novelties. We seem to know that the old world is fragmenting and will disappear; but we seem to have great difficulty in thinking coherently and confidently about the principles which should operate in the new world as it develops. Indeed, we seem to have only the most hazy and unconfident sense of what those principles might be, if indeed any exist, other than a desperate attempt to graft the habits of the past on to the quite different future, hoping against hope that as little as possible has really changed. To anyone who doubts this description I commend the transcript, if there is one, of Monday evening's opening session of this Festival with 'The Insiders'!

This broad caricature is – like all broad caricatures – substantially unfair, especially to numerous individuals who are grappling with great energy and imagination with the opportunities and problems created by the evolving technology of electronic broadcasting and who in the process display knowledge, understanding and optimism about the future. Nonetheless, a society has to be able to think together – though not necessarily to agree – about major trends affecting its own character and evolution. To do so there have to be some shared concepts and perceptions, the building blocks out of which intelligible and coherent debate can be constructed and from which the big decisions about the control and regulation of the activity in question can be made. There could scarcely be a better example of such an activity than the primary means of communication and publication within a society, especially when it is undergoing rapid change.

The modest contribution that I would like to make – and that is my purpose in this lecture tonight – is to suggest that there is a helpful perspective in which current developments can be seen and that, when they are so seen, much of the bafflement and mystification about where we are going in electronic publishing will disappear, while at the same time it will become very much clearer what the basic principles are which society should apply in debating the future legislative, regulatory and institutional framework within which the technological potentialities of electronic publishing should be permitted and encouraged to fulfil themselves over the next several decades. I by no means expect general, still less universal, agreement with the specifics of the analysis which I want to sketch out for you in this lecture. But I shall feel that the effort has been more than worthwhile if it at least contributes to the debate being conducted with a more confident sense of historical perspective and with a more rigorous recognition of the already available criteria for choosing the principles which society should apply in setting and modifying the rules of the game for electronic publishing from here on.

Let me start by inviting you to stand on its head the conventional perception that, in the universe of electronic publishing, it is the world in which we have been living which is 'normal' and the world into which we are now beginning to move which is strange or peculiar. Instead I ask you to consider the hypothesis that, on the contrary, it is the world in which we have been living, for nearly a century now, which is artificial and special and that it is the world into which we are moving which will be much more properly regarded as normal and natural. Let me explain what I mean.

Why do human societies have governments at all and why do they feel, to the extent that they do, the need for them? Whatever may be the factual historical derivation of the institution of government, the broad justification that most of us feel for the existence of governments at all is and only is that, at least in principle, they enable the individuals who comprise a society to live lives which are more satisfactory to them as individuals (though in most cases social individuals) than they would if there were no governments. We tolerate governments and we justify or condemn their actions by this broad criterion, although there is, of course, almost limitless scope for dispute whether any particular act, policy or programme does or does not satisfy the criterion. The broad kinds of activity which have been traditionally accepted as fulfilling the criteria are very well known: political relations with the outside world; defence of the realm; the making and enforcement of such laws and regulations as may be necessary and justified by the criterion mentioned; the exploitation of those 'public goods' and the correction of those 'external dis-economies' which, as is well known, even the idealised workings of the market economy cannot accomplish; the monitoring and modification of the distribution of wealth and income in ways which affect the overall character of the society; and in several other ways. The presumption, however, in societies which adhere to this libertarian and utilitarian conception of government is that government action and involvement is not justified unless it can be positively shown to satisfy the condition that, however measured, the sum benefit to individuals will exceed the cost. The notion that a government action could be justified because of some independent right or interest of government itself, conceived as something above and beyond the sum of the individuals in whose name it governs, is strongly rejected, in contrast with other political philosophies which do see government as the embodiment of some other or higher force or purpose than simply the welfare, however broadly interpreted, of the individuals who comprise the society.

A classic example of an activity which is normally presumed not to require government intervention is communication. Second only, perhaps, to the right of individuals to think privately what thoughts they wish comes the right of individuals to communicate those thoughts with one another. The historic battles to establish this right after the invention of the printing press and the perception of the power and potentialities of what by the standards of those days may be called mass communication was, to be sure, long and bitter. But, for those who adhere to the libertarian and utilitarian tradition, it is not seen as a battle between two arguable propositions or legitimate interests, but rather as a simple struggle between a sound and fundamental ideal on the one hand and dark forces motivated by interest (or occasionally mistaken bigotry) on the other. We now regard it as axiomatic that mass communication of the printed word should be a free activity which does not require any general framework of government regulation or sponsorship, although according to our varying different individual points of view we may be more or less inclined to accept certain general marginal constraints on this freedom for such reasons as sedition, blasphemy, libel, race relations and national security.

When communication and in due course mass communication by the new technology of wireless telegraphy became possible, the natural presumption of a liberal utilitarian society must surely have been that this raised no new question of principle so far as the legitimate role of government in the regulation of mass communiucation was concerned. What in fact brought government and the law-makers into the picture was not and should not have been any general perception that the character of mass communication by wireless telegraphy was so fundamentally different from mass communication by the printed word that it required a form of regulation not thought necessary or appropriate for the printed word, but instead was a simple fact of broadcasting technology. Since two signals could not be broadcast on the same wavelength in the same area at the same time without interfering with one another, some kind of wavelength policing was needed; and, therefore, some act of government was felt to be justified in the interests of the private individuals who comprise society for exactly the same reason that we feel government is needed and justified in imposing a 'keep left' or 'keep right' rule for driving on the public highways.

The nineteenth century Wireless Telegraphy Acts, culminating in the 1905 Act, had this essential purpose and justification; and it has essentially been on this very narrow and specific foundation that the whole inverted pyramid of government and parliamentary regulation of broadcasting has since been built. There was and to some extent still is an inescapable need for someone to decide who should – and therefore who should not – broadcast on any given wavelength at any given time in any given area. In the absence of the theoretically possible alternatives of a lottery or an auction, the only available authority to make this decision was, in one form or another, the government.

But of course, having once got into the act on this genuine but narrow

222

technical pretext, it will surprise no one that even in a pluralistic country governments and Parliament have moved forward from this bridgehead to what is, by the standards of print communication, a massive control and regulation of the dominant forms of electronic publishing. I am not, of course, here talking about the kind of editorial control and crudely propagandist exploitation of radio and television which we associate with Eastern European and other totalitarian societies. Nor am I speaking of the kind of government regulation which is being hotly debated in the framework of UNESCO between the spokesmen of the Western 'free' societies and other societies who feel that governments are entitled to much more positive editorial control of radio and television, to say nothing of newspapers as well.

What I have in mind is simply the contrast between the basic freedom to publish, to create a new publication, to contain in it any material whatsoever within the general laws of blasphemy, libel, national security, race relations etc., the contrast between all of that, whether in newspapers, magazines, books or any other form of printed publication, and the broadcasting framework as it has evolved through the granting of successive charters to the BBC, the creation of the Independent Television Authority and its development into the Independent Broadcasting Authority with responsibilities for commercial radio as well as television. I leave on one side the draconian regulatory powers and monopoly position of the Post Office, now British Telecom, in relation to almost all other forms of private use of the airwaves and other telecommunication facilities for communication and even limited publication. It is quite simply impossible, as things stand, for any individual or private institution to communicate with his fellow citizens by way of broadcast radio or television unless he has either been appointed by a chartered or statutory body to do so or invited by someone else who has been so appointed. Moreover, any such communication has to conform, not merely to the broad general law affecting such matters as blasphemy, libel, national security and race relations, but also has to conform to a most elaborate series of formal and informal codes affecting the content, balance, timing etc, of such publications.

My purpose at this point is not to evaluate or criticise these arrangements. I am aware that many people think they are justified and that there are some who even think that they still permit too much freedom to those who are allowed access to the airwaves. My aim here is simply to bring out the profound difference between the framework of law, regulation and government as it applies to print publications and as it applies to electronic publishing, at least insofar as electronic publishing takes the form of broadcast material.

Against this background, let us now begin to look at what current technological developments are doing to the potentialities of electronic broadcasting and thereby to our existing apparatus of concepts for controlling and regulating it. So far, we have had a world in which for most practical purposes electronic publishing was authorised broadcasting, both radio and television, in the strict sense of broadcast transmissions by authorised bodies across the airwaves to privately owned receivers. To this in recent years and increasingly have begun to be added a whole catalogue of actual and potential devices for enabling the public to enjoy the same or similar services by other means. It began with purely 'pirate' transmissions, which involved no technological innovation at all, but simply exploited jurisdictional or enforcement loop-holes in the existing system of regulation. These were variously dealt with by ignoring them on *de minimis* grounds, as in the case of Radio Luxembourg, or by gradual suppression by methods which were at least as indirect as the pirates' own circumvention of existing regulations, as in the case of Radio Caroline and its emulators.

The advent of audio tapes was treated as if it were an extension of the gramophone record market rather than as violating the broadcasters' domain and therefore as not coming within the purview of the broadcast regulators.

When cable television, under its original guise as 'pay television', first entered the debate a decade or so ago, nobody doubted that this belonged squarely in the regulated area of electronic publishing or, indeed, that it was entirely a matter for government decision whether or not the practice of such a black art should be permitted at all. Fortunately for the upholders of the *ancien régime* of regulated electronic publishing such experiments as were permitted were never sufficiently successful to force a major social decision on whether or how pay television should be controlled. Moreover, even pay television continued to present a solid, though narrow, pretext for official involvement in that the necessary cables to make it possible could not legally or practically be laid without the consent and probably the assistance of public authority.

But now we are well and truly in sight of a world in which significant parts of electronic publishing can both legally and practically take place

without coming within the existing purview of the broadcasting regulators and, indeed, subject to one major once-and-for-all decision without
the acquiescence of public authority in any of its other guises, whether as
the guardian of wavelengths, way-leaves, the public purse or any other
existing basis of gevernmental control. Video – both in its tape and disc
manifestations – is already the most highly developed form of this new
wave. Cable, satellites (especially Direct Broadcast Satellite services),
teletext and other innovations are all contributing to what, from the
cosy perspective of the 'closed circle' of the 'authorised' broadcasters, is
regarded as the 'fragmentation' of the audience. Even moderate developments such as the Fourth Channel, the Welsh Fourth Channel and
breakfast television, which involve no technological innovation whatever and which are twenty-four carat card-carrying creations of the
traditional regulated system, are seen in some circles as threatening
because they let newcomers, new ideas or new languages into the
business or even, more simply, because they might cause the existing
stock of jam to be spread yet more thinly. I will not dwell on the wetness,
let alone the simple-minded fallaciousness, of that kind of reflex
protectionism.

This picture of an existing world of electronic publishing, dominated
by authorised broadcasting, being gradually eroded and fragmented by
technological changes which pare away cumulatively significant marginal slices of the traditional broadcaster's market – and predictably
stimulate the historically familiar catalogue of demands for extended
regulation, if indeed not prohibition, on every pretext of public interest
known to man save the true one of resistance to competition – allied to
the usual desire of every politician, busybody and self-appointed cultural
and moral nanny to lay down what other people may and may not
communicate to one another, this picture itself grossly underestimates
the enormity of the change which is coming about. Quite simply, we are
within less than two decades technologically of a world in which there
will be no technical pretext for a government-appointed policeman to
allocate the airwaves at all; and therefore, in turn, there will be no
technically based grounds for government or legislative interference in
electronic publishing, except insofar as the general laws of blasphemy,
libel etc, which apply to print publishing are applied also to electronic
publishing.

To put it technically, 'spectrum scarcity' is going to disappear. In
simple terms this means there will be able, in effect, to be as many
channels as there are viewers. At that moment all the acrimonious and

difficult debate about how many channels there should be, who should control them and have access to them and what should be allowed to be shown on them – to say nothing of which and how many traditional and new pressure groups are needed to squabble over these issues – all this can disappear. But it will only disappear if we all work, indeed fight, extremely hard to ensure that, once the technical pretext for policing electronic publishing has gone, the whole inverted pyramid of regulation and control, going way beyond the mere prevention of mutually jamming transmissions, is in fact dismantled. It will be an extremely hard fight because, the habit of regulation and control once formed and the vested interests which benefit from it once established, the regulators and beneficiaries are extremely reluctant to give up their role and their territory; and the politicians and legislators will be extremely reluctant to abdicate power and influence in a field which they know is important and which they are accustomed to enjoying. Let me add in passing that the beneficiaries of a regulated world are not by any means confined to the regulators themselves or to those whose commercial interests are thereby directly protected. All the other armies of lobbies and special interest groups, whether they represent shareholders, managers, creators, various echelons of employees or countless special geographic-al and other categories of consumers, all in varying degrees live off a world in which regulation occurs and in which it is thereby possible – whether by lobbying, negotiating, persuading or even attending solemn conferences – to seek to determine the way in which the regulations are framed and enforced. But take away the honey-pot and the bees will disperse. There are only pressure groups if there are pressure points. Were we not being told on this very Monday evening that yet another new body was needed in order that the voice of the broadcasters themselves should be more loudly heard in the privileged arena of centralised regulation and control, a club to which every interest group belongs, but in which not a single ordinary producer or ordinary viewer is to be found? Also Jeremy Isaacs, whom I greatly revere and who said many wise things, remarked *en passant*, 'Of course, we don't want unregulated Babel here.' But I would say to him that the term 'Babel' can much more properly be applied to the squabbling of the politicians and the special interest groups over the control of the regulated system of authorised broadcasting than it can to free communication, whether electronic or not, between private authors and private consumers.

Now let me try to sketch how this wondrous emancipation can occur, if not today, at least the day after tomorrow in terms of the eras of electronic publishing; and I make only a small apology here for drawing on some evidence I gave nearly five years ago to the Annan Committee, evidence which must rank as one of the most purely solipsistic experiences in the history of the written word. Rather before the end of the century, subject only to a very large initial capital outlay which could only be borne by society as a whole in the first instance, it will be possible by fibre-optic technology to create a grid connecting every household in the country, whereby the nation's viewers can simultaneously watch as many different programmes as the nation's readers can read different books, magazines, newspapers etc. The only constraints, technically speaking, will be the obvious ones that no one television set can simultaneously display more than one programme and that it may be necessary to watch any given programme at a stated number of minutes past the hour. There will doubtless also continue to be somewhat fewer sets than people, though by the year 2000 we may even have the wall-size screen, for multiple simultaneous images, in general use, with the viewers simply choosing which source he wants.

In other words a television set (or radio) will be like a telephone in that the user selects for himself the connection he wants; and it will be quite immaterial what connections other users wish to make for themselves. In contemporary parlance, the number of channels will become, if not infinite, at least indefinitely large – certainly as large as the number of receivers.

Imagine each set equipped with a telephone dial on which the code number of the desired programme or connection can be dialled. Imagine also the equivalent of a telephone meter monitoring receptions on each set, linked to the code number of the item received. Imagine finally a central 'black box' maintained by British Telecom into which an indefinitely large number of programmes can be fed (either by lodging a tape or by direct feed for live transmissions).

The rest of the conditions for a free electronic publishing market, with consumer choice and freedom of access, falls quickly into place. No general laws are required other than those which already govern publishing (libel, copyright, obscenity, common law, etc.), though there is nothing in the system to prevent Parliament making special laws for electronic publishing; and some special laws may be needed to deal with copyright in a world of satellite transmissions and cassette copying. The only necessary function of the State is to lay a duty on British Telecom to provide and operate the technology of the system, to accept all programmes which conform to the law, to collect charges from the viewing public and, after deducting its own costs and any other approved taxes or charges, to pass what remains over to the publisher of each item. This, indeed, is the framework already adopted for the Viewdata system.

Large and small wholesale publishers will be free to establish themselves. Many of them might well be best organised as workers' cooperatives rather than as limited liability companies. They, the publishers, will arrange and finance the preparation of the programmes, set the charges for them, advertise their availability and their code numbers and reward the authors and participants under freely negotiated contracts. Individuals who wish to make their own programmes will be free to do so though, as with books, they will either have to find a publisher or bear the costs and risks of publishing themselves.

There is nothing in this system to prevent the State continuing to subsidise any particular categories of electronic publishing which are considered virtuous or in the public interest, even to the extent of ensuring that the equivalent of one or more whole channels of regular transmissions are available to the public without direct charge.

Nor is there anything to prevent any other patron or sponsor from subsidising meritorious, or indeed meritless, productions. The BBC and the independent broadcast companies would presumably continue as major publishers on the new scene. But the IBA would disappear; and the BBC would cease to be a broadcasting authority with (self-) regulatory powers and duties, insofar as Broadcasting House can at present be said to exercise over the rest of the BBC analogous supervision to that which the IBA exercises over the ITV and ILR programme companies. As large independent producers the BBC and ITV programme companies would doubtless continue to set their own policies and standards; but these need not reflect any general state policy for broadcasting.

The news and party political broadcasts could be catered for either under the general provisions above or by special provision. On the face of it there is no reason why the news should not justify itself commercially; but, if it is felt that it needs to be subsidised, this could be done by raising through the British Telecom charging mechanism a small levy on all other transmissions, which would be earmarked to finance news services.

Party political broadcasts should presumably be financed by the parties (one would suppose at a loss), though Parliament could require British Telecom to make them available free to the viewer and to collect the cost direct from monies voted by Parliament.

The treatment of advertising raises no insuperable problem. Either Parliament could disallow advertisement altogether. Or it could require British Telecom to accept programme packages which included advertising material in natural breaks, in which case the charge to the viewer would be lower – or nil. It would then be up to individual publishers to decide whether or not they wished to include advertising material at intervals during their programmes. The viewers would be free to decide whether they thought this interruption worth the saving in charges or not.

This extremely compressed sketch of a future market in electronic publishing is designed only to show that there is nothing God-given or immutable about the familiar duopolistic regime, a conclusion which can also be reached from other premises. At present, cumbrous giants battle for franchises of the air; and, between their occasional encounters, they are themselves besieged by multiple special interests trying to steer programme time and programme content more to their particular way of thinking. This process in no way guarantees, or even necessarily tends towards, the maximum satisfaction of viewers' preferences. Indeed, that is not even the objective of the present institutions.

The addition of an extra channel, or even two or ten, would not change this essential pattern. Indeed, so long as electronic publishing is confined to a limited number of channels, there is a plausible argument that consumer choice is maximised by giving one or two authorities the duty to provide choice rather than by forcing several rival organisations to vie with each other for a limited mass audience.

The argument so far has sought to show that, on certain assumptions about the development of telecommunications technology, a radically different organisation of broadcasting, seen as electronic publishing and modelled partly on print publishing, would be possible. But technical feasibility does not entail financial feasibility, still less desirability, (despite the widespread belief to the contrary).

There are in fact two distinct financial questions about the scheme of electronic publishing sketched here:

(a) Would the huge investment in the necessary telecommunications grid and in the change-over of the nation's receivers to the new system be justified after allowing for the earnings of the other non-publishing chargeable services which could be carried on such an electronic network?

(b) Would the system of meter charging for viewing, augmented by specific subsidies on merit and, if allowed, by advertising receipts, generate the revenue necessary to support the required level of broadcasting?

The first question is legitimate and important. The answer to it depends on many variables, whose values are certainly not known and some of whose values are probably extremely difficult to assess. Fortunately, society does not have to give a precise answer now, since final decisions will not be needed for a decade or so. But it is important to form a view about whether such an investment is likely to be within the realm of the possible or whether it is pure science, or rather financial, fiction.

This will partly depend, of course, on the cost of the investment. British Telecom are able to give sketch estimates of this, at least in terms of orders of magnitude. It will also depend on how many other users there will be, in addition to what we now think of as television services, for the new telecommunications infrastructure. The more there are and the greater the prospective yield from such other users, the smaller will need to be the specific return from sales of grid capacity to the broadcast public.

Much may also depend on the rate of society's time preference used in discounting the future flow of benefits from the new facility. The arguments will be familiar to economists.

The question about the adequacy of the revenue to be generated is only meaningful if it is supposed that there can be a difference between what the viewing public, together with public and private patrons and sponsors, as well as advertisers (if they are allowed), are willing to pay for broadcast material and the right quantity of broadcasting. It is possible to construct senses in which there could be such a conceptual difference; but it is not a distinction which is normally held to be generally meaningful in the provision of marketable services to the public, except in areas like national health or perhaps housing where some sense and measurements can be attached to the notion of the public's 'needs' as distinct from what the public will pay for (though some economists dispute even this).

So, the short answer to the objection that the public would not want to pay for the amount of broadcast material which vested interests or wise men think should be provided is the same as the answer to any other entrepreneur who complains that the market will not bear as much as he would like it to: hard luck!

Indeed, the argument can be pressed a little further. One of the great merits of the system adumbrated here for financing broadcasting, as against finance which depends heavily either on the Government's taxing power or on advertising alone, is that it generates invaluable information about the effective demand for broadcast material and therefore about the scale of resources which it is right to invest and to use in supplying the material. Indeed, where this information is not generated, it is common for public authorities either to look abroad to see what proportion of their national incomes other countries spend on comparable facilities, where market choice does operate, or to corral the growth of expenditure into conformity with the average growth rate of the national economy as a whole (cf. the present plight of the National Health Service). Now that GNP growth is nil or negative this stifles what should be, by public preference, expanding services such as health and communication.

Inevitably these proxies for direct evidence of demand lead either to more or to less resources being devoted to the service in question than the public wants; and there is no way of knowing whether it is too much or too little. One may guess, partly from overseas data, that in the areas of national health and broadcasting what we now get is probably less than the public would choose to spend and that in the areas of hard technology, such as futuristic aircraft, it is probably more. It would be better to know than to have to guess.

This then leaves the question whether there are any good non-technological-cum-financial reasons for going on as at present, in the sense of keeping electronic publishing under the degree of statutory supervision which the BBC charter and the Broadcasting Act have laid down even after the historical 'rule-of-the-road' reasons for this involvement of the State have become technically obsolete. People will answer this question according to their different political and social philosophies.

In the circumstances envisaged here for the end of the century there need be literally no limit to what can be published electronically, other than the general law and what the public (and others) will pay for. In those circumstances the only role of supervision is to prevent the publication of lawful material which the public would choose and pay for. Otherwise, supervision is wholly passive and merely reproduces what would happen under open publishing. To believe that such prevention of publication would be desirable it would appear to be necessary to believe one or more of the following propositions:

(a) that a man or woman does not always know what is best for him or her to receive; that someone else does know best (or at least knows better); that Parliament can embody that somebody else's knowledge in some general law or, more likely, appoint him or her and their like to control what is available to the public; that Parliament will, in fact, normally appoint the right people and that the fact that Parliament thinks this someone else knows best gives Parliament and the someone else the right to deny the public access to the forbidden material – in other words, as Jeremy Isaacs put it so vividly 'We don't want unregulated Babel here.'

(b) That free electronic publishing would in practice lead to a narrowing of choice, even in the new conditions described, as compared with what would happen under a benevolent supervision; that the supervision would in practice tend to be benevolent and that by preventing the publication of too many similar programmes of little 'worth' resources can be kept free (or, rather, not too expensive) for more worthwhile or varied productions. Or

(c) that economic activities, of which broadcasting is certainly one in the sense that it uses scarce resources including labour to purvey goods or services to the public, exist primarily or exclusively for the benefit of those who work in them rather than for those who use their output and that workers are likely to have a better time of things working for a benevolent (perhaps malleable) supervisory authority, backed by the State and its taxing power, than they would have supplying a competitive market in which the consumer was sovereign and some big publishers, whether public or private, came to play a large part.

It will be evident that none of these propositions appeal much to me. Few, in fact, would be found today to defend the first proposition as it stands. But there are many who, without perhaps admitting it even to themselves, adopt positions which entail this proposition; and it is better to see it nakedly for what it is, namely a complete rejection of the philosophy of the primacy of the individual and of his liberty on which most people would claim that our society is and ought to be founded.

The second proposition is rather more plausible at first sight. But this is only because the alternative system of electronic publishing suggested here is being construed as though it were still oligopolistic publishing, but writ a little larger. It will be asked how in practice can an indefinitely large number of electronic publishers, to say nothing of countless go-it-alone authors, afford the hugely expensive overheads, such as cameras, studios, editing facilities and so forth, which television production requires. Only the few could do it; and competition among the few leads to homogenised products and neglible choice. Or it leads to domination by big corporations. So the argument runs.

This is mistaken. It will not be necessary for any but the biggest publishers to have their studios, etc., any more than every print publisher and author has to own his own press. It will pay entrepreneurs (as indeed it already does) to provide studio facilities and to hire them out to all comers. Small publishers and go-it-alone authors will rent what they need when they need it. Even that may be more expensive than printing and publishing a limited edition of one's own book; but then no one has a God-given right to use whatever resources he wants to indulge personal fantasies. Either one pays for those resources oneself or one persuades a patron to do so or one persuades a financier to do so in the expectation of a return.

The argument for producer sovereignty, other than in a market environment which makes consumers sovereign, lacks any intelligible philosophical basis for its major premise – outside of certain religious orders which genuinely exist for the sake exclusively of fulfilment in work (i.e. prayer, contemplation, and so forth) and which literally produce nothing beyond their own meals, clothes and shelter that can be of material benefit to anyone (except maybe to God). For the rest the notion seems to be confusion. The exercise of producer power may well be in the selfish interest of individual groups considering themselves as workers in a world in which anonymous millions supply the things they themselves wish to consume; but it degenerates into nonsense if generalised into an economic basis of society.

In practice in the broadcasting industry the argument, whether deployed by executives, 'creative' staff or manual workers, is no different from the special pleading of all manner of groups – from farmers to furnacemen and from opera singers to obsolete printers – to be preserved at the expense of the rest of society in their customary way of life irrespective of whether it any longer serves a useful purpose. Society may judge in some cases that it wishes to make such provision either out of compassion or from other reasons.

But unless such arrangements are by nature exceptions to some more utilitarian general rule, the logical conclusion is the monastic life for all. The notion, therefore, that the unconstrained use of electronic pub-

233

lishing resources should be the sovereign right of creators and producers thus depends either on making a general rule of producer sovereignty or on a special case for adding broadcasting to the list of exceptions to the rule of consumer sovereignty. The general rule leads quickly to absurdity; and it seems hard to think of a less appropriate or deserving exception to the more practical rule of consumer sovereignty in economic affairs. Note also, however, that – given consumer sovereignty in a free electronic publishing market – there is no reason at all why many or even all of the producing units should not be workers' cooperatives, something which I personally strongly favour as a solution to the much broader economic problems of inflation, unemployment etc.

It follows then that, in a world in which central supervision is not an inevitable by-product of some broadcasting rule-of-the-road, there will be no compelling need for continued monolithic (or indeed duo-, or oligo-lithic) broadcasting franchises.

Once this is accepted, it can be seen that most of the problems which preoccupy public debate about the future of broadcasting disappear, at least if the time-scale is extended far enough into the future to comprehend the kind of developments envisaged here. For, most of those problems are problems about allocating scarce publishing opportunities between competing interest groups, whether established institutions, financial vested interests, worker vested interests, evangelical producers, Scotsmen, Welshmen, Irishmen, divines, educationalists, ethnic minorities or any other form of man-in-his-organisations as against man-in-his-home-wanting-to-sit-in-his-armchair-and-watch-the-telly.

Once there is no allocation to be made, there will be no lobbies and so no headaches to be suffered in arbitrating between them. Only consider – the recent strange episodes surrounding the Monopolies Commission gives us a foretaste of what the problems would be if government had to renew, or not renew, *The Times*'s charter, or to allocate the tabloid franchise between IPC and Mr Rupert Murdoch, or if areas of the country had to be exclusively shared out to Macmillan, Cape and Penguin. It is only by looking at it in this way that the liberating effects of escaping altogether from the need to allocate scarce electronic publishing opportunities can be fully appreciated.

At the same time, of course, the power in the hands of the great allocator is liquidated; and Government, as well as the vested interests and busybodies who believe they can manipulate Government, will resist this. But this is scarcely an argument why society should bless such an unnecessary exercise of power with spurious respectability.

In conclusion, let me re-emphasis the obvious fact that this lecture is quite explicitly and deliberately futuristic. It is, as its title states, about the day after tomorrow. It has little or nothing to say about the preoccupations of broadcasters, viewers and regulators today, except in the very broad sense that it would lead those who agreed with the argument of the lecture to welcome the embryonic development over which Jeremy Isaacs is so ably presiding on Channel 4 and to wish him the very best of luck in his efforts. No one, therefore, should be disposed to ask with feigned astonishment how it is that the chairman of a company holding a franchise under the existing system is to be found advocating the eventual liquidation of that system. I have said nothing to suggest that the British system is defective or markedly less satisfactory than available alternatives under the present conditions. But there is, I hope, enough of the existentialist in all of us to permit a man to be both company chairman and to think for himself as a citizen. There is no inconsistency, outside of a world of cardboard caricature functionaries, in operating within the constraints of one system which may be appropriate to one set of circumstances and, at the same time, trying to think about how, in new and different circumstances, a new and different system might serve society even better.

I certainly believe that we shall think more confidently and more coherently about the more immediate and obvious signs of the fragmentation of the system of authorised electronic publishing – video, cable, direct broadcast satellite services, etc. – if we :

(a) realise that these are only the modest precursors of a much more fundamental transformation of the technological base of electronic broadcasting; and

(b) recognise that, as that transformation fulfils itself over the next two decades or so, the world which we will be entering will, in fact, be a much less artificial one in which well known principles of consumer and producer freedom articulated through the proper operation of the price mechanism can and should be invoked to solve problems which have seemed so recalcitrant in the world of authorised electronic publishing and which seem so baffling to those who regard the new world as merely an extension of the old world with complications.

Finally, however, those who care passionately for freedom in communication and publishing, whether electronic, print or simply oral, need now to gird themselves for a prolonged struggle against old habits and vested interests in order to ensure that the new freedoms, which the new technology will make technically possible, are in fact translated into real freedoms for both producers and consumers under law. The belief that electronic publishing, especially by broadcast television, has mystical, hypnotic and unique powers is deeply entrenched in the political mind; and the desire to control and influence it will not be shed like an old skin simply because the technical need for a spectrum rule of the road and, therefore, for a spectrum policeman, has disappeared. The battles that were fought by the great seventeenth-, eighteenth- and nineteenth-century heroes of free speech and free publication will have to be fought all over again. I would foresee – and I hope – that this theme will be a recurrent preoccupation of successive Edinburgh International Television Festivals; and I hope that, by using this opportunity to air the question, I have not only done my modest best to pay tribute to the memory and the inspiring example of James MacTaggart, but have also done something to prompt that debate and to offer some concepts and principles which can give it shape and standards.

The MacTaggart Lecture, Edinburgh International Television Festival, 1981

What is News?

Anyone trained in what was called 'philosophy' at Oxford in the late 1950s is doomed to start a discussion of the question, 'What is News?' with an examination of the question itself. This leads inevitably and directly to the assumption that it is a semantic question, that is a question about the meaning of the phrase 'the news' rather than a substantive, whether empirical or metaphysical, inquiry into what the news is.

At the very least such an investigator will see the question as posing a need for analysis of a concept rather than for examination of some real or palpable object or entity out there in the external world requiring to be discovered or described in the way in which one might seek to discover or describe an answer to such questions as, 'Who are the Poles?' or 'What is the SDP?'.

This is just as well. For, the answer to the substantive question, 'What the news is' would be characteristically ephemeral; and we may presume that the Royal Society of Arts did not organise this lecture, still less entrap me nearly a year ago into giving it, merely in order to be given a preview of tomorrow morning's headlines or, indeed, of this evening's radio and television bulletins.

So, we proceed boldly and without apology to interpret the question, 'What is news? as a question about the meaning of the word 'news' and about the conceptual issues connected therewith and arising therefrom.

A first instinctive stab at a definition of 'the news' might be 'whatever is new' or, more laboriously, 'any newly occurred event'. A brief examination shows that on several counts this definition will not do. In passing I should, perhaps, stipulate that by 'do', when speaking of an adequate definition, I mean quite simply that the definition should successfully accord with the way in which the phrase is commonly used. If a proposed definition would include a meaning that was commonly not intended or exclude a meaning that was commonly intended, then, according to the method adopted here, the definition would be defective.

The definition 'whatever is new' both includes too much and excludes too much. It includes too much because it would embrace all manner of commonplace and predictable events which no one in their right mind – certainly no one in gainful journalistic employment – would include in 'the news'.

The fact that a camellia bloomed in my garden this morning, though not predictable, is too trivial an occurrence to be included in the news (although note in passing that importance is relative to the intended audience for the news, since, if it were my practice to publish a daily news-sheet to my own household, then this floral occurrence might assume quite adequate significance to be included therein). The fact that the sun rose this morning, albeit invisibly behind a bank of clouds, is, though obviously important, too predictable to be included in any news bulletin; and that finding is not disturbed by the fact that the precise timing of this occurrence may be a useful piece of information and worthy of inclusion in almanacs and daily extracts therefrom in newspapers.

So, we conclude that for an event to rate as news it must not be trivial (at least in relation to the interests of the intended audience) and it must not be too certainly predictable. The degree of predictability requires somewhat closer definition. Clearly, if a general election is known to be occurring on a particular Thursday and if the opinion polls and all other relevant predictive signs show in advance that a particular party is likely to win overwhelmingly, it is still 'news' when the official results of that election are declared. This appears to arise because of a combination of the presumed high importance of the event and because of the presumed possibility that the official results still could disprove the predictions however strongly based.

But the conclusion remains that an event which is predictable with absolute certainty (or at least the degree of certainty that attaches to the diurnal rising and setting of the sun) or an event which is wholly trivial will not rate as news.

One may observe, however, in addition that there is some degree of trade-off between triviality and predictability. A very surprising though comparatively trivial event, like a very important though widely ex-pected event, may well rate as news, along perhaps with a moderately important and moderately unexpected event.

It is also necessary to qualify the criterion of 'importance'. A very unimportant event, indeed a wholly trivial one, might still be news not only, as has already been observed, if it were sufficiently surprising, but also if it had other qualities which won our attention or excited our interest.

It was, doubtless, both trivial and in some degree predictable that when the Emperor of Japan visited Disneyland – or was it Disney World? – he should have shaken hands with Mickey Mouse. But I would not be disposed to quarrel with the news judgement of the television news editor who decided to include that event in his nightly news bulletin, although one might presume that in that case the pictorial representation of the event was more than usually important and one might have had less sympathy with a newspaper editor who decided to feature, presumably on the last page, a written report of the encounter. Even in that case one might feel that the newspaper editor was justified if his reporter had a sufficient gift of verbal artistry to match the demands of the occasion.

This qualification need not give rise to any general difficulty in defining 'news'. It reflects no more than the fact that the criterion of importance is not strictly synonymous with audience interest, where interest is taken to include all symptoms of positive audience reaction. Amusement, amazement, fascination, utility, alarm, reassurance, indeed almost any marked *change* in mental state, whether intellectual or emotional, may be presumed to be evidence of interest.

It does not, of course, follow that any item on television or radio or in newsprint that excites such reactions deserves to be rated as 'news', since pure entertainment and diversion achieve those effects by performances which are specifically manufactured with that end in view. To be 'news' there must, for starters, be an event; and that event must genuinely be independent of the processes of observing it and must, therefore, be autonomous, spontaneous and 'real'. Thus, when we speak of a 'media event' – that is an event specifically manufactured by or for the convenience of television, radio and newspapers or of third parties consciously seeking to contrive public attention to themselves or their clients – we quite specifically mean to deny that 'event' the proper status of news and to consign it to the limbo of bogus 'non-events'.

So, our definition so far requires first that to be news an event must *be* an event – and a spontaneous event at that, independent of the contrivances of the news media themselves and of publicists. Secondly, that it must be sufficiently uncertain – in relation to its inherent importance – not to have been fully taken for granted. Thirdly, that it must be – in relation to its predictability – sufficiently important or otherwise interesting to be expected to generate some discernible

239

emotional or intellectual change in the intended audience. The reaction, 'So what?', we normally take as evidence that an event is or was not 'news-worthy'.

But this definition, while excluding some of the events which need to be excluded from the over-catholic definition of 'news' as 'whatever is new', also excludes too much. It excludes, for example, whatever has not newly occurred. Yet, the discovery, if it were newly made, that three thousand years ago the sun on one occasion did not rise – or stood still in the heavens – would indeed be news, just as surely as the fact that the sun obediently rose this morning is not news.

Therefore, we must amend the definition previously reached – namely, in its short form, that 'news' is 'any new event which is genuine, not taken for granted and interesting' – to 'any new discovery or revelation of an event which is genuine, not taken for granted and interesting'. This definition, it seems to me, does, with only trivial borderline qualifications, broadly comprehend everything which would normally be classified as 'news' and exclude everything which would not be so classified.

It is, however, exceedingly important to note that this definition is in part and necessarily subjective. For an element in the necessary and sufficient conditions for an event to be classified as 'news' is its expected impact on the emotional and intellectual state of the intended recipients of the news.

It is true, strictly, that this expected effect on the intended recipients is, from the point of view of the editor and reporter, an objective fact, in the sense that it is a fact, or an expected fact, about the world beyond or outside or independent of their own state of mind in perceiving that world, a real external world which includes the state of mind of other people. And, let me add in haste for the benefit of any of those present who were reluctant or unfulfilled philosophy students in their youth, I have resolved sternly to resist the temptation to make this an excuse for a digression into the fascinating epistemological problem of 'other minds'!

Nonetheless, the dependence of the definition on the expected effect on the mental state of the intended recipients of the news undoubtedly introduces an element which is different in kind, whether or not it strictly justifies the description 'subjective', from traditional purist definitions of 'the news'. These pretend, or at least aspire, to make the definition wholly dependent on the character, including their factual certainty, of the events in question.

The definition proposed here recognises, legitimises and explains the basis for the process of journalistic selection. The necessity for such selection is widely recognised, but only as a regrettable necessity born of limitations of space. It is also generally deplored as a 'subjective' adulteration of the true 'objective' purity of the news.

The truth, surely, is that it is not simply lack of space, ideological perspective or other journalistic prejudice which excludes the flowering of my camellias or the rising of the sun from today's news. Even if the available space were infinite and even if every conceivable ideological perspective and journalistic prejudice were catered for throughout a limitlessly pluralistic spectrum of news media, no journalist or news consumer is going to regard those events as 'news'.

Moreover, the inclusion in the definition of necessary and sufficient conditions which relate to the expected mental state or mental change of the intended recipients of the news does not by any means create a licence for the news editor or the news reporter to be arbitrary or 'subjective' in his efforts to identify and select the news.

From his or her perspective the expected effect on the mental state of others is just as 'objective' a matter as the event itself or its discovery, although it may, of course, be more difficult to ascertain, at least with any degree of certainty, at the time at which his or her news judgement has to be exercised. But the difficulty of ascertaining a fact, including a future fact, has nothing whatever to do – despite widespread confused thought to the contrary – with the 'subjectivity' or 'objectivity' of that event or of reports of it.

The task of the editor and the reporter, in so far as it relates to the expected interest of his or her audience or readers, is to make the most conscientious effort he or she can to estimate that reaction. There is a perfectly clear and straightforward 'objectivity' test of whether that judgement is good or not, namely whether or not the intended readers or audience do in fact find the news as identified and selected to be interesting or not, although, as in the case of the verification of any future event, such verification can only take place after the lapse of the necessary time.

In the great majority of cases there is already plenty of available evidence on which to base a sound judgement of likely reader and audience interest. At the same time, our definition properly leaves scope for complaint, not merely that some particular news judgements were wrongly made on the grounds that they wrongly estimated the likely interest of the intended readers or audience, but also that whole categories of news judgements are wrong on the same grounds.

There is little doubt, for example, in my own mind that newspapers – and, insofar as they tend to be parasitic on the newspapers, radio and television news programmes – rely on inherited traditional news values which are not frequently checked against contemporary evidence of reader audience interest. A good example – and I acknowledge this itself to be a personal and, if you like, 'subjective' judgement – is the massive 'front page' attention customarily given to all manner of natural disasters and man-made accidents, most particularly train and plane crashes, murders, rapes and arson. Another example is the tendency to regard any event, however trivial and predictable, surrounding certain named individuals, who have once become established in this tedious category by some great or notorious achievement in the sometime far distant past, as an automatic candidate for inclusion in the news. Miss Elizabeth Taylor is doubtless the doyenne of this oppressed minority; but there are many other lesser members who could testify to its nuisance.

However, my concern in the present context is not with the plight of such victims, but with the definition of 'the news' and, therefore, with the identification of this particular form of false news-judgement, false because it disregards the criterion, in the definition which I have suggested, of the actual interest of the consumers of the news. Let me remark in passing, unkindly but truthfully, that few human beings lead a less representative lifestyle or are less closely in touch with or exposed to the lifestyles and interests of ordinary people than that select band of nocturnal animals who actually determine the news values and priorities of our great morning newspapers. They rise at about noon, immerse themselves in every known newspaper, seldom if ever listen to the radio or watch television, go to work in the late afternoon where they spend their waking lives in the company of one another. It is scarcely surprising that their ideas of news values are easily out of touch, are commonly inherited from their literal and metaphorical ancestors, powerfully reinforced by the daily evidence of similar news judgements by similar people working for their competitors, and are therefore prone over the years to diverge more and more widely from the actual interests of their readers. If those readers remain nonetheless loyal – and many of them do not – it must be for other things which they like about the titles they buy. It is an evil against which breakfast-time television, as a form of electronic newspaper, will need to guard.

Now let me turn to another aspect of the definition of 'news'. So far we have taken for granted in our definition of 'the news' the definition of 'an event'. But, most of the really difficult questions about the definition of 'news' arise precisely over this. Manifestly, to establish the easy things first, something which has not occurred cannot be an event although, of course, the non-occurrence of an expected event can indeed be 'news' as, for example, with the failure of the sun to rise in the morning. But, even in that case, the story that the sun has not risen can only be news if, indeed, it really is the case that the sun has not risen, that is, if the story is true. Untrue stories cannot be news, however frequently they masquerade falsely under such colours.

But what is 'truth' and, more particularly, how broad can the scope of a 'fact' or an 'event' spread before its telling trespasses out of the true area of 'objectivity' into the suspect areas of opinion and comment or, worse still, into prejudice and bias?

Traditionally, the approach to this problem was very simple and at least claimed to be very clear. News – and therefore news reports, news columns and news editors and reporters – is concerned simply and purely with 'facts'. In the time-honoured slogan of C.P. Scott, 'comment is free but facts are sacred' (*Manchester Guardian*, 6 May 1926).

But what is a 'fact'? Obviously, facts are supposed to be things out there in the external world of empirically verifiable reality. Yet, there is nothing in that world out there which defines and delimits *a* fact.

This becomes obvious the moment one asks, for example, the question 'how many facts are there in this hall?'. The answer, of course, is that there are as many facts as there are true sentences which one can construct describing what is in this hall. 'This man is my father' is, indeed, a fact and in some sense at this moment a fact in this hall; but, as a fact, it is only defined and, so, countable by the identity of the sentence which reports that fact, although perhaps a minor verbal alteration might not be held to create a new fact merely because it created a slightly different sentence.

And what about, 'This man has been my father for forty-five years'? This is a fact and the sentence which states it is true. But is it a fact which is in this hall?

And consider some other sentences, such as, 'This man, having been my father for forty-five years and having been himself a journalist throughout much of that period, has had a great influence on me and is, therefore, in some degree causally responsible for the contents of this lecture.' Or 'This man, though my father, will probably disagree with

243

many of the things said in this lecture.' These are clearly sentences. They clearly claim to make true statements about the external world. Yet, some people may say that they convey explanations, judgements or predictions rather than facts. But why can a statement of causation or a statement of probability or a statement in the future tense not be a fact?

Facts themselves are, of course, incapable of being true or false, despite some muddled usage to the contrary. The sentences which report them are true or false; and if the sentences which report them are true, then what are reported are facts.

What follows from all this is that facts are by no means the simple, self-evident, self-defining bits of external reality that the traditional view of what is the proper quarry of news reporters suggests. If we have to define '*a* fact', then we will have to say something like, 'a fact is whatever it is about the external real world which makes the particular sentence which reports and defines that aspect of external reality true'.

There cannot be, in other words, a definition of 'a fact' which is independent of the identity of the sentence which reports the fact. This, in turn, means that the identity of the fact, though not its status as a fact, is dependent on words and language.

But words and language in their own turn are riddled with presuppositions, interpretations and assumptions about the proper or best ways of looking at and describing the world and about how that world works – in other words, they are never purely factual. The philosopher David Hume long ago pointed out that we can never directly observe one event causing another event. All we can ever observe is that whenever the one event occurs the other follows, in other words, 'constant concommittance'.

He was moved to conclude this, therefore, must be what we meant when we said that one event caused another. Yet, manifestly, that is not all we mean. We mean that the first event in some sense actually produced the second or led it to occur, not merely that the long arm of coincidence is infinitely extended.

This dependence of the identity of facts on the language wherein they are reported leads to an almost infinite extension of the number and type of facts which – given their unexpectedness and interest to the intended audience – are on the news agenda. Not all facts are of the convenient, discreet, dry, sterile and present-tense character of 'the cat sits on the mat', although this is the model always implicitly assumed by the simple-minded, hard-headed, no-nonsense exponents of the traditional view of the nature of news and of its proper agenda.

Moreover, on inspection, even the words 'cat' and 'mat' turn out to involve a large amount of unstated assumption and interpretation running beyond what can currently be observed, namely the presence of a chunk of furriness upon a strip of bristliness. If, after the supposedly pure reporting of this fact – that the cat sits on the mat – the chunk of furriness began to bark, gave birth to a duck-billed platypus and manifested a servile and dependent attitude towards its owner, one might begin to doubt whether it really was a cat.

So, the original description of it as a cat implied an interpretation and, therefore, a prediction that it would not so behave. Likewise, if the strip of bristliness sprouted camellia blooms and complained vociferously of being walked upon, then too one might doubt whether it was a mat and, therefore, whether the original report was correct.

Economic reporting, for example, is redolent of such difficulties, though recognition of them has declined *pari passu* with the general flight from sophistication in all economic discussion in Britain in recent years. You will hear with monotonous regularity that inflation has speeded up or slowed down, that unemployment has risen or fallen or that the balance of payment has moved into surplus or deficit.

Let me tell you, without abusing your patience much more than I already am, that these statements presuppose veritable volumes of assumptions, theories and causal hypotheses. As often as not, they are false even in the sense in which the normal reporter intends to use them.

For example, there is no possible measure of the rate of inflation at any point in time. There are a series of approximate and defective measures, on a whole variety of different assumptions, of the change in the level of prices between a vast variety of pairs of different points in the past. When the evening papers speak of inflation being faster or slower, they are usually referring to the change over the most recently measured twelve months in the 'all-items' index of retail prices. It would be a pure fluke if this reflected the rate at which prices were currently or have recently been rising, even supposing that the index numbers themselves were correct.

Reports of unemployment frequently have to contend with contrary movements in the 'crude' measurement of the unemployed, which also includes school-leavers, and the 'seasonally adjusted' figures, which usually exclude school-leavers. The only generally reliable rule is that the evening and popular papers and the BBC News tend to concentrate on whichever measurement is least germane to the impression which they are giving their readers and audience.

As to the balance of payments, it is always in balance – at zero; and the references to surpluses and deficits relate to certain discretionary, though not necessarily arbitrary, decisions about which items in those accounts to regard as 'autonomous' and which to regard as 'accommodating' of whatever imbalance there may be in the 'autonomous' items. About a decade or so ago a radical change was made in the assumptions which the Government used in arriving at those figures which it chose to highlight. The result was to transform past as well as future deficits into surpluses and vice versa. But the headline writers and the bulletin newscasters never faltered in their stride; and the public continued to be terrorised or elated by the equally mystifying, though totally different, new sequence of surpluses and deficits just as if nothing had happened.

But hardnosed reporters from the muscular school will not be troubled by this. It will merely confirm their view that economic events do not really belong on the agenda of the true news man. Stick, they will say, to simple facts, like rape and natural disasters and wars and the like.

But the difficulty is no less in those time-honoured sanctuaries of, as I once fatally called him, the cub reporter from Gateshead, with his stubby pencil, his tattered notebook, his bowler hat on the back of his head and his vacant, if not vacuous, mind.

(Last time I used this image, let me recall in parenthesis, it lead to an avalanche of outraged letters to *The Times* from Sir Dennis Hamilton, Mr Donald Tyerman, Mr Harold Evans and sundry other leading luminaries of the profession complaining, as a self-evident refutation of my thesis, that they had begun their careers in Gateshead! Let me confess now that the only reason that I chose Gateshead in this notorious remark was that for some inconsequential reason I had a vivid memory from my childhood of my father asking me what was the largest town on the railway between King's Cross and Newcastle and being told, to the total bafflement of my metropolitan mentality, that the answer was Gateshead, a place of which I had then never heard. Ever since it has stuck in my mind, even after visiting it, as the English equivalent of Peioria, Illinois, or of 'Nowhere, USA'.)

But let me return to my thesis. The 'facts' of which natural disasters, rapes and wars are comprised turn out to be no more self-defining and self-evident than the 'facts' of which economic reporting consists. We may think that a report that the Tay Bridge fell down last night is either true or false. There can be no dispute, it will be said, about the identity of the Tay Bridge; and there can be no dispute as to whether or not it fell down.

But there may be. Did it fall or was it pushed? If it was pushed, was it pushed by terrorists or by the culpable negligence of the engineers and entrepreneurs who designed and financed it? And what kind of fact is 'culpability'? It certainly is not the same directly sensible observation that 'furriness' and 'bristliness' are supposed to be.

And consider rape. Whole squadrons of the legal profession and their camp-followers are dedicated to, and gainfully employed in consequence of, the proposition that rape is not a self-evident description of certain physical transactions. On the contrary, limitless vistas of speculation about intention and consent are involved in deciding whether or not the physical transactions in question are or are not properly described as 'rape'. So – our theme in the simple world of Geordie imagination where facts are as discrete, as unconnected and as hard as rounded pebbles on the shore – what is the nature of the 'fact' that rape has occurred?

And, again, wars – were the Patriotic Front at war with the Smith and Muzorewa regimes in Salisbury or were those regimes, or perhaps only one of them, merely engaged in combating terrorism? Are the IRA fighting a war of liberation in Northern Ireland against the British Government or are the British Government engaged, at most, in combating terrorism or even perhaps merely in putting down common criminality on an exceptional scale?

There is, indeed, no need further to multiply the examples. The work was, in fact, all done for us seventy years or so ago by the school of philosophers who called themselves 'logical atomists'. They established for themselves the ambition and programme of showing that all empirical statements, i.e. all sentences which purported to describe the world capable of being observed by the traditional five human senses, were either pure statements of current sensation or were shorthand, compendious statements of a series of such propositions linked together in logical relationships defined by the statement itself.

Thus, something like 'there is furriness on the bristliness' was seen as the ultimate 'atomic' fact, while statements like 'if Napoleon had not had piles at the Battle of Waterloo, Karl Marx would have been a capitalist' were to be analysed back into, presumably very large numbers of, atomic statements about furriness, bristliness and the like.

At the end of many years of intensive work by conspicuously ingenious and dedicated scholars, the only conclusion to be drawn was that almost any act of language contained too many interpretations, presuppositions, assumptions and, indeed, metaphysical preconceptions about how the world works, ever to be fully reduced to these pure atomic statements which would, in turn, be capable of direct observational verification. Every word we use in everyday language carries with it its assumptions, not merely about the presenting symptom available to our eyes, ears and other senses, but also about the way in which the entity in question works.

Cats which give birth to duck-billed platypi are not, we surmise, cats or, at least, not proper cats. Yet, at the moment of observing what appears to be a cat, one cannot subject it to all the tests necessary to see whether or not the description 'cat' actually fits all of its past and potential future behaviour. In that sense, one cannot in the glimpse of an eye – or indeed of a camera – observe a cat as, for sure, a cat. One can only observe what one observes and make the simplifying assumption that it is indeed in the full sense a cat.

If the assumption which we thereby make frequently proved unreliable, then we would probably modify and amplify our vocabulary to deal with this new problem. Meanwhile, our perception and our reporting of feline activity will continue to make the simplifying assumption – and quite rightly so. But it is not an assumption which is compatible with the purist pretensions of the no-nonsense school which aspires to see news as concerned exclusively with facts without benefit of interpretation, analysis, prediction or explanation.

The point was most vividly and most elegantly made by perhaps the greatest of all observers, from within and without, of journalism, namely Claud Cockburn, when he wrote in his classic work, originally entitled 'In Time of Trouble' later incorporated in his full autobiography, *I Claud*.

> To hear people talking about the facts you would think that they lay about like pieces of gold ore in the Yukon days waiting to be picked up – arduously, it's true, but still definitely and visibly – by strenuous prospectors whose subsequent problem was only to get them to market.
>
> Such a view is evidently and dangerously naive. There are no such facts. Or if there are, they are meaningless and entirely ineffective; they might, in fact, just as well not be lying about at all until the prospector – the journalist – puts them into relation with other facts: presents them, in other words. Then they become as much a part of a pattern created by him as if he were writing a novel. In that sense all stories are written backwards – they are supposed to begin with the facts and develop from there, but in reality they begin with a journalist's point of view, a conception, and it is the point of view from which the facts are subsequently organised. Journalistically speaking, 'In the beginning is the word'. All this is difficult and even rather unwholesome to explain to the layman, because he gets the impression that you are saying that

truth does not matter and that you are publicly admitting what we long ago suspected, that journalism is a way of 'cooking' the facts. Really cunning journalists, realising this and anxious to raise the standard of journalism in the esteem of the general public, positively encourage the layman in his mistaken view. They like him to have the picture of these nuggetty facts lying about on maybe frozen ground, and a lot of noble and utterly unprejudiced journalists with no idea whatever of what they looking for scrabbling in the iron-bound earth and presently bringing home the pure gold of Truth. (*I, Claud*, p. 147)

When Cockburn wrote those two beautiful paragraphs forty or so years ago, he may never have heard of Professor Karl Popper, still less of his so-called 'hypothetico-deductive' model of the nature of human cognition and scientific inquiry. Yet Cockburn, with a few deft strokes, arrived at the very kernel of the matter, namely that it is impossible, indeed, meaningless, to observe with a blank mind, to inquire with no hypothesis, to report with no context or explanation, to scrabble indeed in the iron-bound earth with no idea whatever of what one is looking for. It was when I first read those words of Cockburn's fifteen years ago that I first began to understand the true nature of journalism; and they have inspired me ever since.

In contrast with the abortive programme of logical atomism, a more useful, even if ultimately no more philosophically successful, metaphysic was proposed by the philosopher John Locke when he tried to grapple with the manifest asymmetry between what we appear to mean and what we can actually observe when we use words and language to report and describe the world outside our heads.

He sought to distinguish between the 'real' and the 'nominal' essences of concepts. The nominal essence consisted of those we could directly sense; and the real essence was the presumed inner character or mechanism of the phenomenon in question. He drew upon the obvious analogy of a clock – in particular 'the famous clock at Strasburg' – distinguishing the clock-face from its internal mechanism, with the face presenting the nominal essence of the concept of 'clock', while the internal mechanism was its 'real' essence. (John Locke, *Essay concerning Human Understanding*, Book III, Chapter 6, pp. 243 and 246 of Oxford Edition.)

This is emphatically not the place to digress into the philosophical difficulties to which this exposed him. It is, nonetheless, a convenient metaphor for the journalist, more particularly for the journalist who – without any aspiration to excuse bias, prejudice or 'committed' or otherwise evaluative or normative intrusions into the news – nonetheless wishes to challenge at its roots the simple-mindedness of the traditional assumptions on which are based the purist conception of the news as an obvious self-selecting category of self-evident and self-differentiating stories of the here and now.

The clock-face may indeed tell us the what, when and where, which for sure we need to know; and, as Mr Brian Wenham, Controller of BBC2, has rightly reminded us recently in *The Listener*, we must first of all have the answers to those questions. It can, indeed, take skill, intelligence and sometimes courage to discover them; and so we rightly honour the investigative journalist who has the clock-face as his quarry and who is single-minded, ingenious and brave in the quest.

But the why, the how, the whence and the whether are just as much factual questions about the world out there. The clockwork behind the clock-face is just as real and just as newsworthy, even if not so easily visible and so naturally visual, as the exterior manifestation of the inner workings.

Vivid pictures of strangely garbed adversaries gunning one another down in a modernised city of undistinguished skyscrapers on the shore of the universal sea are, no doubt, in some degree both factual and news; and they may even win awards for the doughty cameramen who secured them. But without explanation of who is fighting whom and why, and where this city is anyway, and what may be the consequences for the region in which it is located and, indeed, for the intended audience for the news, we derive very little true information from the pictures and from a commentary which does little other than to establish the identity of the reporter who is, we are given to understand, bravely ducking the bullets.

Moreover, once we allow that explanation and understanding are just as necessary, factual and objective – and therefore legitimate – goals for the reporter as the so-called 'pure actuality' (what Locke called 'uncompounded appearances'), we soon discover that the story requires attention, not only to the gunman in the street and the tank in the desert, but also to the aims and plans and deceptions of the strategists behind the scenes and to the negotiations and entreaties of the peacemaker behind locked doors. And so the skeins of explanation lead us wider and deeper and, sometimes, further back in history.

The journalist, of course, must remember that he can never be an historian. His evidence and therefore his account, his explanation and his understanding can never be definitive. They must always be contemporary, incomplete and ephemeral. This is dictated both by the time at which and by the time within which his role must be performed. But the quest for the maximum achievable explanation and understanding of the maximum discoverable information, within the limits which journalism by its nature imposes, remains the sovereign duty and goal of any true newsman.

Let me give a homely example of what I mean by including the context and causation of events, as well as their surface appearances, in the definition of the 'fact' which it is the task of newsmen to investigate, to report and to explain. We are all familiar with the reporting of traffic news. We are told where the traffic is heavy and light, where there are hold-ups and sometimes even whether they are caused by accidents or roadworks.

Yet we are told next to nothing about the general behaviour patterns of traffic. No kind of model or mental picture is built up in our minds which could help us to understand the daily variations or to know what to expect. But listen to any conversation in a pub, between two ordinary mortals and you will find that they are full of theories, possibly wrong and frequently half-baked, but nonetheless theories about the way traffic behaves.

Everyone knows that traffic tends to be heavier when it is raining. Everyone has a theory about why this should be: more people take to their cars in order to keep dry; people drive more slowly because they cannot see so clearly; people drive more slowly because they are frightened of skidding; etc. But have you ever heard this fact alluded to, let alone authoritatively explained in the course of traffic reporting on television and radio?

Or, to take another theory, I believe, from my own casual observation, it to be a fact that the density of traffic on any given route tends to vary inversely to the way it was at the same time the day before. My explanation of this is quite simply that, where people have experienced heavy congestion one day, they avoid that route the next day.

Now, this lay speculation may be rubbish, either as to the phenomenon itself or as to its explanation; but there are people, for example at the Road Research Laboratory, who study these things in a methodical way. An approach to traffic reporting which included this kind of dimension and thereby built up an explanation and an understanding of traffic behaviour would, I believe, not merely be a proper and more intelligent interpretation of the reporter's task, but would also be immeasurably fascinating to and appreciated by the intended audience.

The lesson of this homely example can, I believe, be extended to almost all aspects of journalism, including even human interest and sports stories. So, let us review the position we have reached in trying to define the news and the scope and nature of the facts which properly comprise it.

The proper agenda of the news includes reporting the new discovery of all facts which are not so certain as to have been taken for granted and which are sufficiently important or otherwise diverting to be of interest to the intended audience for that news. Moreover, the facts in question extend, not merely to the here-and-now visible manifestation of an event – as it were, the freeze-frame snapshot of an instant in the swirling sequence of the great and small historical processes of which all experience is composed, a mere static and meaningless cross-section of the ever-rolling stream of cause and effect, collision and dispersion – but also enough of the historical, geographical and other context of these events and of the causal and purposive mechanisms which are at work within them to make those events intelligible, and therefore more interesting, to the viewer or the reader who, whatever the quality of the reporting offered to him, can only comprehend an event in any significant way in so far as he or she succeeds in placing it in some context which he or she understands and seeing it as part of some process which he or she understands.

This need, deeply and unavoidably, imbedded in the very nature of human cognition, and therefore of viewer or reader perception and interest, may be likened to Kant's categories of perception and of reason which structure the way in which we necessarily observe and arrange our peceptions of the objective world of external reality. Furriness located over bristliness is only a significant and usable fact to us as a cat on a mat, with all the assumptions and interpretations presupposed in that inference.

A two dimensional cross-section of the Thames at Battersea is likewise meaningless to us except as a cross-section of a river whose processes we envisage. This month's Retail Price Index number tells us nothing except as a number in a continuing sequence with a measurable relationship to previous and subsequent numbers in that sequence and, with whatever qualifications, as a reflection of a process which we recognise and, at least dimly, understand as inflation.

A tank on a hill top, a child in a slum, an opinion in a pub, a guerilla in a jungle, a statement by an official spokesman, a leak from 10 Downing Street or even a Goal of the Month have almost no cognitive value insulated and sterilised from their context and from the processes of cause and effect or of intention to which they belong. They leave the mind – the mind of the ordinary viewer or reader – gaping and gasping like a goldfish out of water for the sustenance of context and process which alone nourishes understanding and permits a true feeling of knowledge acquired and curiosity satisfied.

There are, of course, those with a natural distaste for abstractions and a reflex scepticism about theories who will not be persuaded by all this and who will, being cynical as well as sceptical, suspect that there lurks behind it a licence to comment and to blaspheme in the sacred domain of the god of Fact. But, being so distrustful of logic and reason and so confident of the dogmas of their journalistic ancestors they not surprisingly deceive themselves.

Comment, in the sense of normative evaluation of people and events, belongs in a totally different logical category from explanation, in the sense of empirical investigation of the context and causes of events. There is no logical connection whatever between explaining how and why events happen and dubbing them 'good' or 'bad' or 'right' or 'wrong'. Moral evaluation is certainly no part of the task of the news reporter; and comment, in that sense, has no place in the news or in the reporting of it.

It may, however, be the case that the rival explanations of a particular event or type of event have become a matter of active controversy between rival groups or even between political parties in a particular society. It is exceedingly important that journalists should think clearly about what the implications of this are for the proper definition and treatment of the news.

The correct view, in my opinion, is as follows. The news remains the news, whatever disputes there might be in society about the correct interpretation and diagnosis of events, although such controversy may itself become a further fact which itself merits reporting as part of the news.

Objectivity, which means nothing except an accurate correspondence between what is said and what is indeed the case, has nothing whatever to do with taking a half-way position between rival prominent opinions about questions of fact and analysis. There is no grounds for a presumption that the truth lies between, let alone half-way between, two such contending views.

For what it is worth my personal observation, if one needs any such crude rule of thumb at all, is that where there are two strongly contending rival views the truth will most frequently be found to lie at or beyond one or other (occasionally both) of the extremes or in some quite different dimension of understanding altogether. But, whatever the truth about that may be, objectivity owes no obligations to the correlates of rival opinions on such matters. The obligations of objectivity are to truth itself and to nothing else.

However, in certain situations and for reasons which have nothing whatever to do with the definition of 'news' or with objectivity, there may indeed be obligations placed upon the news reporter to be impartial between rival received or canvassed opinions about the way the world or a particular part of it works. These obligations can, in their context, be just as important, just as legitimate and just as onerous as obligations of objectivity. But they are totally different in both their character and in their derivation.

The obligation of objectivity arises directly from the nature of 'news' itself as a rendering of newly discovered *facts*. The obligation of impartiality arises, where it applies, from the nature of the vehicle whereby the news is conveyed.

The broadcasting of news on radio and television, for example, involves – and will continue to involve until the arrival of the golden age of free electronic broadcasting foreseen in my MacTaggart Lecture given at the Edinburgh International Television Festival in 1981 and made possible by the nationwide application of the wonders of fibre optic technology – the exploitation of scarce broadcast wavelengths by privileged individuals to whom a monopoly or oligopoly of such opportunities have been conferred by society through mechanisms established by Parliament. It is perfectly legitimate and proper, indeed desirable, that, where such rare and valuable franchises are publicly conferred, they should be conferred upon condition of impartiality as between strongly held points of view, even on matters of fact and factual analysis, in that society.

This explains why we do, I think correctly, find it proper to impose an obligation of impartiality on news reporters who use radio and television, whereas we impose no such obligation on the proprietors of newspapers and magazines; and it further explains why the rules of impartiality in our society impose an obligation on radio and television reporters to be impartial as between, for example, a Labour and a Conservative view of the utility of Government economic policies, while not imposing upon them an obligation of impartiality as between a Marxist and a liberal analysis of society or between a Judaeo-Christian and an Islamic view of history or again, between a scientific and a superstitious interpretation of natural events.

Objectivity is by its nature an absolute concept. There is and can be only one set of facts, correspondence with which guarantees truth and establishes objectivity. Impartiality is a relative concept, implying nothing more than a suspension of judgement between any given pair of views of a matter, coupled with the perfectly sensible convention that, in the case of news reporting in, for example, Britain, the views between which judgement should be suspended by those news reporters who use public franchises are those views which happen to be prominently and vigorously held in Britain at the time in question.

I believe that this examination of the differences between and the separate issues involved in the various concepts of objectivity and of impartiality as they apply to the duties of the news journalist goes a long way to dispel systematic confusions, leading in turn to bitter controversies, which arise only because of a failure to distinguish the principle of objectivity from the principle of impartiality and, therefore, to distinguish the totally different basis, scope and applications of those two separate duties.

All news journalists have an obligation to objectivity. Some, in addition, have an obligation to be impartial; and that second obligation may on occasions prevent them from pursuing the obligation to objectivity to its uttermost extent. That is a reflection of the limitations of the context in which they are practising their news journalism, not a modification of the aims and role of the news journalist as such.

Whatever, therefore, may have to be left out because of the rules of impartiality in certain contexts is not, therefore, to be excluded from the definition of 'news'. It is simply a bit of 'news' which in certain circumstances reporters are properly not permitted to report.

There are, however, other categories of 'news' as we have so far defined it, which may also deserve to be excluded from the domain of the news reporter, not because the vehicle through which they are reported forbids their reporting, but because something else about their character makes it systematically contrary to the ethics of journalism to report them. I would now like to examine these.

Clearly an editor and a reporter have obligations which flow from the nature of their occupation as editors and reporters. These obligations are to investigate, to report and to explain those facts which are on the news agenda as we have defined them.

This obligation to perform faithfully to the role which one has assumed – and in return for which one may enjoy certain privileges and immunities – flows quite simply from the general moral rule of truthfulness and fidelity in dealings between people. It is the fact that one calls oneself a journalist that obliges one to behave accordingly, just as the fact that one calls oneself a doctor, an architect, a lawyer, a soldier or a merchant imposes upon one – whether or not one swears an oath, enters into a contract or takes on some formal duty at the time – an obligation to behave accordingly.

These obligations are the counterpart to the condemnation we feel for the 'con' man or the huckster who seeks to pass himself or his merchandise off as something other than and superior to what he or it really is.

However, the journalist is also a human individual and a citizen; and as such, he is under certain other and broader obligations which flow, not from the fact that he holds himself forth as a human individual or a citizen, but from the general moral law which applies to all human beings, or at least all human beings who are presumed to be capable of moral discernment (and maybe we would apply it to animals too, if we believed them to be capable of moral discernment). One aspect of that general moral law is, indeed, truthfulness and fidelity in dealings with others; and it is this and this alone which provides the moral basis for such professional ethics and obligations as those in particular occupations claim and recognise. But those particular moral rules – of truthfulness and fidelity – are not overriding of all other moral obligations.

Whether or not one accepts the utilitarian concept of a hierarchy of moral principles all ultimately flowing from and justified by the single principle that every man has a duty to strive for the well-being of all other people as those other people perceive it, and to strive against whatever may threaten that well-being, it is almost universally recognised that, important as truth and fidelity are, they must on occasions give way to other higher or more pressing or more relevant moral rules in particular circumstances. Where, for example, the principle of the welfare of others as reflected in the role of kindness, whose converse is the moral prohibition against cruelty, should take precedence over the rule of truth and fidelity, then that is as true for the human individual who happens also to be a journalist as for any other human individual.

What is News?

No journalist, just as no doctor, no architect, no lawyer and no soldier has a God-given right, still less a God-imposed duty, to violate the general moral law and its obligations as an individual and as a citizen simply because his professional code or ethics, which are themselves merely derivative from the principle of truth and fidelity in dealing with others, points that way.

Consider a deliberately trite example. You are the reporter covering the story of an innocent little girl who has just escaped imprisonment by vile oppressors, who are nonetheless set upon her recapture and hot upon her trail. You discover her whereabouts. Do you publish it the next morning? The answer is so obvious that it deserves no debate. But it serves to make the point that the ethics and the obligations of journalism, just as those of any other professions, cannot override the ethics and obligations of mankind. Another broader example of the same issue is presented by events such as the Moscow Olympics and the current cricket matches in South Africa involving well known English players.

On the one hand, in the intention and contrivance of the promoters they clearly are in a sense 'media events'. But it may also be true that they are in some sense genuine too, because they are of real interest to the potential audience for the news. So, the editor and reporter may not be able to resolve the matter simply on the basis that they are bogus events and, therefore, not on the news agenda, although in the case of the South African cricket this judgement might be justified.

If they are not dismissible as purely bogus 'media events', the editor and reporter will come face to face with a real conflict between the imperatives of his profession and what he may regard as the imperatives of his citizenship and humanity. Having studied the reasons why the Government of the day deplores these events in the context of foreign policy, he may conclude that, even though the Government has not used or sought powers to enforce their view on the press and rightly not done so, nonetheless the reasons of foreign policy are valid and pressing and, therefore, press upon him as a citizen.

His presumption, I think, should be that the onus of proof in his own mind lies on the case for non-publication. But I do not think that he can simply excuse himself from the duty to face the issue, think it through and reach his own conclusion by glibly announcing that as an editor or reporter it is not his business.

If an act of publication will give aid and comfort to villains and blaggards, including villains and blaggards on an international scale, and if the giving of that aid and comfort can reasonably be expected to increase the probability of more villainy to the grave detriment of innocent people and the violation of their rights, then in my opinion the editor and the reporter cannot side-step their responsibility to weigh these consequences of their own actions very carefully, taking full account of their primary presumptive duty to cover the news faithfully and impartially, and reach whatever conclusion their conscience dictates. Even then, they remain, of course, like anyone else open to criticism by other individuals for the conclusions they reach and for the actions they take.

It is true that journalists – in the quest for professional status or for convenient immunities and privileges – sometimes do argue that their professional obligations override other normal moral rules; and they sometimes seek to fortify this with applications of the dubious principle of 'the public's right to know' and the solider principle of 'the freedom of the press'. A free press is an invaluable political institution, but not because it has a God-given right to be free, but because, on the whole, societies in which it is free will be healthier and more agreeable for their citizens to live in. It is valuable, too, that the public should be informed of events and processes which concern, interest or affect them; but this, too, is a broad rule of thumb not an overriding right or universal law.

As a moral agent who is a person and a citizen, the journalist is inescapably responsible like anyone else for all the reasonably foreseeable consequences of his actions and for their net impact on the well-being of others as those others measure their own well-being. Let me give an example which I myself experienced.

At almost any time during the late spring, summer and early autumn of 1967 I, like others, was in a position, as a result of my normal journalistic inquiries, to write a story which would have lead to so massive a run on the pound as to have forced a devaluation. That in itself did not greatly bother me, since I believed then – and now – that such a devaluation was long overdue and would be greatly beneficial to the well-being of my fellow men, particularly in Britain.

However, I also believed – and believe – in the principle of democratically based, representative government. The decision whether or not to devalue was an important one, and one for the Government elected to make such decisions. To force the Government's hand by a unilateral journalistic act, however true the story and however beneficial the resultant policy change, seemed to me then, and would seem to me now, damaging to the principle of democratic government and, therefore, to the long-term well-being of other people; and this probable damage seemed to me to outweigh, not merely my professional obligation to report what I knew, but also, and much more importantly, the benefit to be expected from a change in the economic policy. Therefore, I withheld the story; and I have not the slightest doubt that I was right to do so.

Others might have reached a different conclusion; but I would be shocked if they did so without acknowledging the relevance of both sets of considerations, simply excusing themselves on the facile grounds that the journalist's sole duty is to report what he knows without regard to the consequences. No human being, in my opinion, can ever have an obligation to follow any maxim without regard to the consequences for other people.

Now, it is also true that it is not practical to expect every journalist all of the time to solve a complicated felicific calculus, particularly where much of the time most of the relevant factors will be obscure or unknown, every time that he writes a story. He or she has to work with a presumption that normally and most of the time a journalist must perform his or her proper function. After all, if that were not so, then there would be grounds for doubting whether society should or could afford the presence of editors and reporters amid its ranks at all; and, if that were the case, then it would have been up to society by its appropriate mechanisms to have protected itself against this nuisance long ago.

Where it is generally judged beneficial to society that the journalist's role of inquiry, reporting and explanation should be carried out, then it will follow that it will be best if those who have chosen to be journalists work with a strong presumption that it is their duty to find out, to report and to explain and that the onus of proof in their own minds must lie on any contrary promptings which from time to time they may feel. Nonetheless, it would be unforgiveable and wrong if they were ever to confuse a healthy presumption with an absolute principle; and they can never escape the obligation themselves to make the judgement in every case whether the presumption in favour of their professional ethic should or should not yield in particular circumstances to another or higher consideration which affects them as people or as citizens.

In the last resort it is always more important that you exist as a person than that your professional essence is as a journalist. We all have to be existentialists in the end.

These reflections establish, I believe, that it is possible, though rarely, for there to be events which are indeed 'news' by the definition we have given, but which nonetheless the editor and the reporter should not include *in* the news. But these are cases where the decision should be made by the editor or the reporter himself or herself; and they certainly do not justify the imposition of constraints upon the journalist by others.

There may, however, be other categories of restraint which society *is* entitled to impose upon the journalist in the fulfilment of his role as investigator, reporter and explainer.

It has long been recognised that the right of freedom of speech is not and cannot be absolute. The classic demonstration of the need for some qualification of this principle has always been the example of the man who shouts, 'Fire!' in a crowded theatre. Because this can and may be expected to lead directly to a catastrophe as the theatregoers stampede for the exits, it has always been recognised that to give the alarm, perhaps falsely, under these conditions is, not so much an exercise of free speech, as a reckless and irresponsible act which society cannot afford to tolerate.

Our society recognises other applications of the same principle, such for example as in the case of race relations, where certain kinds of provocative or inflammatory utterances can reasonably be expected to produce disturbance and even social breakdown on a 'macro' scale and which therefore justify restraint at least as strong as the prohibition against utterances which may produce panic in a small and crowded place. The point in both cases is that the utterances in question are themselves, in effect, acts and acts which carry consequences that are too grave for society to tolerate in the overall interests of its own survival and the well-being of its citizens.

These are always difficult judgements to make and it is right that we approach the imposition of such restraints with the greatest reluctance and care, placing the onus of proof on the proponents of restraint. Nonetheless, it is arrogant and simple-minded nonsense to argue that the imposition of such restraints can never be justified merely on the grounds that they collide with another important principle, namely freedom of speech.

Freedom of publication and freedom of the press are merely special cases of the principle of freedom of speech, despite the appearance in American constitutional law to the contrary. They are very important and need to be defended; but they are not sovereign or overriding of all other important principles.

The scope for legitimate restraint is not, however, confined to those utterances and publications which are, in effect, acts which lead predictably to dire and unacceptable consequences. The laws of slander and of libel properly aim to protect citizens against false statements to their discredit which may so damage their legitimate right in society, as for example, to inhibit their ability to earn their livings.

The aim, it appears to me, is just; and it is only the particular formulation and application of these laws in Britain which deserves the contempt and derision into which they have fallen in the eyes of practising journalists, who see them used almost entirely to help powerful scallywags abetted by unscrupulous lawyers rather than to protect innocent victims who really need the strength of law to safeguard them.

One particular aspect of the misapplication of the laws of slander and libel is their concentration on damages, which theoretically aim to make restitution to the individual for the damage which he has suffered, but which in practice often seem to operate as if they are intended as a punishment and a deterrent to the publication of items which infringe the law as written. Since the real damage in many cases is the fact of the report itself, rather than any specific financial or other consequences thereof, there is in my view some justice in the current interest in the concept of a legal or voluntarily offered 'right of reply'. Severe and daunting practical difficulties are raised by it, not least the potential conflict between the interest of the aggrieved party in having his reply aired with equal prominence to the publication originally complained of *and* the criterion of reader and viewer interest as it has developed at the time at which the reply is to be published. Nonetheless, if this problem and the obvious dangers of tedious, vexatious and disproportionate exercises of such a right can be overcome, then such a rule could be more satisfactory to all parties and closer to the real justice of the matter than the current well-meant, but in practice arbitrary and cynically abused arrangement.

Another example of legitimate restraint of free speech and, therefore, of free publication came from perhaps the greatest of all apostles of freedom, from Abraham Lincoln himself. It was he who asked rhetorically, when faced with a plague of desertions by young Union recruits egged on by self-serving agitators – and I paraphrase his words – 'Am I to hang the misguided youth who deserts and to leave untouched the wily orator who makes it his business to procure such desertions?'

Thus, even societies which have been most dedicated to freedom and free speech have had to accept some restraint of incitement to serious wrong-doing as another qualification of free speech; and, since the publication of a report, more particularly a false report, can in certain circumstances have the effect of an incitement, it suggests another curtailment of what 'news' we may publish. Of course, if the report is false, it cannot truly belong in the 'news'; but, since it is possible for an editor and reporter sincerely, but wrongly, to believe that a report is true and since also in sufficiently critical conditions even a true report can have the effect of an incitement, there is scope, however limited, rare and circumscribed, for an imposed restraint on publication of the news in such cases.

It remains of the utmost importance that, in those cases where some degree of restraint is justified on the grounds I have described, this restraint must be expressed in a general rule applicable to all, embodied in the law and testable in open court. What is wholly intolerable, except perhaps in the extremities of total war, is any form of restraint which is imposed administratively, that is which gives any discretion over particular acts of publication to any appointed individual. That must always be wholly unacceptable, because it is the high road to abuse, corruption and arbitrary exercise of power.

So far we have spoken of certain categories of news, or of what may genuinely be news, which should nonetheless not always be published either because the general moral law should restrain the editor and the reporter from publishing them or because society is justified in imposing restraint in order to prevent grave and unacceptable consequences for individuals or for the society itself. There may, however, also be certain categories of potential news which ought not to be published, not because of the potential consequences for individuals or society from publishing them, but because of the content of the reports themselves. And it may even be that the imposition of rules to restrain publication of such stories would be justified, provided that the rules were well drafted, that they were general in character and that their application could be tested in court.

A prime contender in this field is the whole area of privacy. Remember that the moral and social basis of the principle of free speech and, therefore, of a free press derives from a particular application of the general moral law based on the well-being of individuals as they define it for themselves. We uphold the principle of free speech, not because it is in and of itself written on a tablet of stone superior to or co-equal with other parts of the moral law, but because we perceive from experience the general consequences for our society (and not just for those for whose creativity and opinions are frustrated) of suppression of information and circumscription of opinion by governmental authority for its own convenience.

But it follows from *this* derivation of the basis for the principle of free speech that the principle can only be properly applied to the reporting of and comment about transactions which can affect individuals and society without their consent. A wholly 'self-respecting act', as John Stuart Mill called it, cannot of its nature belong in this category; and, therefore, reports of such an act cannot come within the legitimate application of free speech and free publication derived in the way I have described.

It may well be that such an act and a report of it would satisfy the definition of 'news' which I have given – the new discovery of an event not wholly taken for granted and sufficiently important and otherwise interesting to excite that attention of the intended audience. But it does not follow that the principles of free speech and so of the free press give us the right to publish that report.

I would myself uphold the principle that to be eligible for protection under the principle of free speech and a free press, the report of an event must be of an event in the public domain, where the public domain is defined as any act or event which may affect at least one other individual without that individual's prior consent. And I would further say that it is not enough or legitimate, as a way of getting an act or event into the public domain, to say that the mere thought or knowledge of it does or may offend the sensibilities of another person without his or her consent.

In short, I do not believe and have never believed that the private lives and transactions with other consenting parties of any person should be included on the proper agenda of journalism although, of course, any individual is and should be free to consent to such revelations if he or she and the other private parties affected consent.

I am aware that it is customarily argued that, at least in the case of public figures, it is important and necessary to know about their private lives in order to judge of their character and so of their probable behaviour in the discharge of their public responsibilities, which in turn are indeed matters in the public domain. If it were true that there were any reliable correlation between private behaviour and public behaviour, there might be some logical force to this argument. But even the most cursory study of history and of the biographies of great men establishes that, at best, the relationship between private virtue and public virtue is random.

There is, in fact, no empirical basis whatever for the view that knowledge of the private man throws light on the probable behaviour of the public man; and, in my view, the onus of contrary proof should rest heavily on those who glibly, but without evident support, parrot the assertion of such a connection, usually as a transparent excuse for their commercial or salacious motives for intrusion into the privacy of others.

But what, it may be asked, if the private transactions in question are criminal? The short answer is that a crime is automatically in the public domain, since it imposes a duty on the law-enforcement authorities to detect and to prosecute it. Nonetheless, one may retain a very strong reservation about the public status of crime which is a violation only of a law which seeks to regulate an individual's private thoughts or his other self-respecting acts; and reports of it would not, in my opinion, be a proper subject for inclusion on the agenda of the truly ethical journalist, at least unless the case had clear implications for other events which were themselves in the public domain.

So now, in conclusion, let us draw together the threads of the answer we have given to the question 'What is News?'. News is the reporting of the new discovery or revelation of any event which is not too certainly predictable or expected and which in itself is sufficiently important or otherwise interesting to the intended audience. The concept of an event and of the facts which compose it extends to the context in which it occurs and to the historical process and other causal mechanisms of which it is a part and to its future implications; and so the task of the news journalist is to inquire, to report and to explain.

There are, however, certain categories of events which, though they undoubtedly satisfy this definition of news and, therefore, are indeed news, deserve not to be reported. In some cases this arises from obligations of impartiality which forbid even accurate explanation. In some cases it arises from the duty of an editor and a reporter not to forget, in the fulfilment of their professional role and its imperatives, that they are also and overridingly moral agents, human beings and citizens. In other cases society may be justified in imposing restraints on the news journalists because there are some things as or more important to the well-being of all people, as they themselves would define it, as or than free speech, the freedom of publication and a free press.

But, just as a wise journalist, who wishes to uphold both in public debate and in his own conduct the principle of a free press to the maximum possible extent, will recognise that he makes his own position untenable and his argument transparently fallacious if he pushes it to the extreme of denying the justice of any conceivable restraint whether self-imposed or imposed by law, so also will the wise society, recognising that the integrity and sturdiness of the principles of free speech and a free press are of fundamental importance to the vigour and health of the society, confine the necessary qualifications of those principles to categories where the case is overwhelmingly proved and, even then, will take scrupulous care to ensure that the rules are written and enforced in ways which are general, open and testable in court, excluding absolutely (except perhaps in conditions of war) anything which is secret, discretionary or unaccountable.

With this definition and with these principles I believe that decent news journalism can survive and prosper, true to its historic ideals – fearless, fair, truthful and illuminating – winning and holding public confidence in and support for its essential freedoms, and building for itself as a profession an ethic, a self-confidence and a set of standards which can liberate it from some of the tawdriness, the amateurism, the self-satisfaction, the self-indulgence and the pretended immunity from the imperatives of humanity and citizenship, which in this country have too often provided ammunition for the enemies of freedom and which have shocked and alienated the very public whom it is our duty to serve and in whose name alone we are entitled to claim the necessary privileges and immunities of our profession.

RSA Lecture, St Patrick's Day, 1982

Betrayal by Clerks:
The Lessons of TV-am

There are really two quite different aspects of the TV-am story: the specific and the general. The specific is irrelevant here, dealing as it does with the precise history of how the franchise was sought and won, how it was translated into a going concern with real staff and premises, its relations with outside bodies, the only partly availing struggle to be allowed on the air as early as possible, the design and implementation of the primary business strategy, the initial ratings failure in February, the immediate actions and plans to rectify this, the change of command in March and subsequent events. Tempting as it is to the author to set the record straight on all this, it would have no place in this book and would involve a violation of his vow to himself of silence on these matters.

The general, however, is relevant, since it bears upon the question how far certain broad and important ideas may have been held to have been tested and either succeeded or failed. To that extent and to that extent only some of the facts of the TV-am story and the lessons to be drawn from it deserve dispassionate examination. What were the main aims of the protagonists at the outset?

On the IBA's part, the main motive seems to have been willingness, rather than any great determination, to give breakfast-time television (defined as 'primarily but not exclusively news, information and current affairs between 6.00am and 9.15am') a trial, provided that this trial was clearly subordinated in every material way to the higher priority of launching Channel Four and provided that the risks were taken by the appointed contractor, not by the IBA or the taxpayer. There was also, no doubt, something of a wish to spice up the renewal or reallocation of the existing regional contracts in 1980 with some evident innovation, as well as some attraction at that time in the idea of ITV getting in first in Britain and perhaps in Europe with a new service. But it was also known that counsels had been divided within the Authority (members and senior staff) about breakfast-time television; and something of a lukewarm aura permeated its approach to the subject during 1980, 1981 and most of 1982.

On TV-am's part the aims were clear enough, namely in order of importance:

(a) to win the franchise;
(b) to run a successful business;
(c) to implement the central programme philosophy whereby the franchise was won;
(d) to pioneer certain ideals of television journalism; and
(e) to establish a firm, but open and straightforward, style of management which would release the enthusiasm and talent of the staff within a disciplined framework.

By March 1983 only the first of these had been unquestionably achieved, although great strides had also been made toward the fifth, marred by pockets of very poor management communication. It is essential, if the general lessons are to be correctly drawn, to define accurately the state of play of the other three aims at that time and reasons for them. Contemporary press comment seldom achieved this.

The most important, for its own sake and as a precondition of all the rest, was the second – success as a business. TV-am was, as endlessly reiterated in 1981 and 1982, first and foremost a company under the Companies Acts with a primary duty to its shareholders. But it was also a company with a difference. It only came into existence because it held a 'franchise' contract from the IBA, given under the Broadcasting Acts. This had a very specific implication for the whole business strategy of the company. Most successful independent businesses start very small. They grow by degrees and by trial and error. This means that, if an expansion fails, the company usually has the option to retreat slightly to its formerly stable plateau before attempting to expand in other directions. Where, however, the main business opportunity is created, as it were, artificially, as by the sudden granting of a major new public franchise, this is not true. The new business finds itself confronting an opportunity where, not only is there no proven guarantee of profitability at the required level of activity, but also the minimum critical mass at which even the possibility of commercial health begins is large. Given vigorous and competent competition from another breakfast-time channel, this minimum critical mass in the case of TV-am was measured at an initial annual turnover of about £17 million, later revised to £20 million. Below this level of effort, itself a minute fraction of the average ITV cost per hour of television produced (and TV-am, though a small and new company, was committed to producing more weekly hours of television than even the largest ITV company and more networked television than the three largest companies added together with staffs of about 1,500 to 2,000 each), the audience, faced with what was always expected to be strong competition from the BBC, and therefore the advertising revenue could be expected to fall off very rapidly, more rapidly than the associated cost savings. Much above that critical minimum level of expenditure the returns in increased advertising revenue from somewhat higher audiences could only be regarded as speculative. It was only in this 'envelope' of minimal critical mass around £20 million of initial annual turnover that the prospects were good for attracting the target 'spot rate' audience of 800,000 to 1,000,000 (i.e. four to five million people reached per week) and, so, for earning the revenue needed for commercial success.

The implications of this strategic context for TV-am's business were clear and specific:

(a) a fully developed and detailed business plan for at least the first four years of operation was needed;

(b) its shape and rationale needed to be well absorbed and understood by all concerned, especially the financial backers and top management;

(c) large financial resources needed, on that basis, to be committed years in advance and strong nerves would be needed as the plan fulfilled itself, with the usual 'ups and downs' of the unforeseen;

(d) critically important 'charter' negotiations with the broadcasting unions would be needed to open the way for modes of working and levels of reward which would be consistent with the economics of breakfast-time television and which would therefore have to be quite different from the existing pattern in other ITV companies (who had been free to start – and, but for this, would have started – breakfast television any time in the preceding dozen years);

(e) the earliest possible 'on air' date was vital in order to minimise the period of 'high-powered' expenditure without revenue (i.e. when you have both to spend the money and then pay interest on it) and in order to match BBC competition;

(f) the two key unknowns were audience size (both total breakfast and TV-am's share) and advertisers' response to the target level; and

(g) the strain on a very lean staff and resources – and therefore on the quality of management and editorial leadership – was going to be, rightly but importantly, great, since there was no way that the enterprise could be successful on the basis of traditional ITV levels of manning and comfortable use of facilities.

In retrospect, it is clear what went right and what went wrong up to March 1983; and the lessons to be drawn flow only if that accounting is accurately drawn up.

From the very beginning there was just such a business plan, of which the heart was a cash flow and financial projection over the eight-year period of the franchise. It was substantially modified only once, in the autumn and winter of 1982, to accommodate a higher initial level of planned expenditure. Its essential features were: a target 'spot' audience of close to a million on average in the first year out of a total breakfast-time audience shared with the BBC of about 1.8 million; a first year net revenue of about £17 million, rising with inflation and with some modest real growth in the early years; and initial annual total outlay of, originally, £16½ million, revised in 1982 to an internal budget of £20½ million and to an outside projection of £22 million; and an initial capital budget for premises and equipment of £10 million, revised late in 1982 to £10¼ million. This plan aimed at the bottom end of the 'envelope of profitability' described above and showed a thoroughly healthy business over the life of the franchise (to 1991).

Events justified or exceeded all but one of the elements in the plan up to March 1983. The all-important exception was TV-am's share in February and March of the joint breakfast audience. Out of a total 'spot' audience of close to two million for the two channels, TV-am's share fell through February to a low point of 300,000, recovering to 500,000 by the fourth week of March. The total audience was up to expectation; but TV-am's share needed to be built steadily up to 800,000 by early summer. Advertiser response, given the achievement of the target audience, was shown in February to exceed all expectation. It was possible then to calculate that, even with the continued and debilitating dispute between the actors' union and the advertising agencies over fees, an audience of 800,000 would generate a revenue of £20 million (£3 million above the target level) and, without the dispute, a revenue of £25 million or more. On that basis the business would be very profitable indeed. The expenditure required to achieve this remained at £20½ million; and actual expenditure was running within this budget and, so, well within the 'outside' projection. The premises and equipment, with minor exceptions, were bought in on time and all within the £10¼ million budget. Thus, it was clear that, given only the all-important audience improvement, even to a figure rather lower than the original target out of a total shared audience at or above the target level, the plan could be achieved, indeed exceeded.

The second implication mentioned above of TV-am's strategic business context – namely the need for the plan to be well understood by all concerned – was in retrospect less well fulfilled. Although the plan was fully shared with and approved by the board of the company at every stage, it later appeared that, when in the early months of 1983 the cash deficit flowed precisely in line with the planned levels, some of the company's backers were taken aback and started to see worrying 'losses' where a week before and a month before and a year before they had seen acceptable 'start-up costs'. The numbers were the same; but the attitude to them changed, partly because the daily front-page coverage of the poor ratings and other more imaginative stories rattled those who were unused to that kind of prominence and misrepresentation. This meant that the third implication mentioned above – the need for large resources and strong nerves – was prejudiced. The resources were committed; but the nerves frayed, with resulting convulsions and distraction of immediate effort from the priority – and otherwise reasonably straightforward – task of correcting the ratings deficit, or at least completing the already visible ratings recovery.

The fourth implication of the strategic business context – new kinds of union agreements – was fully satisfied by agreements reached in substance two to three months before TV-am went 'on air'; and it proved yet again that union negotiations can be highly constructive and realistic if intelligent management deals sensibly and candidly with union representatives.

The fifth implication – the need for the earliest possible 'on air' date – was never fully recognised by the IBA. When TV-am applied for the franchise it asked to start broadcasting at the beginning of 1982, like the new or renewed regional franchises. When the IBA offered the franchise to TV-am, it said only that the 'on air' date would be some time in 1983, possibly December. In 1981 this was brought forward to May 1983; and in the summer of 1982, after TV-am's pleas to be allowed to start with or before Channel 4 in November 1982, it was brought forward (with some caveats) to February 1983. The gain of eleven months was invaluable; but the loss of thirteen months, in start-up costs and in competition with the BBC, added to the burdens of the new venture. Even so, they were provided for in the business plan.

The sixth implication – the key unknowns – was precisely right. The total audience and the advertisers' response to the target TV-am's share were in line with or above expectations. TV-am's actual share in the first eight weeks was far below target, though in process of recovery; and that proved too much for the suddenly frayed nerves of the backers.

The seventh implication – the strain on staff and leadership – was also right in two senses. The strain on new and young recruits was very great. But their enthusiasm and dedication rose to the challenge and produced prodigies of long hours and courageous improvisation. The management and editorial leadership were more patchy; and somewhat Byzantine editorial structures and odd blockages in communication with pro- gramme staff frequently marred the good general atmosphere of the company.

In short, of all the things required for the planned business strategy to succeed three – and only three – were missing or deficient: the ratings; business nerves; and programme management. The first – which was due both to the inevitable initial trials and errors in presentation (see below) and to the third – and the third were capable of rapid corrrection, for which decisions and proposals had been made. The failure of the second, allied to some natural ambition, proved fatal to a business strategy based on the franchise *as offered*, because it took away the couple of months needed to correct the other two and because it caused the company after March 1983, progressively to fall out of the bottom of the 'envelope of profitability', in other words to stall the aero- plane just when it needed maximum thrust.

This leaves to be examined the state of play by March 1983, of TV-am's other two unfulfilled aims listed on page 267, namely to implement the central programme philosophy and to pioneeer certain ideals of television journalism. The short answer is that they were unfulfilled because they were barely tried and because in their nature they take years, not weeks, to fulfil. They were barely tried because the overriding priority, as perceived at the time, was 'to get the show on the road' and to build the initial audience on which the whole enterprise as a business depended for survival. Naively, as it turned out, it seemed that there would be time enough, once the physical, organisational and programming challenges of getting 'on air' and established with the viewers had been overcome, to refine and develop the technique of the, above all, popular, but also intelligent and illuminating, journalism that

271

according to TV-am's prospectus was meant to share equally with entertaining material in making up the total mix of what was adumbrated as a '*Daily Mirror* of the air'.

In retrospect it may also have been, though this was not detected at the time, perhaps because of very top management's preoccupation with the operational, financial and sales aspects of launching the business, that there was a divergence of opinion about the desirable programme style between those who invented and proclaimed TV-am's programme missions and those who had the task of carrying them out. Once into rehearsal and 'on air' this began to become apparent. But almost immediately the problem deserving first priority was the ratings; and the available research pointed to the need for swift and simple presentational changes, with general improvement of programme standards inevitably requiring a much longer and more painstaking gradual amelioration. Early moves to start the process encountered, perhaps understandably in the atmosphere engendered by the ratings problem and the press blitz on TV-am, exceptionally sensitive and defensive reactions; and more ruthless action was neither necessary in conquering this longer term problem nor possible once the backers' nerves became frayed by the same press blitz and by imperfect understanding of the ratings problem and the actions actually being taken to correct it.

While this is the whole explanation of the fact that no serious attempt was made in the first few weeks to implement the central programme philosophy and even more the pioneering of certain ideals of television journalism, it may still be worth recalling what they were and to consider how successful they could have been.

This philosophy and these ideals were, of course, set out in TV-am's original application for the franchise in May 1980; but they were amplified and refined in the succeeding months and years. They were, perhaps, most conveniently and clearly stated in an interview given by the author on 11 February 1982, a year before TV-am went 'on air':

'The audience which we aim to reach is the great mass of the ordinary British public. It is not targeted on any particular sub-group. It is obviously very much part of our thinking that we are broadcasting at a time of day, 6 o'clock or 6.15 to 9.15am, at which the great majority of people, though not a hundred percent of them – we have to remember that it is not a hundred percent – are getting up, doing whatever they do by way of having breakfast (which, in some cases, is maybe a full breakfast and in many cases probably just a quick cup of coffee or whatever, getting dressed, glancing at the newspaper), having quick snatches of conversation with one another about the day's plans and getting on the road to work, to school, to wherever they go. There is, however, still a big slice of the population, probably not as big as it once was, who are doing all those things, but are not leaving the house. They are going to stay there – the housewives, or as we prefer to call them, the "non-breadwinners".

'What we aim to do, and we are very excited about it, is produce something which in one sense is very unoriginal indeed, namely a newspaper at breakfast-time. What is original is that we are producing it on television and not on paper. I believe that, if we do it very well, the great mass of the ordinary people of our country, who are interested in what is going on, if it is well explained, if it is fast moving and if along the way there is plenty of fun and amusement in the process, if it is entertaining as well as illuminating, will value such a service very much; and I further believe very strongly that the newspapers for various reasons, partly because they have loony proprietors, partly because they have terrible trade union problems and partly for other reasons have not been serving that public very well. Indeed, they are having increasing problems in serving it basically because the technology on which they live is increasingly out of date and the public has already, and has for decades, accepted television and radio as the primary means of mass communication.

'If we can provide them with a breakfast-time newspaper service, not just news but the whole gamut of what a newspaper has to deal in, which includes features and fun as well as useful facts and service information, weather and everything else, then I believe that we shall succeed in attracting a healthy proportion of that audience. By a healthy proportion, of course, we do not mean what would be meant if this were some kind of general election in which you have to get fifty-one percent in order to win. Nobody, except maybe the Royal wedding, ever gets fifty-one percent of the available audience. A healthy, very successful audience would be five percent, five homes in a hundred.

'It is certainly not targeted in any primary or exclusive way at women. It is a newspaper. It is perfectly true, sociologically, that, if you come back three years after we have been on the air and analyse

273

the audience, you will probably find that there are, have been, more, significantly more, women than men; but there are also young people. Our aim is to interest and amuse and entertain the greatest possible number of men, women and very importantly young people, too, including children. When children go to school, they are frequently expected to discuss and to be aware of current issues; and it should benefit them to have been able to watch this on television together with their parents. Reading a newspaper, getting stuck behind a newspaper at breakfast, is a very solitary, isolating affair. Watching television together, which I think will happen in some cases, is more of a shared experience. I certainly find, and I know a lot of people have said this to me, that, when adults and kids watch a stimulating television programme together, it actually provokes conversation between them and brings them more together in ways which might not otherwise have occurred; and that is something in which we take pride. We think that, if we do succeed in our primary mission of explaining and illuminating the world in an enjoyable, brisk, entertaining and fascinating way, then that will be not only a service to the great majority of adults, who will appreciate it, but also perhaps even more importantly, though numerically less important, to young people as well.

'This is all provided, and it is the big proviso, that the programmes we make are really first class – that they are fascinating, informative, explanatory and illuminating – and in addition that the whole process is fun. It is laid down by law that the emphasis has to be, and I quote the phrase, "primarily but not exclusively news, information and current affairs". And we have interpreted that as meaning – and our interpretation has been accepted by the regulatory authority, by the IBA, because it was in our franchise application – that we would aim to be like a popular intelligent newspaper in all of its facets from the front pages to the back. So, if you think of what is on the agenda of a newspaper, which is very wide, not just news, it is everything, well that is on our agenda too. We shall be originating more hours of television than any other institution in Britian apart from the BBC. So, we have a lot of time. Even so, if you compare a newspaper with television, the number of actual words or word-equivalents that you can get through in half an hour of television or indeed in three hours of television is quite modest compared with what you can pack into a newspaper. So we have to be selective and succinct; but all the things newspapers do are on our agenda ...

Question: What about this ideal of serious popular journalism?

'The thing that at the moment fascinates me is that the more time you spend close to government, the more convinced you become that the options open to government and to the whole democratic political process are very, very narrowly constrained by the state of public awareness and understanding. And that is where what I call decent journalism comes in. By this I do not mean high-brow or learned or long-winded journalism or even necessarily the journalism of *The New York Times*. I mean journalism which is genuinely motivated to find things out, to explain them to ordinary people in ordinary clear ways. That is where I think decent journalism has a tremendous role to play.

'Now I do believe very strongly that for a whole series of more or less accidental reasons the newspapers are finding it more and more difficult to play that role. As I say, I think really terrible proprietors who seem to me to have absolutely no sense of the role of journalism or the dignity of the profession, appallingly antediluvian trade union practices in a number of areas and obsolescent technology – and also, I am afraid to say, certain attitudes and practices within the profession of journalism, which I may add would not be tolerated and are not tolerated in the United States and which are very unprofessional, very amateurish, very unethical in my opinion – have all contributed to making newspapers very much weaker and very much less adequate in playing this role that I have described. Secondly, I believe that television, which is overwhelmingly the most important medium in terms of what actually affects people's attitudes, has not seized the opportunity to create a distinctive television journalism of an adequate kind. I think that both BBC and ITV, which to a certain extent follows the BBC pattern, have been hag-ridden by this wholly artificial and destructive distinction between news and current affairs, which has meant that quality journalism has not gone into the basic reporting, which should include the analytical and explanatory process, to the extent that it should. I think that we, because of the nature of our franchise and because of the personal commitments and philosophy that by luck – and I do not kid myself that it is anything other than luck – we have got an opportunity to be what I have called a kind of Noah's Ark for decent journalism. As the floodwaters of an alien environment for good journalism are rising all around us I see us here in this small building as a little ark into which we want to gather in two-by-two or one-by-one representatives of the key elements in decent journalism; and I hope that a more favourable environment will one day come, that those floodwaters will recede and that, when that time comes, people will go out with the seedcorn which we have preserved; and so decent journalism can survive. I believe that good journalism is enormously important for its own sake; but I also believe that it has a role to play in the creation of what academics call a polity and a society which is capable of responsible, understanding and caring political action.

'In the last resort, in my opinion, television like all other productive activities is for the consumer; and it is bad economics, bad democracy and bad morals in my opinion to try to displace that criterion by any other. That is what it is for. The desire to be entertained, the desire to be relaxed, the desire to be amused and the desire to have your mind totally evacuated from time to time are just as legitimate and natural as the desires to be stimulated, uplifted, informed and so on. So, I think all of those things ought to be there in the total spectrum of what television offers. Now, our particular part of it on breakfast television obviously is directed to a particular task, which is the journalistic task, but entertaining, enjoyable, fun, illuminating journalism. Light entertainment is not part of our task; and the way the law is written it is not even something that we would be allowed to do on any significant scale.'

The philosophy and ideals behind TV-am were also stated in a speech given by the author on 27 January 1982, to The Market Research Society:

'Our target audience is the maximum feasible proportion of the general mass of the ordinary British people at that time of day. It is not our intention, with what is essentially a nationally networked service which by law and by stipulation of the IBA has to be, and I quote the phrase, "primarily but not exclusively news, information and current affairs", to seek to cater mainly or primarily for any particular sub-section of the audience. That, as we see it, is more the task of Channel Four, given that they have a rather different charter and rather a different role. Our task is to provide a service in that broadly journalistic field to the general mass of the ordinary viewers at that time of day.

'Another, perhaps even simpler, way of putting what we are trying to do is that we are trying to provide the first newspaper on television and to provide what we call popular intelligent journalism in all of its facets from the front pages to the back. I have sometimes been pressed to identify which particular newspaper or newspaper audience it is that most nearly conforms to the type of audience that we have in mind. I have attempted to abstain from this because there are so many characteristics of any particular newspaper that one might name with which I would not wish to be associated. One is easily misunderstood if one uses a newspaper as a way of identifying a particular audience; but if I am really pressed to say in the very broadest general terms which newspaper would I wish to come closest to emulating, I would say – indeed, I have said – it was perhaps the readership of the *Daily Mirror* in the 1950s, which I regard as one of the highest achievements of mass popular intelligent journalism. That was the paper which, in addition to achieving pretty well the greatest national daily sales of any newspaper in the English-speaking world, was also in my opinion widely entertaining and bright, lively and diverting in all sorts of ways and combined with that the fulfilment of a very decent and honourable and brilliantly crafted journalistic mission of confronting from time to time, sometimes on the whole of the front page, sometimes on the middle-page spread, sometimes in other ways, the serious issues of the day in a way which was successful because it was informative to, illuminating for, the ordinary readers in the ordinary population. So, it is certainly no part of our task, although we have said many things about the mission and the ambition that we have to provide a vehicle for decent journalism and to explain events more illuminatingly and more intelligently than they have been in the past, to follow in the steps of *The Times* or the *Financial Times* or the *Guardian* or even the *Telegraph* in this regard. Our aim is popular journalism for the great mass of the ordinary people.

'To offer to what is still pretty well the greatest newspaper-reading public in the world a popular, intelligent and amusing newspaper at the traditional time of day on what is now the most universally accepted medium of communication, namely television, cannot and should not be regarded as a commercial undertaking of the riskiest kind. It is, in my opinion, broadly and strategically a very sound proposition indeed. Nonetheless, in order to make a success of it we have to make that all-important transition from defining a broad concept which makes a great deal of sense to actually doing it on the air morning by morning by morning, seven days a week, as it will be, fifty-two weeks a year. And in order to do that we believe that, while the programme itself does not break down in this way there are two essential things to achieve. One is that one's treatment of the news, of events in the world, in the nation and locally is (a) reliable, up to date and authoritative and (b) illuminating.

'I could go on for a very long time, but I will not because it would be an abuse of your patience, about my particular theories and convictions about the defects and weaknesses of British journalism in general and British television journalism in particular and about the failings of the forms and ways in which it has traditionally been done. We have to make news treatment come alive to ordinary people by making the events as described intelligible, interesting and related to them, related to their lives, related to what they heard yesterday, to what they might expect to happen tomorrow, related to other items that they hear. The world, the real world, is made up of an almost seamless garment of interacting events; and yet the traditional treatment of journalists is to break everything up into these totally atomised and unrelated little "stories", which are treated as though they had no bearing on anything else whatever, needed no context, no perspective, no history, no geography in order to make them intelligible. I think that, in providing that kind of context and causal dimension and in thus fulfilling what I call our "mission to explain", we have an enormously important task to do. It is not only important for its own sake and for journalists; but it is also a vitally important part of reversing what in British television in recent decades has been evidence of a declining public interest in news and current affairs. I do not believe that that is because the public are becoming less concerned or more despairing or less intelligent or less educated or anything else. I think it is because the way in which the world has been treated by television journalists has, to put it crudely, "turned people off". It has turned people off because we have bombarded them with an endless stream of atomised little gobbets of so-called information, which have no context, no perspective, no meaning, no relationship to anything else; and I think people, like atoms, break up or glaze over when they are bombarded in that way.

'That's the journalistic part of the mission. But the other part which is at least equally important – and certainly equally important in terms of assuring that we do achieve the kind of audience for which we aspire – is that the whole process should be fun. It should be fun, not in the sense of being a part of the entertainment business, but in the sense that it should be, as all good professional popular journalism is, entertaining; and I make that distinction, not just because there is a formal obligation laid on us by the IBA to be essentially in the journalism and the field of pure entertainment for its own sake. So because I actually believe that that is a fair and proper description of the difference between the task, the legitimate task, of popular journalism and the field of pure entertainment for its own sake. So our programmes certainly will not consist of quiz shows and old movies and the things that one might be going into on a limited budget if one were simply doing television on an entertainment basis at an off-peak time. They will on the contrary be conceived as, put together as, edited as, a popular newspaper with lots of fun things in it. We have to develop, and we shall develop and are developing, not merely the television equivalent of the purely reporting part of newspapers but also the television equivalent of political cartoons, strip cartoons and all those other features – woman's page features, city page features, other columns, books, last night's television, tomorrow's television, etc, etc. – which are part of the total agenda of any successful popular newspaper today. And we believe that on that basis – and given of course the very strong team of senior and experienced journalists and presenters with whom we shall launch the new service, in the form of David Frost, Michael Parkinson, Robert Kee, Anna Ford and Angela Rippon – we shall rapidly achieve a decent and substantial audience for this service.'

The speech of welcome to new staff given by the author in November 1982 also sets out the ideals behind TV-am:

'Our overriding editorial task, indeed, is to ensure that by their tone, pace, style, content and timing our programmes infiltrate themselves into the often very rigid start-the-day rituals of our audience so that *Good Morning Britain* becomes as indispensable as a first cup of coffee, a first glance at the papers or – perish the thought – that first cigarette. But for that very reason we are, in *this* respect, building on the very long-established habits of the legendarily conservative British public, namely their addiction for over a century to the tradition of the popular newspaper – that special blend of news, useful information and fun – as the proper accompaniment to breakfast and the start of the day.

'Of course we wish to exploit to the full all the massive advantages of the fact that our newspaper is conveyed, not by the steam-age printing press, but by the wonders of television technology, which is also why we have spent so much money under Geoff Monks's wise guidance in getting the most advanced and effective equipment. But, while the methods are uncompromisingly that of television, the function which the programmes we make ultimately fulfil for our viewers is much more akin to the function of the good popular morning newspaper than to the function of conventional evening entertainment on TV.

'This is just as well since our contract with the IBA obliges us to provide "primarily but not exclusively news, information and current affairs", which indeed is a fair approximation to the agenda of a good popular morning paper. We are therefore essentially in the business of journalism – news journalism, feature journalism, journalism for children – to be sure journalism on television, but still journalism, which is why the IBA recognises us as a news organisation for the purposes of the equipment we use and the rights we enjoy round the world.

'My second point – making a new and different kind of television – flows in part from the first. We are in the business of journalism. But we are practising it in the new framework of a very large number of hours – over twenty a week, more than any other ITV company and over three times more networked output than any other ITV company – very large numbers of hours of live studio-based programmes. It is fundamental to the economics of our operation as well as to the new kind of journalism that we are practising – I shall come to that in a moment – that the studio, the live studio, is the primary and central forum of our work.

'It is why the experience and talent of our five senior presenters are so integral to our formula and why all of us – executives, journalists (on-screen and off-), technicians, sales people and, perhaps above all, studio directors – are going to have to think and work all the time in new ways to adapt to new opportunities and a new environment. It will, as I said, be tough and demanding, but also fun because it will be creative.

'My third point – a new and different kind of journalism – brings me back to what was, I now think, the single most important idea that won the breakfast franchise for TV-am, namely "our mission to explain". We have, of course, an equal mission to entertain – not by traditional "light entertainment", but by entertainingly informing and diverting our audience.

'The "mission to explain", to be sure, does no more than emphasise the third of the three co-equal functions of all good reporting, namely to find out, to report and to explain. And I will not now add – you may be relieved to hear – to the billions of words that I have already seemed to have spilled over the last three years and more about this notion – you are all welcome, if you want it, to copies of my now notorious lecture on the subject, "What is News?" the tedium of which Michael Deakin claims has stunned more sheep at a greater range than even the works of Hegel and Channel 4 combined. I will only say that in everything we do the aim should be, not to impress the audience – still less each other or other journalists – with our knowledge and sophistication, but to reach out for that wonderful moment when the light of understanding is lit in the eye of the viewer as he or she, old or young, says "Oh, *now* I see".'

To implement these programme goals was obviously – and was always intended to be – a medium-to-long-term project. Programme philosophies do not turn into reality on the screen simply by being expounded, however enthusiastically and frequently. What appears on the screen is always an expression of a culture; and that is the culture of the people and of the place where the programmes are made. In order to create the culture which can deliver the intended programmes it is necessary to recruit a team with the right enthusiasm, skills and interests. Then they must be fully imbued with and convinced of the intended programme philosophy. Finally, solutions must be found to the almost limitless set of specific practical problems which arise for producers, reporters, presenters and editors in dealing effectively on the screen, both visually and aurally, with the presentation of scores of items every day in accordance with the intended philosophy.

This raises questions of technique, of facilities, of sheer journalistic insight and fact-finding, of the organisation and rostering of round-the-clock teams, of relations between journalists and technicians, of accepted and novel working practices, of the effective exploitation of wonderous new machinery, especially in the graphics and news computer areas, and of the proper integration of the main studio base with all the external and outlying facilities, teams and 'locations' which give such a programme the essential feeling of freedom and broad national coverage which it needs. These are not things which come fully and smoothly together overnight, however much pre-planning there is. The theories can be honed. The facilities can be planned and, subject to the usual hiccups and delays, delivered. The necessary number of individual-

281

ly talented people can be recruited. Programme structure and items can be planned in advance on paper and certain regular spots designed and contracted well in advance, although there was not in fact enough of this kind of pre-planning of programmes. But while, if these preparations are effectively made, as for the most part they were, they can assure a reasonably competent physical launch on time, the full creation of a working team with a shared philosophy, mutual understanding and effective new techniques for getting that philosophy on the screen must take many months of trial, error, refinement, experimentation, correction and training.

Where the financial facts of life of a new company, living off shareholders' money, rule out any possibility of recruiting staff, installing facilities and running real rehearsals more than a very brief period before revenue starts to be earned, i.e. before the programmes go 'on air', this process of progressive amelioration from initial crude technical competence to higher and higher creative refinement has, willy nilly, to be done on the job. As long as the initial product is strong enough to attract a large enough audience to secure the economic base of the operation, then it is professionally acceptable that the fulfilment of the higher journalistic and creative aspirations should be achieved and judged over at least half a franchise period, i.e. four years, not over six weeks.

This is not the place to discuss in detail the specific production techniques, use of graphics, sourcing of news material and deployment of personnel that are needed to achieve the entertaining popular journalism with an enhanced explanatory dimension that TV-am aimed to achieve. These are important questions and will continue to be debated amongst professionals; but the only important point here is that there is nothing in the TV-am experience, including its initial audience failure, to suggest that these aims cannot be achieved or would not be successful with the audience.

There remains the question of why the programmes, as actually made, were so unsuccessful with the audience in the first month. It is the kind of question to which the complete answer will never be known definitively, although every observer has his own strong private convictions about the 'real' explanation. A reasonable judgement, blending the available preliminary research with professional judgement, would, in the author's opinion, be sceptical of the standard excuses, such as the

BBC's two weeks' head-start 'on air', the habit of modern sets with electronic channel selection of tuning automatically to BBC1 when switched on, some unprecedented public aversion to advertisements and massive error in the BARB ratings. Instead, such a reasonable judgement would, first, pay tribute to the BBC for having achieved the rare feat of launching a major new long-running series with the right tone and balance from the beginning and, secondly, will ask why TV-am, whose general specification of its programme aims was barely distinguishable in all essentials from that of the BBC (though expounded two years earlier), nonetheless missed its target. The key, according to the early research, lay not in contents or agenda, but in presentation, tone and style.

There is much quasi-learned debate about precisely what this means, most of it pretending to a higher degree of certainty than the evidence by itself can possibly warrant. The most plausible interpretation is that it measures viewers' general reaction to the overall character of a programme, without the viewers themselves necessarily being skilled in or bothered with diagnosing accurately the precise elements in the impression which they like or dislike. The professional, however, has to try to carry the explanation further; and that really comes down to two things. The first is the general excellence and sensitivity of production, that is all the things which by experience, by flair, by sound organisation and by the right feel for popular tastes the people behind the scenes do to make the programme. The second is that indefinable and unmeasurable quality of 'personality' which a programme has and which viewers like or dislike.

Weaknesses in the first were undoubtedly an important contributory part of the explanation for TV-am's poor ratings in its first four weeks. Despite the individual quality and enthusiasm of the programme staff at the coal-face, weaknesses in organisation, facilities and editing meant that their efforts, often prodigious, were not as productive as they should have been. This in turn meant that those who were presenting the programmes on the screen did not receive anything like the quantity or quality of support which is normal and which they needed. Indeed, it was only at times their own talent and experience which kept the programmes going despite crises behind the scenes. Specifically, the deployment and rostering of programme staff turned out to be unbalanced. Some editorial decisions tended to be made too late and unnecessarily late. The shape, pattern and regularity of the programmes was insufficiently signposted for the viewer to see within the programmes. Picture editing facilities were over-stretched, as was the early capacity to generate diagrams and other graphics.

There was, also, a fatal tendency, quite contrary to TV-am's stated intention of integrating news and current affairs (i.e. all aspects of television journalism), to separate organisationally and conceptually 'news' from the other journalistic elements in the programme. (The whole point was supposed to be that, on the output side, while it was convenient for the viewer to segregate a brief news *summary* on the hour and the half hour, there should be no segregation of the treatment of important stories between the headlines in the summary and the fuller treatment in the main body of the programmes and that, on the input side, the same people and the same organisation should supply both the headlines for the news summary and the fuller treatment so that the division of labour would be by stories and subjects, not by categories of programme output.) All of these things had their inevitable effect on the 'feel' and quality of the programmes as produced. Despite the most explicit and endlessly reiterated determination from the earliest days to achieve the popular tone of the *Daily Mirror* and to avoid any metropolitan flavour, a certain aura of the *Guardian* and Camden Lock crept in too often.

It is important to recognise these failures squarely. But is is also important to recognise that they were all fairly routine teething problems, which were capable of – and in process of – rapid correction as part of the staple task of management. The first month 'on air' was TV-am's 'shake down' cruise. The probable need for rapid and flexible changes, as soon as it was seen how the programmes were received by the public, had always been recognised as a likely contingency; and one or two drastic moves were needed and decided upon. But there was nothing in any of this that went beyond the normal day-to-day task of management or called into question the validity of the basic conception of the company, the franchise or the programme philosophy and journalistic ideals.

What was called for, on the production side, was not any radical shift of agenda, nor any plunge 'up' or 'down' market (a term seldom used by commercially successful enterprises, such as Marks and Spencer, who succeed precisely because they do not have the condescending, even contemptuous, attitude to their public implied by those uncommercially-minded theorists who deal in such language), still less any systematic violation of the franchise obligation to deal 'primarily but not exclusive-ly in news, information and current affairs'. The need was simply for much greater excellence, flair and common touch in the delivery of the existing agenda, plus a gradual evolution towards the more daring and original programme philosophy as propounded from the beginning. Undoubtedly, the BBC had benefited decisively in the initial weeks from having more readily available the organisational and editorial skills in the programme-making area to ensure that from the earliest days they did what they did to a high standard; and that carried through to an impression on screen which the viewers preferred, even if they did not fully analyse it, under the broad heading of 'presentation, tone and style'.

When one comes to the undefinable element of programme 'personality', it is wrong to see this exclusively in terms of the people who present the programmes, important as they are. To some extent programme personality is an epiphenomenon of all the things discussed just above under the heading of 'production'. In the early weeks, despite the predominantly warm and laudatory reception from the TV critics, programme 'personality' did perceptibly suffer from the inevitable reflection on screen of at least some of the stresses and strains behind the scenes. It is hard to maintain an air of effortless relaxation, gaiety and avid curiosity on screen, when staff are having to work exceedingly long hours and to combat technical teething problems which can easily come to occupy far more time than the strictly journalistic tasks of researching and presenting an item. These things are hard to measure; and impressions no doubt vary. But to this observer there was some tendency, after the colossal enthusiasm and excitement of the first week, for the grim determination and sheer exhaustion behind the scenes to come through in a certain strain and contrivance 'on air' which viewers instinctively disliked, particularly at a time of day when, if they look at television at all, they look to it to cheer them up and thereby help them through the day's most difficult transition, namely getting up.

The other part of programme 'personality' is, of course, the people who actually present the programmes and appear on screen. TV-am had at its disposal a formidable array of talent, experience and reputation in those roles. Sundry myths about their role can be quickly dispelled, for example, that they were originally recruited indiscriminately for their 'star' quality, that this quality dazzled the IBA into giving the franchise to TV-am and that, as founders and shareholders of the company, they did not or could not fit comfortably into TV-am's management and editorial command structures. They were in fact recruited for their journalistic and programme-making skill and experience because that was seen to be a necessary means to the end of the chosen programme philosophy, which in turn was the decisive magnet that attracted them, at significant personal financial risk, to abandon established careers for TV-am. The point was clearly explained by the author repeatedly between 1980 and 1983, as for example in an interview on 11 February 1982:

'Q. Your team of celebrities are quite an astonishing coup – to get all of them.

A. We think of them and they do themselves – it is a very important part of why they are here, though obviously they are celebrities – as working journalists. One of the, indeed the, decisive reason why they wanted to be involved was because they wanted to be fully creatively involved in making the kind of television journalism that they believed to be possible and which they had felt in very different ways, working for existing large institutions, for impresarios, for bureaucrats, for bankers or whatever, they had not been fully free to do. So we always refer to them as programme-makers or presenters. We do not think of them as stars or celebrities.

Q. But the public does.

A. The public, of course, does and we welcome and are proud of their celebrity. But that is not how or why we chose that particular group of people. If you look at their backgrounds and their biographies, you find that they have all been real working journalists and that is what they want to be. Sure, they will be in front of the camera; but they will not just be in front of the camera. They are not just people who read autocues or perform. They are senior members of our journalistic team and that is what has excited them.'

But this point never really sank in with the writing press, who preferred its own home-made image of the 'galaxy of stars', which of course then became a convenient object of irony by those who had themselves invented this very misconception when the early audience results were poor. It is true that TV-am themselves from the earliest days had used the analogy of United Artists to highlight the fact that the original TV-am consortium was composed from many people whose backgrounds were in, as they said, 'the front end of the business'. But this was not meant to – and did not – imply that the well-known names were a random collection of any old top stars. They were a carefully chosen group of proven professionals with a shared commitment to a specific philosophy and with skills and experience to suit.

IBA members must, if they ever feel free to do so, speak for themselves about why they awarded the breakfast-time franchise to TV-am. But the author's own careful researches at the time and subsequently established beyond any doubt whatever in his mind that the decisive factor was the programme philosophy and the enthusiastic commitment of the TV-am consortium to it. Certainly, the adherence of, at that stage, six senior presenters who were clearly ready to take such big risks with their careers for the sake of something so experimental was important because it underlined the seriousness of the commitment to the pro-gramme philosophy. Likewise, the solid financial backing and the sensible technical planning also helped to reinforce the application. But all of these things were secondary to and would have achieved nothing without the programme philosophy.

Even further from the mark was the notion that the presenters' involvement as founders and shareholders created confusion in the executive and editorial operations of the company. It was made abundantly clear from the earliest days when the franchise was written in April 1980, that these roles were distinct; and it was specifically written into the franchise application – and later carried into practice – that the presenters had no executive position and that their contribution to programme monitoring and development should be channelled through a specific Programme Committee, which made no decisions. Naturally their experience and skills meant that their ideas and com-ments deserved to be listened to carefully. Naturally, too, given the very lean staffing and the enormous amount of programme output, their day-to-day contribution to editorial thinking was to be welcomed and valued. But it was crystal clear from the beginning that in company affairs decisions rested only with the executives, in editorial matters the final decision rested with the editors and in the studio the normal discipline of the studio director's authority was absolute. The presenters themselves understood this and kept meticulously to it, although in one case (weekend programmes) a presenter was specifically asked to take on broader editorial responsibility for certain programmes. Indeed, this self-discipline inevitably engendered some intense frustration when things did not go right and the experienced eye could see all too clearly where the weaknesses lay. This frustration did at one point finally erupt in public indiscretion. But at no time were the clear lines of executive and editorial authority challenged by the presenters in any way different-ly from the ordinary dialogue between producers and presenters which is commonplace in all television organisations.

287

Even so, the question can still be asked whether in their strict role as presenters they were able to contribute to the programmes the kind of personality it needed and whether, in so far as they were not, they share in any responsibility for the initial ratings weakness. These are very much matters of judgement. Even where available research throws any light on the matter, it is unable to distinguish that part of the public's reaction to a presenter which relates to his or her own innate qualities and that part which is really a reflection of how well or badly he or she has been supported by the team behind the scenes. It may have been, at most in one or two cases, that the morning environment was not ideally suited to the strong talent and style of the presenter. But even that merely throws responsibility back on to management to ensure that they are making the best possible use of the skills and personality available. It is not uncommon in managing a television programme or channel to have to experiment before finding the right personality for the right role and the right role for the right personality. This was why early experimentation was built into TV-am's initial plans and why it was possible to make swift changes, which quickly established an improving trend in the audience figures from 300,000 at the end of February to 500,000 by late March. The plan was to build thereafter on the proven particular success of Michael Parkinson; and had this decision, made at the beginning of March, been implemented, there is little doubt that the target rating of about 800,000 would have been comfortably reached in April or May, thereby (as explained on page 269 above) ensuring TV-am's success as a business as well as in its programmes. In general, the overwhelming conclusion on the evidence is that there was nothing fundamentally wrong with the presenters. On the contrary they were a great asset. The problem lay in the thinness of the support which they received and in other weaknesses of programme organisation and management affecting programme quality. These were our, the management's, responsibility and, though they were important, they were not unusual or at all intractable in any organisation which was growing and learning rapidly. There was, however, an inevitable temptation, because of the prominence of the presenters, for blame to be shifted quite undeservedly on to them both by external critics and regrettably by one or two within who were naturally fearful of being blamed themselves.

These things are only important in so far as they bear upon the possibility of fulfilling the kind of broad business and journalistic aspirations which an enterprise such as TV-am had. This makes it necessary to clear away and explain misconceptions and false interpretations of events which may otherwise cloud accurate historical judgement.

In summary, therefore, TV-am's failure to achieve all of its starting aims by March 1983, came down simply and solely to the very bad audience ratings in the first few weeks and the effect of this on the nerves of some of those whose money was at stake. Those poor ratings were not due to any flaw in the conception of the franchises or TV-am's application for it or the role and talent of its original presenters. A spot audience of close to two million was shown to exist for the two channels. A one-channel audience of above 1½ million was shown by the BBC to be achievable on a basis very similar in conception to TV-am's franchise application – relaxed, fast-moving, studio-based, popular news, information, current affairs and features, the very 'electronic popular newspaper' of which TV-am had spoken. A revenue well in excess of the budget target was shown to be available, given even slightly less than half that joint audience and given even the IPA-Equity dispute. Necessary (and actual) expenditure was within the budget and was eminently affordable, given that prospective revenue. Presentation, style and tone were proved not to be right at that time of day; but changes could be and were swiftly made, where the evidence pointed to the need for it.

The general lessons that follow, therefore, are that:

(a) the IBA was justified in offering such a franchise;
(b) TV-am's application for it was sound in business terms, given only the assumed programme success;
(c) programme success, as with very many new TV series, can take a few months to achieve;
(d) new ventures that have a large initial minimum critical mass require strong financial and psychological resources;
(e) there is no evidence either way from this experience whether the ideals of television journalism embodied in TV-am's prospectus, in the franchise applicatin and elsewhere could or would be successful with audiences, because they were never tried; and
(f) there is no substitute, not even the strongest presenting talent, for strong and competent editorial leadership with a sure popular touch and for good programme organisation.

289

Personal
and Philosophical

Religion – That's the Only Cloud
in Civilisation's Sky

Any view about the future of civilisation is tenable – just because any definition of that elusive entity is permissible. Which makes it just as well that this is a strictly personal testimony.

My opinion, in short, is that 'our civilisation' is in excellent shape and improving still further every day. Only one cloud hangs in the sky; and to that I shall come.

I should make it clear, lest I be thought callously complacent in the face of the grosser political and economic injustices in every nation, that in speaking of 'our civilisation' I am confining myself to a much shallower view of the world.

If I am looking a little beyond my personal way of life, my horizon is still well this side of the great social issues of man's cosmic condition. I am concerned, let us say, with the scope and the affronts offered in England today to the sensibilities of a youngish man with conventional education, normal appetites and as much money as he and his wife can earn.

There are, it must be straightaway admitted, impressive incivilities whose assaults have to be endured. There are 'skin-heads' and motorway-mad official engineers. There are the Concorde aeroplane and Vice-President Spiro T. Agnew. There are the Northern Line and the New English Bible. There are Commercial Television and the Common Market. There are Mr Tom Jones and Lord Hill. There are the life-insurance business and *Punch*, the dentists' weekly. There are Plaid Cymru and the Conservative Party. There are the Rev. Ian Paisley and the vocabulary of space travel. There are Mr Wedgwood Benn and – if it comes to that – the dawn chorus of my neighbour's Black and Decker drill.

There are many other lesser vexations, such as the decline without the fall of the mini-skirt and the pestiferous nature of all creditors. But these are not the things of which civilisations die, nor on which prophets of their doom please to dwell. Such seers warm to much grander themes.

Civilisation is typically portrayed as a kind of wedding cake,

293

composed of a rich and sturdy centre iced with culture. The economic and military base is acknowledged only as an essential foundation to the coating of civility which is nonetheless the purpose and vindication of the whole. The cake is baked that the exterior artistry may shine securely.

This view was most elegantly developed in Clive Bell's celebrated essay, 'Civilization', which he dedicated to Virginia Woolf in 1927. He sets out in it to prove that 'a civilized society is nothing but a society that has been coloured by a group of civilized people'.

Armed with such epochal findings as that 'the savage rarely smiles; he grins', Mr Bell affirms that 'that only a leisured class will produce a highly civilized and civilizing elite is an opinion supported by what seem to me incontrovertible arguments and borne out by history'. Lest any in the 'upper', professional or managerial classes should begin to feel heartened by this doctrine, they should note that Mr Bell judges it 'difficult, if not impossible, for anyone immediately and deeply con- cerned with the exercise of power to be completely civilized'.

He also warns his readers not to 'mistake a crowd of big wage-earners for a leisured class', adding that 'men who earn several thousand pounds a year by their trade, profession, or calling are generally nothing better than overpaid helots'.

Indeed Mr Bell will happily leave to the 'jolly alliance of great and small money-makers' their tug-o'-war for 'the plums of barbarism' under any form of government provided only that their productive efforts generate an adequate surplus to endow 'a sufficiency of children with the most thorough and liberal education wit can devise or money buy, provided it support these through life with an income adequate to their cultivated wants, provided above all it ask nothing of them'.

He accepts the logic of his ban on civic and economic involvement, admitting that 'the perfectly civilized are essentially defenceless'. It is not hard, therefore, to see how someone who held this view of civility as mere cultivated urbanity might be somewhat uneasy about civilisation's prospects.

But to me the whole conception is not only effete, avowedly elitist and rapidly decadent, but also essentially uncivilised. For it involves the arbitrary and arrogant exclusion of much the greater part of any community from the fullest possible development and gratification of their sensibilities.

Since to Mr Bell civility resides precisely in recognising the moral primacy of the intelligent pursuit of pleasure, it is at least ungracious of him not to count towards his own restrictive measure of civilisation the fruits of the generous provision which he himself, as despot, would make for the leisure, education and pleasure of the producers. To me, the progress made in just these regards are the greatest glories of 'our civilisation'.

More seriously-intended books are written, published, bought and read than ever before. More plays are produced on stage and television. More concerts are performed. More gramophone records of all musical kinds are sold. Painting and sculpture thrive. Architectural innovation is faster, more original and more experimental than in previous centuries.

More people attend universities and leave school later. There is more leisure and it is more diversely used. More people travel for pleasure and farther. More people probably than ever sail boats, climb mountains, explore the countryside, experiment with cameras, tape-recorders and hi-fi equipment and cultivate beautiful gardens.

Much more important, greater numbers of people feel, and are more nearly, free to express themselves in their own way. This appears in how they eat, dress, live, decorate their homes, cherish one another and find their pleasures. An incurably authoritarian mentality calls this 'permissiveness' and condescends to, where it does not openly condemn, 'pop culture', hippiedom and the younger generation.

Yet, 'permitting' is merely the obverse of 'being permitted'; and that is what freedom, especially cultural and personal freedom, is. Some will argue that this new vitality of self-expression and independence in styles of life is barren hedonism, leading nowhere and signifying nothing but decay for civilisation. Even if that were true, I should still acclaim it.

For hedonism is the only honest religion, even if it is also the only religion which to practise successfully you must not too consciously believe. As Tennyson was right that 'there lives more faith in honest doubt . . . than in half the creeds', so too there lives more joy in honest pleasure than in all the virtues. Sensuality is a great gift; and, like any talent, it should be put to work.

But it seems to me that the vigour of the present renaissance amongst those who have been born mostly since Munich goes beyond a gloriously exultant Bacchanalia. The discoveries that to be alive is more important than to aspire to some status, that today is more important than tomorrow because it is now, that to live in gay houses, to look marvellous, to spend money, to enjoy oneself are better than to be respectable – all these discoveries are profound ethical advances.

They liberate the human spirit. From this almost anything could come and it cannot but be creative. Refinement will follow; and it will not be the dead refinement of an ossified gentility, but the vital development of an experimental creativity.

To me this is the acme of civilisation, both moral and aesthetic. The only problem for the over-thirties is how to get in on it. But I spoke of a cloud in the sky.

There is one real threat to civilisation; and that is the possibility of a religious revival. In the last chapter of *The Decline and Fall of the Roman Empire* Edward Gibbon wrote simply that 'I have described the triumph of barbarism and religion'.

And, despite Professor Arnold Toynbee's elaborate sophistries in his war-time essay on *Christianity and Civilization*, I believe that Gibbon was profoundly right to bracket barbarism and religion as twins, indeed as Siamese twins, in his story of the ruin of a civilisation.

For religion abhors the alliance of pleasure and reason as utterly as, say, capitalism abhors intelligent social purpose allied to government. Each fears being put out of business by such dangerous combinations. Hedonism always provokes its own backlash. There are always those for whom the pleasure of others is a very present personal pain. That St Paul should have returned so carefully upon his hour in the guise of Mr Malcolm Muggeridge is, perhaps, what is known as 'one of history's little ironies' – in more senses than several.

But the power for wreckage of such worthies should never be underestimated. They gain great sway over men's minds. As even Mr Bell recognised, 'Puritans, for all their good intentions, are the enemies of good, because they . . . attach to what were once means to good an importance due only to the end, and on these obsolete means insist often to the detriment of means more hopeful because more appropriate.' He cites, as an example, a primitive version of Mr Muggeridge's fascination with 'the pill'; and he might have added 'pot' as well.

Gibbon himself, in his unrivalled chapter XV on the five causes of the spread of Christianity, recalls yet more topically the attitude to pleasure and luxury of Mr Muggeridge's forerunners in the early Christian church. The Early Fathers, who presided with such gleeful severity over the conception of a millennium of cultural darkness, 'despised all knowledge that was not useful to salvation' and even – alas for Mr Muggeridge – 'considered all levity of discourse as a criminal abuse of the gift of speech'.

Worse still, Gibbon tells us, 'our devout predecessors, vainly aspiring to imitate the perfection of the angels, they disdained, or they affected to disdain, every earthly and corporeal delight'. In the necessary minimal use of our senses for our preservation 'the first sensation of pleasure was marked as the first moment of their abuse'.

Music and art were to be studiously ignored. 'Gay apparel, magnificent houses and elegant furniture were supposed to unite the double guilt of pride and sensuality,' Gibbon writes. Then in a passage that might also serve as a Pauline anathema of our times, Gibbon records that 'in their censures of luxury, the fathers are extremely minute and circumstantial; and among the various articles which excite their pious indignation, we may enumerate false hair, garments of any colour except white, instruments of music, vases of gold or silver, downy pillows (as Jacob reposed his head on a stone), white bread, foreign wines, public salutations, and the practice of shaving the beard which, according to the expression, of Tertullian, is a lie against our own faces, and an impious attempt to improve the works of the Creator.'

On the question of sex, Gibbon found that 'since desire was imputed as a crime, and marriage was tolerated as a defect, it was consistent with the same principles to consider a state of celibacy as the nearest approach to the divine perfection'. 'It was with the utmost difficulty,' he adds 'that Rome could support the institution of six vestals; but the primitive church was filled with a great number of persons of either sex who had devoted themselves to the profession of perpetual chastity.' How gratifying for Muggeridge; but how tragically absurd.

Gibbon presses remorselessly onward to find that 'the Christians were not less averse to the business than to the pleasures of this world'. But his eighteenth-century intelligence observed that 'in this situation likewise, the situation of the first Christians coincided very happily with their religious scruples' and that 'their aversion to an active life contributed rather to excuse them from the service, than to exclude them from the honours, of the state and army'. They would, no doubt, still have got into the Sunday papers and on to the television on Sunday evenings, peddling their joyless morality.

The fate of Rome is the *locus classicus* for students of civilisation in decay. If Gibbon rather than Toynbee shall be our guide, the maggots for which we should be on the watch are not the 'hippies', but the devout ascetics. And they are stirring.

Just before writing this I heard a chirpy radio preacher declare, 'Cheer up! The whole history of the Christian church is full of doubts and sorrows.' He appeared to feel that he had made a telling point.

Illustrated London News, 2 May 1970

Who's Left,
What's Right

I label myself a 'market socialist'; and as such I have, perhaps, particular reason to regard the conventional Left–Right spectrum of political classification as unsatisfactory.

By 'market socialism' I mean the following combined beliefs:

(a) that the role of government in society should be confined to the traditional minimal functions plus a negative income tax and specific corrections of market mechanisms through taxes and subsidies where a specific 'public good' has been clearly shown to be achievable thereby;

(b) that macro-economic policy should be directed to securing a non-inflationary expansion of the money supply, related to the estimated underlying growth of the productive potential of the economy, a balance in the budget and a cleanly floating exchange rate;

(c) that regional imbalances in an economy should be seen as suppressed exchange-rate adjustment problems within an excessively large common currency area and should be tackled by actual or simulated exchange-rate adjustments depending on whether it is practical to introduce separate currencies within the larger area;

(d) that, for the rest, governments should confine themselves to extending the role of the market as widely as possible and to ensuring a high degree of competition within such markets;

(e) that all enterprises employing more than (say) a hundred people should be self-owned and managed under the sovereign authority of the people who work in them, each having a single vote for membership of the main board or council; and

(f) that such enterprises should raise capital both from retained profits and from a freely operating capital market, where they would borrow both at fixed interest rate and on equity-like terms (giving a share of the profits and a mortgage on assets in the event of break-up, but carrying no freehold of the assets or power of appointment of directors).

I may be wrong, foolish or even mad. But how does it add to my or anyone else's understanding of my position to describe it as Left or Right? I feel the greatest affinity to those Conservative 'extremists' who are extreme for individual liberty even at the expense of corporate power and to those Labour 'extremists' who are extreme for workers' democracy even at the expense of Government and trade-union power.

I feel the greatest antipathy to those 'moderates' in the Conservative, Labour and other parties – like Heath, Jenkins and Healey – who see Britain's salvation in some national combination of interest groups (Government, CBI, TUC, the NCC, etc.) who will arrange matters over the heads of individual voters, consumers and workers. I am sometimes shunned as subversive, as often denounced as reactionary. I find myself more interested in knowing whether I am right.

Encounter, February 1977

The Great Fastnet
Disaster

Book Review
1. *Fastnet, Force 10* by John Rousmaniere. W. W. Norton & Co. Price $12.95
2. *Fastnet – One Man's Voyage* by Roger Vaughan. Seaview Books. Price $10.95

The greatest disaster in ocean racing history occurred last summer when a severe storm struck the more than three hundred yachts competing in the Fastnet race. The turmoil of that night of 13/14 August has left three questions which sailors and experts will be debating for many a long year: what happened; why did it happen; and what could have been and now should be done about it?

John Rousmaniere's and Roger Vaughan's studies of the race and the storm are only two of the many books it will produce. The primary document remains for the moment the report of the inquiry into the race conducted by the Royal Ocean Racing Club and the Royal Yachting Association, published December 1979.

John Rousmaniere's book is a useful, readable and thoroughly sane introduction to the basic facts, individual experiences and underlying issues of the 1979 Fastnet disaster. Although the material is badly organised, jumping suddenly from anecdote to analysis and back to anecdote, it is written in the good muscular style of a competent journalist with all the necessary sailing experience and specialist knowledge.

Roger Vaughan's book, though containing some fascinating insights and yarns, is much too self-indulgent, autobiographical and slangily written to be appreciated by anyone reared in the best tradition of nautical writing, which prefers bald accounts, understatement, simple prose and minimal 'philosophy'.

What happened on that terrible night – and the present reviewer, who witnessed it from the comparative safety of a small Irish harbour six

300

miles from the Fastnet rock keeping anxious anchor watch in wind speeds which consistently exceeded the 60-knot maximum reading on his boat's anemometer, will never forget it – can now be starkly summarised. The biennial Fastnet race is the crowning event of Cowes Week, the premiere event of British yacht racing.

The course runs six hundred miles from the Isle of Wight in the middle of England's south coast, round Land's End at the south-western tip of England, up to the Fastnet rock off the south-west corner of Ireland and back round the Bishop rock, off the Scilly Isles, to the finish at Plymouth on England's south coast. In all 303 yachts of between 28 and 79 feet overall length started the race. 85 finished, after 194 had retired, 19 had been abandoned and 5 had sunk.

Out of 2,700 crew members fifteen were lost; and 136 were saved from sinking yachts, life rafts and the sea itself. Nothing remotely comparable had ever occurred before in the more than fifty years of popular ocean racing. Less that forty people have died in ocean racing in a total history of over a hundred years. In the fifty-five year history of the Fastnet race there had been one previous death – forty-eight years earlier.

More astounding still, of the 180 yachts under 39 feet in length, only 13 finished the race, 144 retired and the rest were abandoned or sunk. Almost half the boats in the race were at some point knocked flat in the water or almost flat; and one-third were knocked down beyond horizontal or rolled right over through 360 degrees.

Even the largest boat in the race, Jim Kilroy's *Kialoa* with an overall length of 78 feet, was knocked flat; and she was not at that time in the area where the most vicious seas developed, namely a circle with a 40 mile diameter centred 70 miles west-north-west of Land's End. The reason why most of the damage in the race occurred to smaller boats was not that they were smaller, but that they happened by bad luck to be concentrated in this particular area during the worst of the storm.

The direct cause of this catastrophe is clear. Sea-going is in essence a horizontal activity and on the night of 13/14 August the marine environment between Land's End and the Fastnet rock became effectively vertical.

The damage was done by the waves – up to forty feet in height, almost vertically steep and frequently breaking over boats caught in their path – and not by the storm-force winds. The wind, however, caused the high seas.

The cause of the very high winds – a steady average of force 10

(48–55 knots) and frequent violent gusts above 60 and possibly as high as 70 knots – was a small, fast-moving and eventually deep depression (below 980 millibars), which was born in the northern Great Plains of the United States on 9 August and swept into the Fastnet sea area during the night of 13/14 August. The ferocity of the seas which resulted was a direct consequence of the strength of the winds, blowing over open ocean for several hours, and of the fact that the direction of the wind swung from south to north-west in twelve hours, thus causing wave motions coming from many directions at once.

More than half the participants in the race believed that the steep seas were also caused in part by the Labadie Bank (depth 40 fathoms, with 21-25 fathom patches, compared with an average depth of 65 fathoms in the Western Approaches).

A long tradition of sea-faring lore corroborates this opinion. But Britain's Institute of Oceanographic Sciences told the official inquiry that the Labadie Bank could not have influenced wave height or shape.

In the wake of the disaster much nonsense was talked on all sides about how it could have been avoided. Grave errors of weather forecasting were alleged.

Skippers were accused of bad judgement in taking to life-rafts. Inexperience in handling small boats in storms, excessive racing zeal, excessively light and defective design of boats and rigging, and general weaknesses of character and fortitude were all alleged against the less fortunate boats by those who were safely on shore or who were lucky enough to survive without serious damage.

Careful examination of the facts shows all these charges to be unfounded. There were only two ways to avoid disaster that night: either not to be there at all or to be lucky.

There was no way that the storm and the resulting sea-state could have been forecast in time to make a significant difference to the number of boats affected. The racing authorities had no reasonable cause to cancel the race. No differences in radio communication or boat design or sea-faring experience would have significantly altered the outcome.

The plain fact was that a storm of extraordinary, though not totally unprecedented, force happened to strike a small sea area in which there happened to be an extraordinary – and unprecedented – concentration of small boats and for many crucial hours created a marine environment in which, for the unlucky, it was simply impossible to avoid disaster.

John Rousmaniere well summarises the sensible findings of the official inquiry:

Neither two-way radios nor a smaller fleet nor any other single factor would have forestalled disaster, the committee appeared to conclude. This was an experienced group of sailors exposed to an exceptionally severe sea condition. Some of the boats may not have been quite as stable as they should have been, and some equipment should have been stronger, yet as elucidated in the report's last paragraph, the lesson was: 'in the 1979 race the sea showed that it can be a deadly enemy and that those who go to sea for pleasure must do so in full knowledge that they may encounter dangers of the highest order.'

The only people to emerge with discredit from the whole tragedy are the busybodies and wiseacres who, after the event, claimed that this, that or the other reasonable precaution could have prevented the disaster or that some new bureaucratisation or regulation of sea-faring is necessary in order to prevent the minute risk of repetition. The truth is, as with so many others of the hazards of contemporary life which the sedentary 'committee' mind cannot tolerate, that the costs of reducing such risks to zero greatly exceed the benefits to the human spirit and personal fulfilment of cheerfully accepting them.

There is not a good seaman who would have been in the sea area between Land's End and the Fastnet rock that night if he had *known* what the sea conditions were going to be. But also there is not a seaman who would not have been there on the evidence that was reasonably available at the time or who would wish to be prevented from being there by some new regulation imposed over his own sea-faring judgement.

The story of the Fastnet disaster is thus at one and the same time a series of fascinating individual dramas, a fascinating meteorological and oceanographic puzzle and a fascinating microcosm of the perennial moral and political problem of the proper balance between the individual's right to incur risks and the duty of government and other authorities to protect people from the possibility of misfortunes which may overtake them.

The most difficult thing in the world for committees, for politicians, for the media and for other experts to accept is that such-and-such a disaster occurred and absolutely nothing should be done in future to prevent it happening again. Yet, the Fastnet disaster may have done a service to mankind by demonstrating that there are indeed occasions when this is the right thing to say and that, if they exist in ocean racing, they may also exist much more widely than is recognised in other aspects of society where the mania for 'absolute' safety is involving us in a

Personal and Philosophical

greater and greater risk of 'absolute' regulation and 'absolute' inactivity.

The Washington Post, 23 April 1980

Index

Acheson, Dean 133fn
Acton, Lord 14
Ackley, Gardner 100
Afghanistan, Soviet intervention in 141, 144-5, 148, 149, 152-3, 181, 182; US and Western Europe's reaction 168, 169, 172
Africa, black nationalism in 144; Carter administration and 142, 144; human rights in 139; US interests in 143
Agenda for the Nation (Kissinger) 130fn, 135fn, 183
Albu, Austen 113
Allen, Sir Douglas 112, 119, 120, 121
American Employment Act 1946 38
Amin, President Idi 139
Annan Committee 22, 85, 227
Armstrong, Sir William 119
Atlantic Alliance, erosion of 134
Atlantic Charter 165, 166, 167

back-benchers, role of 18
Baghdad Pact 149
balance of payments 62; concepts of 122; deficit in 42; disequilibrium of 106
Ball, Professor Jim 68
Bank of England Bulletin, The 122, 123
banks, role of 60
bargaining, collective 2, 7, 40-1, 42, 48, 49, 57, 59, 79, 82; abstention from 69; advance of 70; and capitalism 74; and workers cooperatives 66, 71; corollary of 57-8; disappearance of 63, 84, 87-8; effect on labour costs 83; influences of 54-5, 70; outlawing of 50, 58, 59, 69
bargaining, individual 42, 44, 69
bargaining, monopolistic 84
Basle sterling area 122
Begin, Menachem 147
Beijing's Democracy Wall 140
Bell, Clive 294, 296
Berkeley, Unviersity of California 19, 167
bipolarity, military 132, 135fn
Birt, John 25, 26, 191 *et seq.*
Birt-Jay thesis 191 *et seq.*
Bokassa, Emperor 139
Bolivia, human rights in 140
borrowing, fixed interest 71
Bretton Woods 129, 165, 171
Brezhnev, President 150

Britain, and US 160-1, 168 *et seq.*; cyclical trends in 162-3; disinflation in 162; friendship for US 158-9, 164; interests in S. Africa 143, 163; pay restraint in 162; realism in 160-4
British Broadcasting Corporation 25, 228; Acts 267; Charters 209, 223, 231; news 202, 204-5, 207
British Council of Economic Advisers, need for 102
British Employment Policy, White Paper 1944 98
British Telecom 223, 227, 228, 229, 230
Brittan, Samuel 3-5, 6, 10, 77, 79-81, 92, 124fn
Brook, Sir Norman 94
Brown, Secretary Harold 145
Brzezinski, Zbigniew 131, 131fn, 147
Bullock Committee 88; Report 74-5, 91
Butskellite era 13
Butt, Ronald 111fn

cable broadcasting 22-3, 25
Callaghan, James 29; White Paper of 95
Camp David 146, 181
capital, entrepreneurs of 60, 64, 65, 73
capitalism 2, 7, 35, 59, 63, 64, 65, 73-4; and collective bargaining 74; collapse of 45; mixed 53; state 47-8, 53; world market 69, 72
Capitalism, Socialism and Democracies (Schumpeter) 12
capital markets 35, 60-1, 63, 65-6; and workers cooperatives 67
capital productivity, maximising 68
Carey, George 27
Carrington, Lord 144
cartels 69, 78, 79, 80, 81
Carter, President/Administration 131, 133, 147, 150, 168-9, 173, 179; achievements in 1979 152, 154, 156; and Namibia 143-4; and Nicaragua 140; and Philippines 141; and southern Africa 142, 143, 144; and South Korea 141; and SALT 134; and Third World 138-9; and Zimbabwe/Rhodesia 143-4; at Camp David 146-7; errors of 151-2, 153; foreign policy of 181-2, McGovernite policymakers of 142; position with Iran 144-5; recognition of

Red China 150; support for human rights 134, 138-41, 169; Tokyo pledge of 169
Castro, President, pro-Soviet posture 140, 141
CENTO 149
Channel 4 25, 225, 235, 276; Welsh 225
Chile, Carter Administration and 140
Christianity and Civilization (Toynbee) 296
Churchill, Winston 163, 165, 167, 171, 172, 186
civilisation 293-7; incivilities of 293; religion in 296-7; threat to 296
Clarke, Sir Richard 113, 114
class warfare 35
Clayre, Alasdair 90
Cockburn, C. 196, 248-9
Cold War 130, 139, 151, 173, 183
collective ownership, *see* workers cooperatives
committees, deliberative 8-10, 16; parliamentary 16
commodities, changes in price of 5
communism, spread of 130
competition, and economic resources 47; and new enterprises 73; and working people 50; between cooperatives 63, 78; enforcement of laws of 82-3
Concorde, US landing rights for 161
Conference of the Nonaligned, Havana 132, 154
Congress, United States 97-8; committees of 111; Economic Report to 97-8
Conservative Party 4, 53
Constitution for the Commonwealth of Great Britain (1921) (Webbs) 87
cooperative ventures *see also* workers cooperatives, ownership of 51; redundancy problems in 52; sale of assets 51-2
corporatism 47-8
Council of Economic Advisers (Great Britain) 101, 102-3
Council of Economic Advisers (US) 97-8, 100
Cuba, Castro in power 140, 141; pro-Soviet posture 140; Soviet activity in 150, 151
Curran, Sir Charles 202

Dacko, David 139
Daily Mirror 26, 277, 284
Daily Telegraph, The 277
Deakin, Michael 281
debate, parliamentary 9-10; public 9, 16, 18
Decline and Fall of the RomanEmpire, The (Gibbon) 296
de Gaulle, General 14
Delusion of Incomes Policy, The (Brittan and Lilley) 86
demand deficiency 85; efficiency 84; management 2, 38-9, 40-1, 83, 84
de-nationalisation 14
d'Estaing, President Giscard 134, 186
détente, and US 132, 149, 150, 151, 153, 183; as high alliance priority 152

deterrents, need for 178
Diamond, John 116
disinflation, British 162
dissidents, liberation of 169
Domestic Credit Expansion 122
Douglas, Senator Paul 10, 100
Downie, Jnr, Leonard 173fn
Dubs, Ambassador, murder of 150
Duchy of Lancaster 53
Dulles, John Foster 130, 131, 133fn, 140, 142

Economic Consequences of Democracy (Brittan) 3
Economic Indicators 98
Economics and Industrial Relations of Producer Cooperatives in the United States 1791-1939 87
Economic Trends 122, 123
Economist, The 24, 90, 187
economy, and workers cooperatives 67, 87, 90; capitalist 73-4; free enterprise 71, 76; labour managed 87, 88; threat to Western 135-6; workers cooperative 67, 71
Ecuador, human rights in 140
Egypt, and Palestine 147
elections, parliamentary 3-4, 6, 12-16
electoral reform 4
Employment Act (1946) US 97-8
employment, full/high 3, 4, 38-9, 42, 55, 57; and inflation 43, 45, 48, 84; and workers cooperatives 72
Employment, Inflation and Politics (1976) (Jay) 73, 78
Encounter 22, 85, 299
Essay Concerning Human Understanding (Locke) 249
Estimates Committee 10
Ethiopia, US 'loss' of 142
Eurodollars 122
Europe, single currency for 177; Soviet threat to 171, 172; unification of versus nationalism 173-4; United States of 174, 180
European Economic Community 107, 122, 171, 182-3; and US 175-6; Britain as member 160, 163; common agricultural policy in 175-6; industrial policies in 175; political tensions of 175; White Paper on membership of 110
European Monetary System 176-7
European Parliament, 136, 185
Evolution of Giant Firms in Britain, The (Prais) 75
exchange controls 62; abolition of 135
exchange rates, adjusting 83, 298; control of (US) 100; influence on cooperatives 66; use of 107
Exchequer and Audit Department 18

Falklands affair 4
Fastnet disaster 300-4; possible service to mankind 305-6

Fastnet, Force 10 (Rousmaniere) 300
Fastnet, One Man's Voyage (Vaughan) 300
Feudalism 2
Financial Times 33, 124fn, 277
Financial Statistics 122
First World, *see* West, the
Ford Administration 141
Ford, Anna 279
Foreign Affairs 157
free enterprise, working of 63
Friedman, Professor Milton 40, 72, 100, 162
Friends of the Earth 70
Frost, David 279
Fulton recommendations 102

Gaitskell, Hugh 30
GATT (General Agreement of Tariffs and
    Trade) 165, 171; and European
    Community 175
*General Theory of Labour-Managed Market
    Economics, The* (Vanek) 56, 87
geopolitics 127 *et seq.*
Gibbon, Edward 296
Gilbert, W.S. 14, 15
Good Morning Britain 279
Gordon, Kermit 130fn
government as provider of capital 70-1
Granada Television 11
Guardian, The 26, 277, 284

Hamilton, William 110
Healey, Denis 4, 29, 299
Heath, Edward 4, 29, 81, 299
Hee, Park Chung 141
Heller, Walter 100
Horizon 215
House Appropriations Committee (US) 111
Houthakker, Henrik 100
Howell, David 121
human rights 134, 141, 154; as counter to
    Marxism 141; British support for 163; in
    Africa 139; in Latin America 139-40; in S.
    Korea 141; US policy of 138-9, 169
Hume, David 244
Hunt Committee 25
hyper-inflation 41, 44, 58

I Claud (Cockburn) 196, 248-9
Illustrated London News 297
incomes policy 2, 5, 49, 50, 58, 59, 69, 84;
    results of 81
Independent Broadcasting Authority 191,
    209, 223, 228, 266, 267, 270, 279, 280,
    285
Independent Television 228
Independent Television News 25, 204-5
individual wants, satisfaction of 36-7
Indochina 150, 151
industrial societies, foundations of 36
inflation 3, 4, 5, 6, 38, 40-2, 53; accelerating
    45-6, 48, 58, 63, 70, 83-4, 87; and market
    forces 46; in US 44, 99; monetary demand
    and 83, 84; reduction in 160; stability in 57

information, shortage of for Opposition 11,
    17-18
Institute of Economic Affairs 57, 86
Inter-continental Ballistic Missile (ICBM)
    178
interest rates 84
International Monetary Fund 100, 165, 171,
    176
investment, industrial 35, 59, 60-3, 64, 71;
    cost of 65; equity-type 61-2, 65, 66, 73;
    few incentives for 70; fixed interest
    borrowing for 65; overseas 62, 66; returns
    on 64-5, 70
Iolanthe (Gilbert) 15
Iran, hostages incident 147-8, 169;
    overthrow of Shah 144, 15; US
    involvement in 145, 146-9
Isaacs, Jeremy 226, 232, 235
isolationism, in US 170, 171, 179, 186
Israel, and Camp David 147; peace with
    Arabs 149

Jacobson, Sydney 26
Japan 128, 182; economy of 133
Jay, Peter 124fn, 132, 189 *et seq.*
Jenkins, Roy 4, 29, 299; White/Green Papers
    of 95
Johnson, Paul 21
Johnson, President 129
Joint Economic Committee (of Congress) 8-
    10, 11, 97-100, 111-12; roles of 98-100;
    sub-committees of 99
Jones, Professor Derek C. 67, 86
journalism, *see also* television journalism *and*
    news; 19, 22, 191*et seq.*; ethics of 255-6,
    264; nature of 249
journalists, *see also* television journalism;
    191*et seq.*

Kee, Robert 279
Kennedy, President 100, 129
Kennedy Council 100
Keynes, John Maynard 38, 39, 58, 72, 83,
    85; revival of his ideas 84
Khomeini, Ayatollah 141; anti-Americanism
    of 144, 147-8; barbarities of 145
Kissinger, Henry A. 130fn, 131, 131fn, 132,
    133, 133fn, 134, 135fn, 137, 137fn, 139,
    140, 142, 145, 150, 154, 155, 168, 169,
    183-4; and *détente* 151
Korea, South, Carter Administration and 141

labour, as entrepreneur 57, 64-5, 73; cost of
    64
Labour Government in Britain, and Carter
    Administration 142
labour market 54, 59, 73; American 44; and
    trade unions 69; and workers 57; freedom
    of 45-6; frictions in 73; imperfections in
    39, 40, 48; *laissez faire* 69; monopoly in
    41, 74
Labour Party 6, 35, 53; leadership of 4
labour productivity, and workers

cooperatives 66-7; influences working on 67, 68; maximising of 68
Latin America, human rights in 139-40
Law of Global Chaos (Jay) 132
law, rule of international 170, 171
legislation, anti-trust 78, 79
Lilley, Peter 86
Lincoln, Abraham 261
Locke, John 249, 250
London Weekend Television 25, 26

Macias of Equatorial Guinea 139
Mackintosh, John 120, 121
Macmillan, Harold 21, 29, 30
Mactaggart Lectures 22, 23, 254
Manchester Guardian 243
Marcos, President Ferdinand 141
market economy, extension of 85-6
market socialism 63, 75, 78, 81, 82, 83, 86, 89-90, 92; beliefs of 298-9; in Yugoslavia 89
Marshall Plan 129, 165, 171
Marx, Karl 54
Maudling, Reginald, White Paper of 95
McCracken, Paul 100
Meade, Professor James 56, 86
Mercer, Derrik 26
Meriden Cooperative 90
Middle East, necessity for US support 148-9; regionalism in 144*et seq.*; Soviet/Western competition in 149
Midweek 192
Mill, John Stuart 263
Mitchell, Austin 207
monetarism 2, 3, 13, 21, 29, 40, 58, 84, 106
monetary reform, international 107
Money Programme, The 194
Monks, Geoffrey 280
monopolies 56, 59, 69, 75; and trade unions 77-85; as workers cooperatives 77; legal operation of 80; statutory 77; technical 79
Monopolies Commission 234
Moynihan, Patrick 155
Muggeridge, Malcolm 296, 297
multipolarity, problem of 130, 132
Murrow, E. 172
Mussolini, Benito 136

Namibia, and Carter Administration 142-4
National Economy Group (Treasury) 115
National Institute Economic Review 106
National Economic Development Council 101, 106
National Institute of Economic and Social Research 106, 118
nationalisation 14
nationalism, economic 170, 173, 175, 186; in Europe 136-7, 170, 171, 174, 184, 187
NATO (North Atlantic Treaty Organisation) 134, 135fn, 137, 150, 165, 169, 171, 173, 177, 181, 186; and US 128, 151, 152; meeting in Brussels 152
NEDO (National Economic Development

Organisation) 70
news, and the moral laws 256-8; facts, definition of 243-4, 246-7, 248-9, 251; freedom of speech 260, 261, 262-3; impartiality, obligation of 254-5, 264; intrusions on privacy for 263-4; logical atomism 247, 249; nature of 237-65; newsmen's obligations 251, 254-5, 256, 258-9; reporting, difficulties of 245-7; restraints on 260-2
News at Ten 207
New Statesman 87
New York Times, The 275
Nicaragua, expulsion of Somoza 140; Sandinista regime in 140
Nixon Administration 8, 100, 132, 141, 153
Northern Ireland 14
North Sea, profits from 162
nuclear weapons 134, 138, 166; deployment of 178-9; modernisation of 134, 138, 150, 152, 169, 175; symmetry of 178
Nyerere, President Julius 139

OECD (Organisation for European Economic Development) 57, 58-9, 70, 165, 167
Okun, Arthur 100
Organisation of African Unity 143
Organisation of American States 140
Owen, Dr David 162, 164

Pakistan, arms for 148
Palestine 147; Carter's fight for rights of 182; problem of 149
Palestine Liberation Organisation 147
Parkinson, Michael 279, 288
parties, differences between 17
Patman, Congressman Wright 98
pay restraint, British 5, 162
pay settlements, public and private sectors 82
Pearl Harbour 172
Peking, recognition of 149
Philippines, Martial Law in 141
Phillips curve 38
plebiscites 15, 16
Plowden Committee 94, 104-5; Report of 95, 113
pluralism 130, 131, 131fn, 154, 187
policy-making, democratisation of 11-13, 15
Political Quarterly 207
Popper, Professor Karl 249
Power of Parliament, The (Butt) 111fn
Prais, Professor S. J. 75
Press, the – *see also* journalism *and* journalists – 10; alleged failure of 95
Pretoria 144
prices, stability of 57
Privileges Committee 109
producer cooperatives, records of 86-7
production, democratisation of 47
prosperity, erosion of 34
protectionism 166, 170, 175, 184, 186; demands for 183

Index

Proxmire, Senator William 10, 98
Public Accounts Committee 18, 109, 114

QUANGOS 23

Radio Caroline 224
Radio Luxembourg 224
Reagan, President 20
recession, domestic 84
'Red China' 130; recognition of 150
referenda 15, 16
reflation, wish for 83
regionalism 127*et seq.*
Regional Employment Premium 107, 117-18
regional problems 19-20
Reuss, Congressman Henry 10
Richardson Committee on VAT 110, 118
Rippon, Angela 279
Rippon, Geoffrey 180
Robertson, James 103, 112
Role and Limits of Government (Brittan) 3, 6
Rome, Treaty of 174; US support for 174
Royal Commissionon on Taxation 118
Royal Ocean Racing Club 300
Royal Yachting Association 300
Roosevelt, President Franklin 165, 167, 171, 172, 185, 186
Rousmaniere, J. 300

Saatchi and Saatchi 14
Sadat, President 146, 147
SALT I and II 134, 149, 150, 151, 152, 177, 178
sanctions, democratic 13, 15, 16
Sandanista Government, Nicaragua 140
Saudi Arabia, US and 145-6, 151
Schmidt, Chancellor Helmut 134, 175, 186
Schumpeter, Joseph 13, 36
Scott, C.P. 209, 243
Scottish Daily News 67, 90
Second World 128
Second World War 129
security, budgetary 117-119, 183; collective 170, 171, 172, 187; regional 171
Select Committee on Economic Affairs 10, 93, 124; and Joint Economic Committee of US 97, 100; and the Treasury 94, 112-24; case for 100, 101, 103, 104-5, 107, 121, 124; objections to 108-24; prematureness of 123-4; role of 95-7, 100, 107, 110, 115
Select Committee on Estimates 94
Select Committee on Expenditure 11, 101, 103-4, 109, 110, 123
Select Committee on Nationalised Industries 105-6, 109
Select Committee on Procedure 10, 11, 94, 109, 124, 124fn; Report of 101, 103, 108, 109
Senate Foreign Affairs Committee (US) 8-10
separatism 35
Smith, Adam 37
Snow, Peter 27

Social Contract 195
Socialism 2, 7, 44-5
Somalia, Soviet action in 142-3
Soviet Union, activity in Cuba 150; and the Arabs 147; arms build-up of 152; influence on NATO 137; invasion of Afghanistan 141, 144-5, 148, 149, 152-3, 181, 182; involvement in Ethiopia 143; loss of Somalia 142-3; preoccupation with US 127-8; US, possible threat to 178
Spain, democratic elections in 139-40; US landing rights in 151
St Paul 296, 297
stability, foreign exchange 176; of price 44, 70; search for 2, 3, 4, 5, 18, 19
Stamp Memorial Lectures 114
Strauss, Ambassador Robert 147
strife, multipliers of 165-7
superpowers 20, 137, 142, 143, 148, 153, 173, 174, 187; credibility of queried 154
Swann, Sir Michael 202
syndicalism 56

'Task Ahead, The' (Green Paper) 105, 115
taxation, and social security 107; changes in 114, 117, 118; levels of 63, 71, 105, 115-20; structure of 105, 114; use of 115
Tax Reform Bill (1969) (US) 117
Taylor, Elizabeth 242
technology, growth of 70, 72
television 9-10, 22-3, 191*et seq.*
television journalism 19, 22-5, 26-7, 191*et seq.*; audience attraction of 207-8; bias in 191-218; 'capsule analysis' 213; current affairs 195, 196, 199-205, 213; documentary influence on 197, 199, 201, 206, 213; editors 203-4, 206, 217; 'fact' versus 'comment' 209-10, 211-12; 'fallacy of composition' 213-14; feature 191, 192-3, 195, 199, 200-1, 203, 205; integrated news system 216-17; issue 191, 193-4, 200; morning 27, 225, 242, 266-89; news 191, 192, 195, 196-208, 213, 228; news analysis 198-9, 200, 202-3, 205, 206, 209, 213, 216; news and current affairs 203, 204, 206, 207, 208, 209, 215, 216, 217, 278; news-room, influence of 197-9, 206; on-the-spot reporting 215; party political 228; programmes for 202-3, 206; staffing for 203-4; story 194; studio discussions 194, 213
Thatcher, Margaret 21, 29
Third World 128-9, 173; and decolonization 129; and US 138-9, 155; problems of 132; stability in 132
This Week 192
Thorneycroft experiment 106
Times, The 5, 8, 26, 107, 124fn, 191, 196, 201, 205, 206, 218, 234, 277
Tito, Marshal 89
Tobin, Jim 100
Tonight 208
totalitarianism 45, 58; avoidance of 54

Toynbee, Professor Arnold 296
trade unions 2, 35, 42, 48, 50, 53, 55, 69;
    and capitalist supplies of labour 69; and
    collective bargaining 58, 67, 88; and
    workers cooperatives 67; as bargaining
    agents 48, 64, 67; power of 49, 77-85;
    prohibition of 59, 69
Trollope, Anthony 14
Truman, President 153
Turkey, US landing rights in 151
TV am – *see also* under television journalism
    – 22, 24, 25, 26-7, 189, 266-89;
    advertising revenue for 268, 269; BBC/ITV
    competition 268; business plan for 267-
    71; failures of 282-5, 288-9; lessons
    learned 291; motives for 266-7, 271-4,
    276; presenters' role 287-8; programme
    philosophy of 267, 272-4, 276-82, 287;
    ratings 270, 271, 272; studio as central
    point for 280

ul-Haq, President Zia 140-1
under-employment 59, 72, 73, 84
under-investment 71
unemployment 3, 5, 6, 40, 44, 46, 53; and
    collective bargaining 57-8; avoidance of
    38; European fears of 136; incidence of
    39; reduction in 84; relationship to
    inflation 38, 42, 44, 47, 54, 58; rise in 59,
    166; tolerance of 46, 54
unilateralism, US 135fn
United Nations 165, 171
United States, and Australasia 128; and
    détente 132, 149, 150, 151, 152-3, 169,
    183; and Japan 128, 176; and NATO 128,
    151, 152; and Saudi Arabia 145-6; as
    anticolonial power 129; as anti-
    communist champion 129-30;
    consumption of imported oil 169, 176;
    economic power of 177, 181; focus of
    European rivalry 181; friendship with
    Britain 160-1; growth of anti-Soviet
    feeling 154-5; inflation in 176;
    involvement with W. Europe 137-8, 168-
    70, 171-2, 177*et seq.*; 'loss' of Ethiopia
    142; moves in N. and S. Yemen 146;
    preoccupatin with Soviet Union 127-8;
    problems with Iran 145; relations with
    Africa 143; reliance on the Shah 148;
    response to invasion of Afghanistan 173;
    rivalry with W. Europe 135

Vance, US Secretary Cyrus 141, 147, 161
Vanek, J. 56, 87
Vaughan, Roger 300
Vietnam, War in 8, 129, 132, 181; Chinese
    invasion of 151

Washington Post 173fn
wealth, redistribution of 38
Webbs, the 87
Weekend World 191, 194
Wenham, Brian 250
West, the 128, 133; aims of 138; as coherent
    entity 129, 136, 173, 177, 183; economic
    system of 135-6, 170; lessons of the
    thirties 170-1; opposed to Marxism 132;
    security order of 133; W. Europe's reliance
    on health of 168, 175, 181, 182
Western Europe, and human rights 163; and
    Soviet invasion of Afghanistan 168-9, 172;
    and US 168-9, 173*et seq.*; British
    cooperation in 163; economic adversity in
    184-5; economic power of 133; fear of
    Soviet Union in 166, 172, 177;
    reconstruction of 129, 136; relationships
    within 161; reliance on 'the West' 168;
    search for identity 135
White House Years (Kissinger) 133fn, 184
Wilson, Harold 21, 29, 30, 53, 95
Wincott Foundation 33
Wincott, Harold 33
Wireless Telegraphy Acts 222
Woolf, Virginia 294
workers cooperatives 7, 56*et seq.*; and
    collective bargaining 66; and labour
    productivity 66-8; and trade unions 67;
    cost of capital for 65, 66; definition of 56,
    60; disadvantages of 86; 'equity-type'
    finance for 61-2, 65-6, 73; exchange
    control for 62-3; factors against 67-8;
    founder-owners' rights 73; government
    finance for 70-1, 78; investment for 59,
    60-3, 64; lower productivity of 68;
    management in 67; *modus operandi* of 59,
    60; optimum size of 59, 73, 74-7; profit
    distribution from 61; redundancy in 68;
    relations with investors 73; role of banks
    60; shareholders in 60, 62, 65, 66;
    tendency to under-employ 72, 73, 84, 89;
    unwillingness to invest 72
workers, as entrepreneurs 49-50; break down
    of 74-5; combination of 69; desire for
    cooperatives 91-2; monopolistic action of
    77-8; 79; rights of 51, 55
World Bank 165, 171
World Court 171

Yemen, North/South, and US 146
Young, Arthur 143, 155
Yugoslavia, experiences in 72, 73, 89

Zeit, Die 172
Zimbabwe/Rhodesia, and Carter
    Administration 142-4